Real LOVE *in* PARENTING

A Simple and Powerfully Effective Way to
Raise Happy and Responsible Children

Greg Baer, M.D.

Real Love in Parenting — The Truth About Raising Happy and Responsible Children
Copyright © 2004 by Greg Baer, M.D.

Baer, M.D., Greg
    Real Love in Parenting
    ISBN 1-892319-18-7
    1. Relationships 2. Self-help 3. Psychology
Second Edition
Published by:
Blue Ridge Press P.O. Box 3075 Rome, Ga 30164
www.GregBaer.com

Also By Greg Baer, M.D.

Real Love — The Truth About Finding Unconditional Love and Fulfilling Relationships
    —Gotham Books
Real Love — The Truth About Finding Unconditional Love and Fulfilling Relationships, Unabridged Audio Book — Set of seven 60 Minute CDs
    — Blue Ridge Press
The Real Love Companion
    — Blue Ridge Press
The Wise Man — The Truth About Sharing Real Love
    — Blue Ridge Press
Real Love in Marraige — The Truth About Finding Genuine Happiness in Maraige
    — Blue Ridge Press
Real Love in Parenting — The Truth about Raising Happy and Responsible Children
    — Blue Ridge Press
The Truth About Love and Lies — Set of three 60 minute CDs
    — Blue Ridge Press
The Healing Power of Real Love — set of two DVDs, total running time 2 Hours, 20 Minutes
    — Blue Ridge Press

Printed in the United States

REAL LOVE in PARENTING

The Truth About Raising Happy and Responsible Children

Introduction

Every day our children demonstrate with their behavior that something is seriously wrong in their lives. Our older children are angry, rebellious, sulking, avoiding interaction with us, using alcohol and drugs, and having sex and babies at an age when they're just babies themselves. Our younger children are whining, disobedient, irresponsible, and having difficulties in their relationships with siblings and classmates. And despite our ability to send men into space, manipulate DNA, and move mountains, we're often reduced to a state of utter helplessness and frustration by the tears, tantrums, and defiance of our children.

We all want our children to be happy and responsible, but we don't seem to be clear about how to accomplish that goal. When they misbehave, we struggle in confusion to regain their obedience and cooperation. We lecture them, punish them, manipulate them, beg them, bribe them with nice things, and take them to counseling. We've proven with extensive personal experience that none of those approaches produces the genuinely happy and responsible children we really want – but in the absence of something better, we keep trying.

Our children are screaming for help, and we're looking for answers. We blame the schools, television, the government, the music industry, peer pressure, and the generally declining morals of modern society. And of course we blame our children. We blame anyone but ourselves because we don't like seeing the truth: our children are unhappy because they haven't received what they need from **us**, their parents.

Rottweiler puppies are adorable, and if they're treated well, they remain playful and affectionate — even when they become enormous and physically capable of ripping a man's throat out. Let's suppose I bring such a puppy home and chain it to a stake in the middle of my backyard, next to your house. And then I completely ignore the dog except to feed it and occasionally yell at it and kick it when it barks and annoys me. One day when the dog is full grown, I neglect to feed it for several days, something I've done several times before. While I'm at work, he pulls up his stake, tears through the fence, and eats your cocker spaniel.

Something must be done. We could shoot the dog. We could enact legislation that requires stronger fences for all dog owners. We could demand the registration and periodic inspection of all dogs. Or we could order the destruction of all Rottweilers. Each of these approaches has some merit in preventing another disaster, but they all ignore the real problem: **me**, the irresponsible owner of the dog.

And so it is with our children. When we care for them properly, they're happy. When we don't, they're miserable and react with all the behaviors we call "bad." As much as we hate to admit it, we don't give our children what they really need (Chapter 1). And it's no surprise that we don't — although no job in the world is more important than being a parent, we're not trained for it. In school, we learn algebra, history, and grammar instead. Where do parents ever get serious instruction for the most important job on the planet? We don't.

That's the bad news. The good news is that we can all learn to be great parents. *Real Love in Parenting* will help us understand what children need to be happy and responsible — and how we can give it to them.

I recommend that every parent read two books — in the following order:

1. *Real Love—The Truth About Finding Unconditional Love and Fulfilling Relationships* (published by Gotham Books, a division of Penguin Group). This can be found at all major bookstores, or on Amazon, or by going to the website at www.gregbaer.com and clicking on the "Books" tab on the navigation bar to the left.

Most of us don't understand what a genuinely loving relationship is. Instead, we protect ourselves from people and manipulate them to get what we want. That always leaves us feeling empty, disappointed, angry, and alone. In that condition, we cannot be loving and effective parents. I'll be talking much more about that in Chapters 4 and 5. *Real Love* teaches us how to have profoundly rewarding relationships where unconditional love is freely given and received. When we parents are whole and happy ourselves, we're naturally able to give our children what they need most, and then we can make an enormous difference in their lives.

2. *Real Love in Parenting*

If you haven't read *Real Love*, don't stop reading *Real Love in Parenting* now. The first five chapters of this book are designed to summarize most of the principles found in *Real Love*. After finishing the parenting book, however, I strongly advise reading *Real Love*.

Chapter 1

**What Children Need:
Real Love**

Imagine that you and I plant a healthy seedling in the ground, but then we don't water it. In a few days, of course, it begins to wilt and turn brown. What should we do now? We could blame the plant. We could yell at it for failing to grow as we had expected. But that would be foolish when we only need to water the plant.

Children are no more able to tell us what they really need than plants are able to speak up and ask for a drink of water. Like plants, children express their needs indirectly, with their feelings and behavior — with anger, disobedience, worrying, tears, violence, bad grades, rebellion, drugs, alcohol, etc. How foolish we are to then criticize or control their behavior while we ignore the *needs* they are communicating with that behavior.

What our children need more than anything else is the feeling that they are *unconditionally* loved. Without that feeling, they cannot be happy or function productively, just as a plant cannot be healthy without water. Whenever children behave badly, or when they appear unhappy, it *always* means that they don't feel sufficiently loved. As parents, we don't like to hear that because the responsibility for loving our children rests primarily with us. Most of us cannot even begin to admit the possibility that the love we give our children might be deficient in some way. But their troubled *behavior* is undeniable proof of that. We don't need to feel guilty about it. We *have* loved them as well as we could. Our children are only unhappy because we couldn't give them what we didn't have ourselves: Real Love.

REAL LOVE

Real Love is caring about the happiness of another person without any concern for what we'll receive in return. We give our children Real Love when we care about *their* happiness, without any regard for our own convenience. When they're ungrateful, disobedient, and inconvenient, we're not disappointed, hurt, or angry. Real Love is unconditional.

When we unconditionally care about our children's happiness, they feel a powerful connection to us. They feel included in our lives. They feel whole, safe, and not alone. Each moment of unconditional acceptance creates a living thread between us and our children, and those threads weave a powerful bond that fills them with a genuine and lasting happiness. Nothing but unconditional love creates that feeling. Real Love determines the happiness of our children. "With Real Love, nothing else matters; without it, nothing else is enough." (*Real Love—The Truth About Finding Unconditional Love and Fulfilling Relationships*) It's that simple.

THE CONSEQUENCES OF NOT LOVING OUR CHILDREN UNCONDITIONALLY

How many of us can say that we love our children unconditionally? It's critical that we honestly examine that question. When our children stay quiet and clean, get good grades, express their gratitude to us, give us kisses, say they love us, clean their rooms, don't fight with their siblings, and otherwise do what we want and make us look good, we love that, don't we? And then we smile at them, pat them on the head, hug them, and tell them we love them. *That's easy.*

But do we behave the same toward them when they get bad grades, when they're ungrateful, when they whine, when they fight with each other, when they're irresponsible, when they wreck the car, and when they're noisy, messy, and disobedient? No, we don't. Without thinking about it, we frown, roll our eyes, sigh with disappointment, and speak to them with an impatient tone of voice. We feel irritated when they don't do what we want. *Disappointment and anger are feelings that we experience only when we're primarily concerned about what **we** want.* We do not have these feelings when our principal interest is the happiness of our children — the definition of Real Love.

I emphasize that disappointment and anger establish without doubt that we love our children *conditionally.* We don't mean to. We say we don't. We wish we didn't. We know we shouldn't. But we do. And no matter how we justify our disappointment and anger, what's important is the effect these feelings have on our children. Regardless of the time, effort, and money we spend on our children, every time we communicate disappointment or anger, they feel separated from us and alone. The damage is unspeakable. Without Real Love, children can only feel empty, afraid, and miserable. If you have any doubt about that, look carefully at the face of any child while he's the object of a parent's disappointment or anger. This will be especially impressive if you can briefly detach yourself from an unpleasant interaction that you're having with your own child and look honestly at the effect you're having on him.

A child who has not been sufficiently loved unconditionally is without the most important thing in life. Without Real Love, he does not feel connected to other people. He can only feel **alone**, *which is the most painful condition of all. Every "bad" behavior we see in children is simply a reaction to that pain.*

We wonder why our children are angry and rebellious, and why they fight with each other. We can't understand how they could use drugs and have indiscriminate sex when we've told them about the dangers. They do all those things because they don't feel loved by *us*. Each of those behaviors distracts them and protects them from the insufferable anguish of feeling unloved and alone. We'll discuss this much more in Chapters 2-3.

I am *not* advocating permissive parenting, which has terrible consequences. Children do need to be guided and corrected. But when we correct our children with sighs of disappointment and annoyed facial expressions, we communicate to them that our interest is in *ourselves, not them*, and *they feel that*. **That** is what hurts them. When our concern is genuinely for the happiness of our children — when we love them unconditionally — we are not disappointed or angry at them. Truly selfless teaching is never accompanied by those feelings.

In Chapters 11-22, 24-26, and 29-30, I'll be discussing in great detail how to correct children and how to teach them to be truthful, loving, grateful, and responsible. They *must* learn these principles before they can be happy. But first we must begin to fill their primary need to feel loved. If we don't do that, they can't learn anything else we try to teach them. Children without enough Real Love can only be empty and afraid. They can't be effectively corrected and taught. We must learn to give them Real Love first. Does this mean that we have to become perfectly loving ourselves before we can correct or teach our children in any way? No, but we do need to *begin* the process of loving them. We'll talk more about that in Chapter 11.

Thousands of parents have implemented the principles of this book and have learned how to unconditionally love their children. The effect on their children has been astonishing. It's a gradual and simple process that we can all learn. An important part of that process is acknowledging the truth about how we treat our children now, how we have treated them in the past, and how that has affected them.

Taking Responsibility As Parents
For Not Loving Our Children Unconditionally

We *must* see the effect of our behavior on our children and be willing to shoulder the responsibility for it. Until we do that, we can't do anything meaningful to help them, and isn't that why we're here as parents?

Imagine that you come to visit me at my home while I'm working in the garden. I give you several bushes and ask you to plant them in another part of the yard. And let's suppose that you don't know the first thing about gardening. After half an hour, I walk over to where you're working and discover that you've done everything wrong. You've planted the bushes in the wrong place and at the wrong depth; you've spaced them incorrectly; you've used the wrong soil; and you've broken several branches as you handled the plants.

With a huge smile, I thank you for helping me and apologize for not explaining what needed to be done. And then we work together until it's all perfect, laughing and having a great time. How do you feel? Relieved, of course – even delighted. Despite all your mistakes, you can see that I care only about *your* happiness. There's no better feeling in the world. Most of us can't imagine a scene like this, being completely accepted by someone after we've caused such an inconvenience. We've usually been the object of criticism and irritation under these conditions.

Now imagine the same scene again from the beginning. You come to see me, and again, you do everything wrong. But this time, when I see what you've done, my face falls to the ground. Although I don't say anything, I quietly sigh and drop my shoulders in that expression of profound disappointment that no one could fail to recognize. And then I silently repair the damage you've done.

How do you feel now? Happy? Hardly. The moment I communicated my disappointment, you knew that my concern was for *myself* and for what *I* didn't get, not for *your* happiness at all. That is *always* what disappointment and anger mean. And the effect on you was devastating, even though I didn't say a word. I might as well have yelled at you and screamed that you were an idiot, because that's what you heard and felt.

That is how our children feel every time we feel disappointed or irritated with them. We may think that we hide those feelings from them, but we deceive ourselves. The difference between unconditional acceptance and disappointment is unmistakable. Every child can feel it. The effect of our disappointment — however mild — is awful, even though we don't do it intentionally. Now imagine the effect of unbridled anger.

I know exactly how hard it is to swallow the concept that parents are the cause of all the bad behaviors in their children. For many years, I did the best I could as a father, but I did not love my children unconditionally. I *couldn't* have — I'd never felt unconditionally loved myself. I couldn't give what I didn't have. So I gave my children the best I had – I gave them conditional love. I praised my children and "loved" them when they were obedient, successful, grateful, and otherwise "good." But when they were "bad," I was disappointed, critical, and often angry.

Regrettably, that kind of love is worthless to a child. As a result, my children felt empty, unloved, and miserable. They reacted with anger, rebellion, withdrawal, alcohol, drugs, and other indications of their unhappiness (Chapters 2 and 3).

I tried everything I could think of to change their behavior — reason, discipline, pleading, manipulation, bribes, consequences, and spending more time with them — but nothing worked until I finally realized that they didn't feel loved, and that I was the reason they didn't. I then took the steps to find Real Love for myself (Chapter 5) and shared it with my children. As I did that, their bad behaviors began to disappear without me doing anything to directly control or eliminate them. When children feel loved, they don't need to do those things, which are just reactions to their emptiness and pain.

Why We Don't Love Our Children Unconditionally

If our children need Real Love from us so badly, why don't we just give it to them? I mentioned the answer to this question briefly a moment ago: because we can't give what we don't have.

As a child, I enjoyed it when my mother smiled at me, held me, and spoke softly to me. On those occasions, I felt connected to her and not alone. And from the beginning, I noticed that she did those pleasant things more often when I did what she liked — when I was quiet, grateful, and cooperative. In other words, I saw that she loved me more when I was "good," something that almost all parents understandably do.

When I was "bad" — noisy, disobedient, and otherwise inconvenient — she did not speak softly or smile at me. In fact, she frowned, sighed with disappointment, and often spoke with a harsh tone. *Although it was unintentional*, she clearly told me with those behaviors that she loved me less, and then I felt disconnected from her and alone.

Nearly all of us were loved that way, and of course, that's how we love our own children. We pass on what we received ourselves. It's natural that we "love" people more when they make us feel good and that we "love" them less when they don't. It's natural, but it's not unconditional — it's not Real Love.

Real Love is, "I care how **you** feel." Conditional love is, "I like how you make **me** feel." That's what we do with our children. We like them more when they make us feel good, or at least when they don't do anything to inconvenience us, hurt our feelings, or make us look bad. We don't consciously withhold

Real Love from them. We just don't have it to give because we don't feel unconditionally accepted ourselves. We'll talk more about this in Chapter 4.

Again, loving children unconditionally does not mean spoiling them. Children do need to be corrected, and they need to be taught to be loving and responsible. We'll address that in later chapters.

BUT—

It's understandable that many parents protest, "But *I'm* not responsible for everything my children do. They make their own choices. And there are other influences in their lives: television, school, their peers, and lots of other people and things." All right, let's play the blaming game. First, we'll blame our children, and then we'll blame everyone else.

Blaming our children

Before we start blaming our children for their bad behavior, we must first be certain that *we* are blameless. After all, we *were* given the responsibility of teaching and guiding them. We *are* supposed to be older and wiser. Before we can properly blame our children, we must first claim that we have perfectly discharged our responsibility as parents — that we have instructed them flawlessly and have loved them purely, selflessly, and without exception. We can't really place the blame for their behavior on them until we're certain that none of the blame is ours. Can any of us make that claim?

Blaming everyone else

We love to blame other people when anything goes wrong. The more we do that, the less responsibility we have to assume ourselves. So let's blame everyone else for our children's problems and see where that takes us.

How much shall we blame television for our children's behavior? Laying aside the fact that *we* are the ones that allow them to watch television in the first place, we still don't *know* how much blame to place, do we? We just don't know, so blaming immediately becomes absurd. But because blaming is so popular, let's do it anyway. Let's blame television for 14% of our children's behavior — a generous figure, I think. And we'll blame the schools 9%, their peers 12%, and popular music 8.27%. We can't leave out the government, so let's blame them 6.73%. That's at least 50% of our children's behavior that we can blame on other people. Isn't that a relief?

Now what? There's no sense starting this blaming thing unless we stay with it. So now we'll devote all of our time to changing television, the schools, our children's peers, the music industry, and the government. With the doubtful exception of a local school here and there, the most likely outcome of all that effort will be very close to zero. Several million of us have proven that already. We can therefore only conclude that blaming other people and things for our children's behavior is worthless — stupid, I might add, since our goal is to help our children.

So are we *really* entirely responsible?

So is it really all our fault? Are we entirely responsible for our children's feelings and behavior? If we perfectly loved a child unconditionally from birth, would he be guaranteed to be happy, loving, obedient, and responsible? Is every child's problem a result of our mistakes? Probably not.

Do other people play a role in how our children turn out? Don't in-born genetic responses make a significant contribution? Yes. Then why do I focus on our role as parents? Because there is nothing in the world more essential to the emotional health and happiness of a child than Real Love, and we *are* primarily responsible for giving that to our children.

Being responsible is simply the most *effective* approach

I strongly suggest that even though other factors are involved, we still make the *assumption* that we are completely responsible for the feelings and behavior of our children. We need to do that for one simple reason: it's the most *effective* course we can take as parents. When we blame anyone else, we unwisely divert our time and energy from the essential effort of loving and teaching our children. In short, when *we* take the responsibility, we can *do* the most to help our children be happy, and isn't that what we want as parents?

The only disadvantage of taking all the responsibility ourselves is that we might feel guilty when we see the evidence of our mistakes in our children's behavior. Fortunately, there's no reason to feel guilty. We've done our best. We simply can't give our children what we didn't get ourselves (again, more about that in Chapter 4). Once we get over the hurdle of feeling guilty, being responsible for our children is a joy.

THE JOY OF BEING RESPONSIBLE

We have learned from a lifetime of experience that when we make mistakes and people learn about them, they think less of us. That's especially unfortunate when it comes to parenting because we waste so much effort denying our mistakes instead of helping our children.

When wolf cubs cry out in hunger, do their parents argue with each other about who is at fault? No. Do they blame the cubs, or the hard winter, or other wolves? Ridiculous. If the cubs are hungry, it is their *parents'* responsibility, and they do whatever it takes to find food, even if they die in the attempt. There is no question about that. Nor do the parents seem to feel any shame about it.

We could learn from this example. We are primarily responsible for the happiness of our children. If they are angry, rebellious, or otherwise declaring their unhappiness, who could possibly be more responsible than we are? Eventually, at some undetermined age of maturity, they do become responsible for their own feelings and behavior, but for a very long time, *we* must accept that responsibility. If we are willing to do that, we can begin to give our children the greatest gift in the world.

I was speaking one day at a seminar on relationships, and during a break I was approached by a woman who described her son. He was becoming increasingly difficult for her to handle as he displayed his anger, rebellion, disobedience, etc. She was obviously irritated when she asked, "How can I get him to stop acting like this?"

It was clear that she was looking for a technique to *control* her son's behavior and make her own life more convenient. I explained that her son was reacting to the lack of Real Love in his life, and that it would take a considerable change on *her* part before she would be able to *help* her son become happy enough to stop doing the things that were troubling her. Early in our discussion, she said, "So you're saying this is *my* fault?!"

"Of course. When it comes to our children, that's the only productive way to see things. However, I wouldn't use the word *fault*." I explained to this mother that it had simply been her *responsibility* to love her son, and that she had been unable to give him sufficient Real Love only because she hadn't been given enough herself. She refused to consider the possibility that she could be responsible for her son's behavior, and she walked away from our conversation determined to find someone else who would help her control her son.

I have seen so many parents deny their responsibility for their children's happiness in this way, and the consequences are awful. They blame and attempt to control their children, which makes their children feel even more unloved. Their children react with even worse behavior, and the parents react with more blaming and controlling. This cycle never has a happy ending.

There is a way out. I have now seen many parents accept the responsibility for loving their children – acknowledging all the mistakes they've made as parents, but without feeling guilty – and that creates the possibility for change. These parents have learned how to unconditionally love and teach their children. The reward is well worth every sacrifice we could ever make. I speak from personal experience.

THE PRIMARY RESPONSIBILITIES OF PARENTS

We have three principal responsibilities toward our children, and we succeed as parents only as we fulfill them:

1. To love our children (Chapter 9)
2. To teach them how to love other people (Chapter 13)
3. To teach them responsibility (Chapter 14)

More simply, we're responsible for loving our children and teaching them what's right. When we do that, they can begin to choose to be happy and loving instead of being empty and miserable. We need to keep these three responsibilities in mind as we discuss all the details of parenting in subsequent chapters.

HAPPY AND RIGHT

Since we're responsible for teaching our children what's *right*, and for helping them be *happy*, let's define those terms.

The entire goal of life is to be happy. When I talk about happiness, I mean a profound peace that does not come and go with changing circumstances. Real happiness comes from feeling loved and from loving other people, and that feeling stays with us through struggle and hardship. It does not come from being entertained or getting people to do what we want.

Since happiness is the central goal of life, a behavior is right when it contributes to genuine happiness — in other words, when it leads to being unconditionally loved and to loving others. Any behavior which interferes with feeling loved and loving others is therefore wrong.

We're All Little Children

In the following chapters, as I talk about the behaviors that result from a lack of Real Love in the lives of our children, keep in mind that *those same principles apply to us as adults.* Most of us are still living with the effects of not getting the Real Love which is essential to the emotional and spiritual health of every human being.

Chapter Summary

Real Love is unconditionally caring about the happiness of another person. Children can only be happy when they receive that kind of love from us.

Each time we're disappointed or angry when we don't get what we want from our children, we prove that we love them conditionally — we love them more when they're "good" and less when they're "bad."

Children without Real Love can only feel alone and unhappy, and all their bad behaviors are nothing more than indications that they're missing the Real Love they need.

We can't be better parents until we recognize that we are primarily responsible for the happiness and behavior of our children. We must learn how to love them unconditionally.

Chapter 2

What Children Use Without Sufficient Real Love: Imitation Love

In the absence of Real Love, children can only be empty and afraid. To eliminate these intolerably painful conditions, they use whatever makes them feel better: anger, disobedience, whining, the approval of their peers, sex, alcohol, drugs, violence, etc. All of these things briefly and superficially fill their emptiness or protect them from their fears, giving them a pale *imitation* of the genuine happiness that can only be produced by Real Love. When these things are used as substitutes for Real Love — as they so often are — they become forms of Imitation Love.

We must understand that all the things our children do which we find unacceptable — anger, rebellion, sex, drugs, etc. — are just forms of Imitation Love. Although they're not consciously aware of what they're doing, our children use Imitation Love to distract them from the pain of not feeling unconditionally loved. If they can't have Real Love — which is what they need — they fill their lives with Imitation Love, which at least feels good temporarily. When we understand that, our children's behavior is no longer puzzling, nor is it as frustrating to us.

All of the forms of Imitation Love that our children use fall into one or more of only four general categories: praise, power, pleasure, and safety.

PRAISE

What children need is to be loved unconditionally. But if they can't get that, they quickly learn that it feels wonderful to be praised for doing what other people like. Children wriggle like scratched puppies when they're told that they're a "good boy" or "good girl," and they'll do virtually anything to hear words like that.

The quest for the overwhelming satisfaction of approval and praise then becomes the central driving force in most children's lives. In early childhood, they do whatever it takes to please their parents and earn their praise. Eventually, unloved children devote themselves to winning the praise of their peers. That motivation determines what they wear, how they speak, the way they wear their hair, the music they listen to, the friends they choose, and so on. This pattern of winning the praise of others then continues on through adulthood. Most adults base their decisions around the approval of others, something they learned as children. That dependence on approval can be crippling.

On the surface, complimenting children appears to be a good thing. However, unless we're filled with Real Love ourselves, there are serious dangers commonly associated with praising a child:

1. We praise children as a form of manipulation to get what *we* want.
2. Children learn to seek praise as a substitute for Real Love (Imitation Love).
3. They feel pressured to keep earning our praise.
4. They feel responsible for our happiness.
5. They continue to use praise as a form of Imitation Love for the rest of their lives.

The Manipulation of Praise

Tony was six years old. When he was cheerful and helpful, his mother said, "Oh Tony, you're such a good boy." But on the occasions when Tony was messy, loud, and inconvenient, she did not praise him. In fact, she was often critical and angry when he failed to please her. Without meaning to, Tony's mother praised him much more when he did the things that *she* wanted. Almost all of us do this with our children, and with everyone else, which is understandable — but it's not unconditional love, and our children feel that.

I cannot over-emphasize how much damage is done when our children feel that our love for them is conditional. No matter what else we provide for our children — a beautiful house, a great education, nice cars, lots of money, endless entertainment, the finest clothes, the best cultural environment — they will not be happy if they sense that our love for them is conditional. And virtually all children do feel that, since we do praise them more when they do what we want. I recognize that conditional praise and conditional love are the standards everywhere we look, but that doesn't make them right. And our acceptance of those standards explains why there is so much unhappiness in the world.

Without realizing it, we often praise our children to get something for ourselves. When a child cleans his room and we say, "Oh, what a good boy you are!" our motives are rarely pure. Sure, we want to reward him for doing a good job, and we want to teach him to be responsible. But we also have a selfish desire to get that filthy room cleaned up because it personally offends *us*. We praise him to get something for *ourselves*.

We tend to have similarly mixed motivations when we praise our children for their good grades, athletic achievements, physical appearance, and other accomplishments or behaviors. We do want them to succeed and be happy for their own sake, but we also want them to make *us* look good and feel good. Praise is a way to encourage them to keep doing that for us. Tony's mother discovered — mostly unconsciously — that he did the things she liked when she praised him for doing them.

You may be thinking that *you* are different, that when you praise your children you're not trying to get anything from them. Before you claim to be different from almost every parent on the planet, be honest and ask yourself this question: What happens when your children behave badly and fail to meet your expectations? Are you disappointed or irritated? Sure, on many occasions. And then do you withhold your praise? Of course, and when you do that, you prove that your praise is *not* as selfless as you thought.

Our children can *feel* that our praise is conditional and self-serving, and the effect is terrible. I'm not saying we should never praise our children. I am saying that when we don't feel unconditionally loved ourselves, we tend to use praise as a form of Imitation Love to manipulate them. We need to be aware of that. As we find Real Love in our own lives (Chapter 5), we learn how to unconditionally love our children. *That* is what they need and want from us, not our praise.

If praise isn't what they need, what exactly *should* we say to our children when they do something well? Shouldn't we say something to reward them for a job well done? And what should we say when they behave badly to discourage them from repeating that behavior? The remainder of the book is devoted to answering those questions. There are far more productive ways to teach our children than praising them. Praise only seems important to us when we're missing what really matters: Real Love.

Seeking Praise as Imitation Love

Tony's mother praised him more when he pleased her, and less when he didn't. Naturally, Tony preferred his mother's praise

— another word for approval — to her criticism, so he did whatever it took to please her. Since her approval made him feel so good, he believed that when she gave it to him, he was truly happy. It certainly felt better than receiving her disappointment and anger.

Unfortunately, conditional acceptance fails to give children a genuine connection to anyone. Children have to *buy* such acceptance with their behavior, and no matter how much of it they purchase, they remain painfully empty and alone. Only Real Love creates the connection between human beings that results in genuine happiness. They may not realize it immediately, because even conditional approval can feel pretty good temporarily, but eventually the pleasure of purchased acceptance *always* wears off and leaves them feeling empty and alone. An ocean of praise lacks the power to create the happiness found in a teaspoon of Real Love.

Children readily learn what earns positive attention from the people around them, and they learn to do those things well. One praise-earning approach they learn is to give praise to others. As a child, Tony obviously didn't know how to flatter his mother in the sophisticated ways that adults would, like, "You look great, Mother. Have you lost some weight?" But he did learn that if his mother was angry at him, he could make her anger go away by saying, "I love you." He could also make her happy by kissing her before he went to bed each night and by always being very grateful for everything she did for him.

Although Tony didn't realize what he was doing, he was manipulating his mother by making her feel important, which is a form of praise. Tony made his mother feel good, and in return, she praised him and made him feel good. They were trading Imitation Love.

Praise, like all forms of Imitation Love, is bought and sold, traded, exchanged, negotiated, and even stolen. I praise you so that you will praise me. We do what other people want so they will praise us, and we praise other people to get them to do what we want. There are endless variations on the commerce of praise, and our children are very young when we begin their training in the way the game is played.

The Pressure of Praise

Children soon discover that they get more praise — which they understandably perceive as more love — when they're good. They like the attention, but they also learn that the feeling is brief and that they have to keep doing good things to continue receiving the praise they enjoy. They feel an enormous pressure to please us. Tony felt that, knowing he would not get the praise he enjoyed if he didn't keep earning it.

Our children want to please us and receive our approval. But that's exhausting if they feel forced to do it, and without meaning to, we do push them to please us. Eventually, they feel trapped by their obligation to constantly earn praise, and they come to resent us for making them do that.

Responsibility for Our Happiness

If we smile and praise our children when they're good, but frown and get angry when they make mistakes, we unintentionally teach them that they're responsible for how we feel. Sometimes we even say out loud, "You make me angry," or "You make me so happy." The effect is disastrous *either* way because the burden to make us happy — or at least to not make us unhappy — is unbearable for a child. With the responsibility of making *us* happy, no child can feel unconditionally loved by us.

A Lifelong Pattern of Using Praise as Imitation Love

As he grew older, Tony discovered that if he dressed a certain way, listened to the right music, associated with the right people, and behaved in a way that pleased his peers, he received their praise and approval, and he liked that very much. It was the same pattern of earned approval he'd learned from his parents. When his friends drank alcohol or smoked marijuana, he naturally went along with them. There was no peer *pressure* — he was *eager* to please them and retain his place in the group. When having sex became the manly and praiseworthy thing to do, he willingly complied with the expectations of the people whose acceptance he valued.

It's ironic that we parents wonder why our children are so eager to please their peers when *we* are the ones who taught them the importance of earning the approval of other people. It started with us. Praise, like all forms of Imitation Love, becomes every bit as addicting as any drug. In the absence of Real Love, we simply can't live without some form of artificial happiness, and praise is a great source of that.

As an adult, Tony tried to please the women he dated, and he was good at it. When he found one that lavished sufficient praise on him in return — as his mother had done — he was certain he'd found true love, and he married her. He also worked hard at his job to please his supervisors. Tony's entire life became established on a foundation of praise and approval.

The Emptiness of Praise

Praise is just like an addictive drug to those who use it as a form of Imitation Love. The first doses are exciting, but they wear off quickly, and the same dose from the same source soon becomes insufficient to produce the same effect. People require more and more praise to get the same thrill they once did.

The initial excitement of Tony's marriage soon disappeared. Tony began to live for the approval he received at work, but eventually, it became obvious that he would go no higher in his company. Now what could he do? Tony was conditioned to find happiness by earning the praise of other people. He had done everything he could and his supply of praise was disappearing.

When people don't feel unconditionally loved and they run out of their only source of Imitation Love, their emptiness and fear become overwhelming. Some switch to another form of Imitation Love (power, pleasure, safety). Many become depressed or develop panic disorders. They acquire physical problems like high blood pressure or ulcers. They have affairs. They turn to alcohol and drugs. Some take their own lives.

POWER

In the absence of Real Love, children feel alone and helpless. They don't like that feeling, and they quickly discover that they feel less powerless when they can control anything at all. They start with little things. Infants are delighted to learn that when they push an object, it moves; when they cry, people come running; when they push food off the table, it splatters on the floor and people scurry to clean it up. A three-year-old utterly controls his mother while she chases him through a grocery store, and he loves it. These exercises of power aren't mean-spirited, just fun.

As children get older, they continue to explore their enjoyment of power. Disobedience, defiance, and rebellion are all ways that children are able — usually unconsciously — to achieve a sense of power over us and other people. It gives them momentary relief from the painful feelings of loneliness and helplessness that always accompany a lack of Real Love. It's no mystery why children go through the "terrible two's." A child that age discovers the exhilaration of the power he has when he says the word "no." Power over other people is a seductive pleasure, one that our children often learn to use all their lives.

Go to a football game, and as the last-second winning touchdown is scored, look at the facial expressions of the players and the fans on the winning and losing sides. Our children can easily see that we *love* the sensation of power that we get from beating down our opponents. They learn to get the same enjoyment from winning, in sports and everything else. We teach them from a very early age to seek Imitation Love in the form of power.

When we attempt to control the behavior of other people in any way, we are enjoying Imitation Love in the form of power. How often do we attempt to *get* people to do things our way? Or *get* them to change their minds? Our children see that. Our children see us do that with them. How many books advocate the Power of This and the Power of That, and teach us how to *get* more from other people? Though we may not like to admit it, we teach our children that success and happiness are found in exercising power over other people. And then, curiously, we're offended when they practice their growing powers on *us* as they dare to resist us in any way while we're trying to control *them*. We're a bit hypocritical, are we not?

Jason's parents both had careers and spent little time with him. Although he couldn't describe it in words, he felt unloved and alone, and he felt helpless to do anything about it. As a young child he got some praise and attention by doing what his parents wanted, but that was short-lived, unpredictable, and required a lot of work. In time, he found it enormously satisfying to simply defy his parents and do whatever he wanted. Where his parents had often ignored him in the past, they now instantly paid attention to him when he was angry and rebellious. The attention wasn't loving, but it felt much better than being ignored, and he felt in control. He enjoyed the sensation of power.

One reason we tend to love babies and small children is that they're mostly willing to do anything to please us and earn the praise that we generously dole out if they do what we want. But we find many older children — especially teenagers — more difficult to like for the sole reason that they're often not willing to do what it takes to earn our praise. They're no longer willing to give their lives to experience the very brief and unpredictable pleasure of our conditional acceptance. Instead they prefer the sensation of power, which they can more consistently control. Who can blame them?

PLEASURE

In the absence of Real Love, we eagerly pursue anything that feels good. Sex, food, travel, and other forms of entertainment temporarily diminish the discomfort of feeling unloved and alone. As parents, we enjoy these pleasures ourselves, and we give them to our children as a form of Imitation Love.

We really do want our children to be happy, and we feel sad — often guilty — when they're not. When we can't give them what they really need — Real Love — we give them the pleasure of toys, television, money, cars, stereo systems, and free time instead. We do this because we hope:

(1) we can make them happy;
(2) we'll look like good parents;
(3) we'll earn their gratitude, however brief; and
(4) we'll avoid the complaints we hear when a child doesn't get what he wants.

Pleasure feels good for a moment, but it never lasts, and it can't take the place of Real Love. In addition, when we try to satisfy our children with pleasure, we teach them to spend the rest of their lives trying desperately to find happiness in excitement and entertainment — and that approach always fails.

SAFETY

The absence of Real Love is painful, and children will do anything to prevent any additional discomfort, like the pain that accompanies our criticism and disapproval. That's why they lie to us, get angry, sulk, and avoid us — all to avoid the sting of our disappointment and anger. In order to feel safe — from *us* — they engage in the very behaviors we dislike. In effect, we teach them to seek safety as a form of Imitation Love.

In many cases, children who appear to be obedient and cooperative are really buying safety from their parents by doing what they're told. Those children don't feel genuinely loved, just safe. Many of them grow up feeling manipulated, alone, unhappy, and resentful that they were imprisoned by fear. Safety does feel temporarily better than the acute pain of fear, but it is no substitute for feeling loved.

Children who don't feel unconditionally loved *will* fill their emptiness with Imitation Love of some kind. If they can't get enough praise, power, and pleasure, they will do whatever it takes to ensure their safety. We often teach our children to pursue safety as a form of Imitation Love when we inappropriately protect them as they interact with other people. For example, if our children experience an injustice at the hands of a teacher at school, many of us jump in and "save" them from the situation. We often give them safety much like we would give them a piece of candy or a pacifier. We make them feel better for a moment, while we neglect our primary responsibilities which are always the same: to love them, to teach them to love other people, and to teach them responsibility.

Children are often cheated as we give them safety instead of providing them invaluable opportunities to learn. Children need protection far less than they need love and guidance. We'll discuss how this is done throughout the book, especially in Chapter 21.

CATEGORIZING IMITATION LOVE

When a child does something for the purpose of winning our approval, it's obvious that the payoff is praise, which is *one* form of Imitation Love. Some things that our children use — and which we use as adults — as substitutes for Real Love fall into *more than one* category of Imitation Love. For example, when a child gets angry at another child and wins an argument, the angry child gets a sensation of *power* over the losing child. If he consistently intimidates others and gets his way — especially if he does it cleverly — he may be *praised* for his behavior. People tell him that he's strong; he's a winner. He also gains considerable *safety* for himself. Thus, from one behavior, he obtains Imitation Love in three categories.

This pattern is seen with many behaviors. Sex is an abundant source of Imitation Love in the form of power and praise, not just pleasure. From money we get praise, power, pleasure, and safety.

Please understand that I divided Imitation Love into four categories – praise, power, pleasure, and safety – only to help you see some of the ways that your children find relief from the lack of Real Love in their lives. Perhaps you will see some of the ways that you do that, too. Don't focus too much on intellectual things like categories. In the end, it doesn't matter *which* form or category of Imitation Love a child uses as a substitute for Real Love. What we do need to understand is that any time we (or our children) use anything to take the place of Real Love, that thing becomes a form of Imitation Love, and it cannot make us happy.

REAL LOVE VS. TRADING IMITATION LOVE

If we don't feel unconditionally loved ourselves, we unavoidably give our children the only things we have. We give them what we were given and what we learned. We praise them when they're good. We encourage them to be strong and independent (power). We give them as much pleasure in life as we can. We protect them and make them as safe as possible. There is potential good in all those things, but not when they're used as a substitute for what children really need, which is to feel unconditionally loved.

If Imitation Love is all we have to give, and if we call it "love," our children naturally believe it's the real thing, and they work hard to get all of it they can. Imitation Love does feels good, and to ensure a steady supply of it, they give *us* Imitation Love, too. They give us gratitude, displays of affection, and obedience, which in the absence of sufficient Real Love we receive as praise and power. The more Imitation Love our children give us, the more we give them. I stress that we're quite unaware that we're doing this, but we still *trade* Imitation Love with each other, and we prove that it's not Real Love every time we're disappointed or angry with our children. There is no disappointment or anger in Real Love. This trading of Imitation Love does feel good temporarily, but our children don't get the Real Love they badly need, and that leaves them feeling empty and alone.

THE PROBLEM

The problem with every unhappy child is the same: they don't have enough Real Love in their lives. It really is that simple. We "love" them when they're good and we love them less when they make mistakes and inconvenience us. No matter how much praise, power, pleasure and safety they accumulate, they cannot be genuinely happy. Imitation Love is deadly. It provides enough pleasure that our children hope they'll be happy if they get enough of it from us and other people. That mistaken belief often ruins their entire lives. The frantic search for Imitation Love is guaranteed to leave everyone feeling frustrated, alone, and miserable.

THE SOLUTION

As we learn how to unconditionally love our children and teach them, they find the kind of happiness that is genuine and lasting. And then they have no need to fill their lives with Imitation Love.

In the presence of Real Love, Imitation Love becomes useless and therefore loses its seductive power.

IMITATION LOVE AND CONDITIONAL LOVE

Conditional love is the approval that people give to us when we do what they want. Throughout the book, I will use *Imitation Love* as a term which describes everything that takes the place of Real Love and makes us feel good in its absence — praise, power, pleasure, safety, *and* the conditional love of others. Because the term *Imitation Love* **includes** *conditional love*, I will use the first term rather than the second to describe those interactions where love is conditional.

Chapter Summary

Children without Real Love are unhappy. To fill their emptiness and to protect themselves, they use praise, power, pleasure, and safety, all forms of Imitation Love.

Imitation Love feels good temporarily, but it never lasts and never leads to the intimate connection and happiness that result from Real Love.

When parents are without Real Love themselves, parents and children unavoidably trade Imitation Love with each other.

Chapter 3

How Children Behave Without Sufficient Real Love:
Getting and Protecting Behaviors

Nothing can compensate for a lack of Real Love. Without it, children can only feel *empty* and *afraid*, and they'll do anything to get rid of those feelings.

EMPTINESS

To fill their sense of emptiness, children use Imitation Love (Chapter 2). It doesn't make them genuinely happy, but it does feel good temporarily and helps them forget the pain of feeling unloved and alone. To get Imitation Love, they use **Getting Behaviors**: lying, attacking, acting like victims, and clinging.

FEAR

Feeling unloved and alone is unbearably painful. In that condition, children are afraid of anything that might add to their pain, and they understandably see the potential for that in virtually every experience. They do many things to protect themselves: lying, attacking, acting like victims, and running — the **Protecting Behaviors**.

HOW EMPTINESS AND FEAR DETERMINE OUR

BEHAVIOR

We'll discuss the individual Getting and Protecting Behaviors below. They include all the behaviors we call "bad," and we need to remember that *our children do these things only because they're empty and afraid.* Their Getting and Protecting Behaviors are not primarily intended to hurt anyone. Contrary to what we often believe, they don't behave badly for the sole purpose of inconveniencing and irritating us. They only use these behaviors to protect themselves and to get the Imitation Love that temporarily makes them feel less unloved and alone. When we believe that fact, our attitude toward our children changes dramatically.

LYING

Lying is both a Getting and a Protecting Behavior. Children don't lie because they're bad. They lie because they don't feel loved. With lies they hope to get people to like them. And they lie to protect themselves from being criticized, ridiculed, spoken to with anger, and otherwise not loved.

Lying as a Protecting Behavior

At an early age, our children discover that when we are inconvenienced, we frown, sigh with disappointment, raise our voices, physically and emotionally pull away from them, etc. They desperately want to avoid the pain of that disapproval, correctly interpreting it as a withdrawal of our acceptance and love. One of the first things they learn to do to protect themselves is to lie.

Three-year-old Kimberley played in her mother's bedroom while eating a peanut butter and jelly sandwich. As she played with one of her mother's dresses, she dropped her sandwich and made quite a stain on the fabric. When her mother came into the room and saw what had happened, she scowled and spoke harshly about her daughter's disobedience and carelessness.

Scenes like this are a daily occurrence with most parents and children. Kimberley's mother thought she was teaching her daughter to be responsible, but Kimberley only learned this lesson: "When I do something my mother doesn't like, she turns into a monster that yells at me and scares me." Teaching the lesson of responsibility was *part* of her mother's motivation, but with her anger Kimberley's mother also selfishly communicated that *she* had been inconvenienced and that Kimberley was "bad." The moment Kimberley sensed her mother's disappointment and anger, she could only feel unloved and alone — and then she learned nothing about responsibility.

A few days later, Kimberley played in her mother's room again, and this time she spilled grape juice on another dress. Eager to avoid what happened the first time, she hid the dress in a closet. And her lie worked: there was no frowning or yelling from her mother.

After several days, her mother found the dress and angrily looked for the offender. On previous occasions, Kimberley had noticed the behavior of her older siblings in similar circumstances. Even when they *were* responsible for a mess or an accident, they had avoided punishment when they responded to their mother's questions by saying, "I don't know. It wasn't me." Kimberley did not want to experience her mother's anger, so she denied responsibility for the stained dress. And her lie was effective — her mother grumbled something under her breath about how it "had to be somebody," but she didn't yell at Kimberley.

Unconsciously, Kimberley learned that with lies she could avoid her mother's disapproval, the thing she feared more than anything else. Almost all children learn the same lesson. We sometimes say to our children – with exaggerated pain in our voice – "How could you lie to me?" If our children had the insight and courage to correctly answer that question, they would say, "Because when I *don't* hide my mistakes, and when I dare to inconvenience you, you're selfish, unloving, and make me feel terrible. I lie to you because you have made the price of telling the truth too high." Every time we're disappointed and angry at our children, we unintentionally teach them to lie and use the other Protecting Behaviors.

We also teach our children to lie by our own example. Whenever we hide our flaws, minimize our mistakes, or make excuses, we're lying — even though in most cases we don't realize we're lying. Following are just a few of the lies that most of us tell every day.

- We're usually lying when we say that traffic made us late. The truth is, we simply prepared poorly and *chose* to do other things until it became impossible to arrive at our destination on time. If a million dollars had been offered as a reward for being on time, would the traffic have "made" us late?

- We lie when we're asked why an assigned task isn't completed and we say we "didn't have time." The truth is, we chose to do the things *we* wanted to do, and we avoided the task that was assigned to us until it became impossible to finish in the allotted time.

- We lie when we want to avoid talking to someone on the phone and instruct our spouse or children to tell the caller that we're not home.

- We lie when we blame other people — including our children — for the mistakes we make instead of taking the responsibility ourselves.

- One of the most common lies we tell is about our anger. How often do we express our anger *at* another person, including our children? We do it with our words, our facial expressions, and with other behaviors. The strong implication, of course, is that the person toward whom we are expressing our anger is the *cause* of our anger. We want that person to know they have *made* us angry. Mostly we imply it silently, but we often come right out and say, "You make me so angry." This is a lie. No one *makes* us angry, and we claim otherwise only because we don't have the courage to admit that we always have a choice. We can always choose to be loving toward someone, no matter what they do, or we can react with anger. We'll talk more about anger being a choice on pp. 100-7. Sometimes we deny our anger by saying that we're only *annoyed*, or *irritated*, or *frustrated*, rather than angry. These are more lies we use to hide our anger.

Most of us lie many times every day, largely unaware that we're doing it. Our children see this and learn to do it themselves.

Lying as a Getting Behavior

It was obvious that Kimberley lied when she denied staining the dress. She used lying as a Protecting Behavior. Other lies can be more subtle. Whenever we do anything to get someone to like us without telling them what we're doing, we're lying. Lying is then a Getting Behavior which is used to obtain Imitation Love in the form of praise, power, and pleasure. We lie a great deal, and it's usually quite unconscious. We're lying when:

we try to think of the "right" things to say in a conversation so that someone will have a favorable impression of us.
we style our hair, dress fashionably, put on make-up, and try to make our bodies look good, all for the purpose of attracting other people to us.
we flatter people insincerely.
we give gifts to people with any expectation of gratitude, affection, or a future favor in return.

These are all lies because we don't tell people that we're trying to win their approval. And we're often not conscious of our own deception. Most of us tell these lies so often that we've come to accept them as normal. Our children follow our example and lie to win *our* approval. It then becomes a habit that they carry with them as they lie to earn the acceptance of other people for the rest of their lives.

As I have talked with people about lying – using the examples above – many of them have said something like this: "Oh come on. That's not really lying. Everybody does those things to create a favorable impression of themselves. That's natural – what's the big deal? What's wrong with it?"

I certainly agree that it's natural. We want people to like us, and if a little deception will help us achieve that goal, we'll do it without hesitation. But it's still lying. We could call it by another name, but it would still be the same. We're not telling the truth. We don't like the word *lying* – and avoid admitting that we lie – because there's usually an implication that lying is intentional and that those who do it are "bad." Contrary to that belief, most lies are told reflexively and unconsciously. That doesn't make them right, but we tell them without thinking, to protect ourselves and to fill our emptiness.

And yes, lying is also very common. From the time we're quite young, we're all told to "put your best foot forward," which is just a fancy way of saying, "Lie, but we won't call it lying. Instead, you'll just be telling *some* of the truth – the truth about the good parts of you. Hide the truth about the rest of you. That wouldn't really be lying. Hide your flaws and show only your assets so that people will like you."

Suppose that a grocer had a bushel of oranges, half good and half rotten. If he put the good oranges on top for the purpose of attracting a buyer, would we say that he was "putting his best foot forward," or would we say that he was lying?

It's understandable that we want to create a good impression.

We want people to like us, and we're willing to do a lot to make that happen. So what's wrong with that? Let me tell you a story.

THE WART KING

Once there was a rich and beautiful kingdom that stretched beyond the horizon in all directions. But the prince of that kingdom was very unhappy. He had warts all over his face, and everywhere he went, people teased him and laughed at him. So he mostly stayed in his room, alone and miserable.

Upon the death of his father, the prince became king and issued a decree that no one — on pain of death — would ever laugh at his warts again. But still he stayed in his room, ashamed and alone. On the rare occasions that he did go out, he put a cloth bag over his head, which covered his warts but also made it difficult for him to see.

After many years, the king heard about a wise man living on the top of a nearby mountain. Hoping the wise man could help him, the king climbed the mountain and found the old man sitting under a tree. Taking the bag off his head, the king said, "I've come for your help."

The wise man looked intently at the king for several long moments and finally said, "You have warts on your face."

The king was enraged. That was not what he'd come to hear. "No, I don't," he screamed. Ashamed and angry, he put the bag back over his head.

"Yes, you do," said the wise man, gently.

"I'll have you killed!" shouted the king.

"Call your guards then," said the wise man.

"My guards aren't here!" shrieked the king helplessly. "I

climbed all the way up this mountain to get your help, and now you tell me I have warts on my face?! How cruel you are!"

Angry and frustrated, the king ran from the wise man, falling repeatedly because he couldn't see very well with the bag on his head. Finally, the king fell down a steep slope and into a lake, where he began to drown. The wise man jumped in, pulled the king to shore, and took the bag from his head so he could breathe.

The king was horrified when he saw the wise man staring at him. "You're laughing at me," said the king.

"Not at all," said the wise man, smiling.

With his eyes fixed on the ground, the king said, "The boys in the village laughed at me."

The old man immediately responded: "I'm not your father or the boys in the village. That must have been hard for you, being laughed at."

"Yes, it was," admitted the king, with tears in his eyes.

"As you can see, I'm not laughing at you," repeated the wise man.

Somehow this did feel different to the king. As he looked into the lake, he saw his reflection. "I really do have a lot of warts."

"I know," said the wise man.

"And you don't find them disgusting?"

"No, and I don't find my own warts disgusting anymore, either."

The king noticed for the first time that the wise man also had warts. "Why do *you* not wear a bag over your head?"

"I used to," replied the old man. "But with the bag on my head, I couldn't see. And I was lonely. So I took it off."

"Didn't people laugh at you?" asked the king.

"Oh sure, some did. And I hated that, like you do. But gradually I found a few people who didn't laugh, and that made me very happy."

The king was thrilled. No one had ever looked at his warts without laughing at him or showing their disgust. "I think I won't wear the bag when you're around."

The wise man smiled. "When you go home, you might even leave the bag here."

The king wondered aloud, "Will I find other people like you, who won't think I'm disgusting?"

The wise man laughed. "Of course you will. And with the love of those people, you won't care when other people laugh."

The king dropped the bag on the ground and went back to his kingdom, which was far more beautiful without the bag on his head. And he did find many people who didn't mind his warts at all. He was very happy.

THE PROCESS OF FEELING LOVED:
TRUTH → SEEN → ACCEPTED → LOVED

Before telling the story of the Wart King, I asked what was wrong with telling "little" lies now and then to get people to like us. Or what is wrong with telling lies to keep people from *not* liking us? It's the same question. The Wart King's experience answers that question. It wasn't the king's warts that made him unhappy; it was his hiding them – lying about them – that made him miserable.

As parents, surely there is nothing we want more than for our children to feel loved and happy. To help them accomplish that, we must understand the importance of telling the truth about themselves. We must help them see the terrible dangers of lying.

When the Wart King was hiding the truth about himself – his warts – he was alone and miserable. He didn't feel like the Wise Man cared about his happiness (**Real Love**) until three things happened:

1. He allowed his warts to be seen (he told the **truth**).
2. He knew the Wise Man actually saw his warts (the king was truly **seen**).
3. The Wise Man **accepted** him *with* his warts.

After the Wart King told the truth about himself, a very simple process led to his feeling loved, as summarized below.

Truth → Seen → Accepted → Loved

When we hide who we are — figuratively wearing bags on our heads — we can only feel alone and miserable, even when people claim to accept who we pretend to be. When we lie, people can only love our lies, not *us*, and *we feel that*. We feel unloved and alone when we hide ourselves. When we tell the **truth** about ourselves, we can finally be **seen** by others as we really are. And then we can feel genuinely **accepted** by people and believe that they actually care about *our* happiness, which is the definition of **Real Love**. In short, we create the opportunity to feel loved when we tell the truth about ourselves, as the Wart King did.

I suggest re-reading the above paragraph. I'll be referring

to the process of feeling loved many times. We must be loved *for who we really are* before we can *feel* genuinely loved. Only when we take the bags off our heads — when we tell the truth about ourselves, especially about our mistakes and flaws — can we find people to accept and love us as the Wise Man did with the Wart King. The effect of such love is miraculous, for our children and for us.

The Wart King and Our Children
Why Children Lie

Almost all of us have loved our children conditionally. We certainly didn't intend to hurt them in any way, but when they didn't do what we expected of them, we were disappointed, and we communicated that to them, mostly unconsciously. The effect was terrible. They heard that we didn't love them, and *they were right.* We did love them as well as we could, but we didn't love them unconditionally, and that's the only kind of love that counts.

Unable to bear the pain of seeing our disappointment and anger, they quickly learned to hide their mistakes. They wore bags on their heads, as the Wart King did. They learned that we expressed our criticism far less when they hid their mistakes and flaws. That's why they lie to us now about their mistakes, as Kimberley did (pp. 34-5). And it works. When they successfully hide their mistakes, we are less disappointed and angry.

Children are terrified that we'll withdraw our affection from them when we see who they really are — with all their warts. Without our love, they're alone, the condition they fear more than any other. Their fear is understandable because on many occasions, we *have* withdrawn our approval when they've inconvenienced and disappointed us, and then they *did* feel unloved and alone.

Unfortunately, hiding — lying — *causes* them to feel alone, the condition they hate most. And unless our children find a source of unconditional love, they will continue to wear bags on their heads for the rest of their lives — like most of us parents do now.

The Cost of Lying

Let's suppose that in a conversation you tell me several flattering things about yourself for the purpose of getting me to like you. That's not difficult to imagine because most of us do exactly that without thinking every day. And let's suppose that your lies are successful, and I indicate in some way that I like you. You might get a brief sense of satisfaction from that, but it's worth nothing because deep inside, you *know* that I don't really see *you*. Even if the things you tell me are true, you know that I only see the small part of you that you have put on display to make me like you. You have "put your best foot forward," and now you have to hide the rest of you — the part that's selfish, angry, and afraid — so I won't see who you really are. Under those conditions, you can't possibly feel genuinely accepted by me, even if I express positive feelings about you – even if I love you unconditionally. You're alone. Your lies make it impossible for you to feel truly loved.

Truth → Seen → Accepted → Loved. Real Love can only begin with telling the truth about ourselves. When you lie to me, the immediate and disastrous consequence is that you're alone, the worst condition of all for a human being. Every time we lie, we feel separated from people and alone. Our children pay the same price. *That* is why lying is so bad for a child — because it makes *them* feel unloved and alone. As parents, we selfishly feel personally offended when our children lie to us. We fail to see the terrible effect that it has on *them*.

Kimberley's lie (pp. 34-5) kept her mother from being angry at her. But Kimberley knew what would have happened if her mother *had* learned the truth: she would have experienced a great deal of disapproval and pain. So Kimberley knew she was not unconditionally accepted and therefore *felt* unloved anyway. Although her lie prevented a real attack, she still *felt* the crushing disapproval of her mother, as though her mother had actually found out the truth about her "crime" and punished her.

It's tragically ironic that when our children lie to keep us from not loving them, they make it impossible to feel genuinely loved. Their lies make them feel safe temporarily, but then we can't see who they are, leaving them feeling unloved and alone, the most painful condition of all. The Wart King discovered that. He achieved a superficial safety by hiding his warts (lying), but then he felt unloved and alone because he knew what would happen if people saw him without the bag on his head. He knew he was not loved unconditionally, and that's all that really matters.

OUR BLINDNESS

Truth → Seen → Accepted   → Loved. It is essential that our children tell the truth about themselves. But the next step is just as important. *We* must be able to see them clearly. We can only do that when we see who they really are, not just who we want them to be or who they pretend to be. If we don't feel unconditionally loved ourselves, we can only be empty and afraid. In that condition, we can't see our children or anyone clearly. We can only see what they can do **for** us (because of our desperate need for love) or what they might do **to** us (because of our fear of being unloved and hurt). Emptiness and fear, which come from an absence of Real Love, make us blind to our children. And then they can't feel loved by us. When we don't feel unconditionally loved ourselves, we *cannot* be loving or effective parents.

PARENTS AS WISE MEN

We have the opportunity to change our children's lives. We can learn to become wise men and women for them. We can learn to accept and love them as the Wise Man did for the Wart King. It's not difficult or complicated. But it's also not just a technique or a collection of words. It involves a real change of heart on our part, a change in who we are. When we take the steps necessary to feel unconditionally loved ourselves (Chapter 5), our emptiness and fear disappear. We can then start accepting and loving our children (Chapter 9).

As our children begin to feel our love for them, they feel safe enough to throw away the bags on their heads and share with us who they really are. And then they can truly feel loved by us. We'll discuss how we can become more loving, and how we can teach our children to be more loving, throughout the remainder of the book.

When I talk about loving our children, I re-emphasize that I am not advocating permissive parenting. When we love our children, we are not giving them whatever they want. We are not allowing them to "get away" with anything. Real Love means caring about their happiness, which means teaching them to be truthful, responsible, and loving. That certainly eliminates permissiveness. In the example of Kimberley, for instance, I would certainly not recommend that her mother ignore Kimberley's irresponsible behavior. Kimberley has to be taught that what she did was wrong, but she has to be taught without disappointment or anger.

Starting with Chapter 11, I'll talk in much greater detail about how to *teach* and correct our children. At this point, I'll be concentrating more on *loving* them simply because they must have their primary need to feel loved first. If they don't have Real Love, emptiness and fear rule their lives. They constantly use Getting and Protecting Behaviors to fill their emptiness and protect themselves from pain. In that condition, they can't hear what we're trying to teach them.

ATTACKING

Attacking is any behavior which motivates people with *fear* to do something we want. Anger, criticism, withdrawal of approval, intimidation, sarcasm, guilt, and using authority and power are all forms of attacking. We attack when we're afraid, hoping to scare people away who might hurt us. Attacking is then a Protecting Behavior. We also use attacking as a Getting Behavior, to manipulate people to give us what we want when we feel unloved and empty. The most common form of attacking is anger.

Anger

When Mike was a baby, everything he did — his first step, his first word, etc. — was the subject of endless praise and admiration. He was too cute for words, and he loved the attention he received. But then Mike's younger sister was born, and he discovered that he wasn't nearly as cute as he used to be. Suddenly, his sister was getting all the attention, and he didn't know what to do about that.

And then at about the age of two, Mike discovered something useful. One day when he was being told to do something he didn't want to do, he dug in his heels and shouted, "No!" In an instant, he got a great deal of attention from his parents, more than he'd received in some time. On another occasion, when he didn't get something he wanted, he furiously demanded it — and his mother gave in to his demands, after spending quite a bit of time discussing the matter with him. He repeated these behaviors often, and his parents were utterly baffled by the change in this child who had once been their little darling. There was nothing mysterious about his transformation. Mike hadn't become a little devil. He had simply learned that anger is a powerful tool, and he continued to use it simply because *it worked*. Two-year-olds are not malicious, just practical.

Mike continued to use anger to protect himself and to get what he wanted for the rest of his life. Why wouldn't he? We all tend to do what works. Mike used anger with his classmates and became the class bully. With time, he refined his techniques and became an aggressive and successful businessman. He intimidated his employees, who scurried to obey his every command. His competitors both admired and feared him. His wife and children were afraid of him, although they wouldn't have used that word openly to describe their feelings toward him. He got whatever he wanted from people because they were afraid of his disapproval and anger. But he was alone. People will do things to please an angry man, but they don't want to be around him. He was on two blood pressure medications and on the verge of his second heart attack. Mike was not a happy man.

Why Our Children Get Angry

We must understand that our children get angry only because they don't feel loved. They get angry to protect themselves and to get Imitation Love in the form of praise and power. They discover at an early age that when they're angry, they don't feel as empty and helpless, two feelings they hate. When they're angry, they can also get people to do things for them and to stop hurting them. Watch how adults move and do things for a child who is pitching a fit. Children certainly notice that, and that's why they throw those tantrums. Children who feel unconditionally loved and genuinely happy have no *need* to get angry. With Real Love, anger simply has no purpose.

Our Response to The Anger of Our Children

If we don't already feel unconditionally loved ourselves — as most of us don't — we become afraid when a child is angry and defiant. What are we afraid of?

1. We're afraid of losing control over them. Without sufficient Real Love, we enjoy the sense of power we get from

influencing or determining what our children do. That's not a pretty thing to see about ourselves, but it's still true.

2. We're afraid of losing their respect (another form of power and also praise).
3. We're afraid of losing their approval and affection (praise).
4. We're afraid of looking like bad parents — to our children and others (praise).
5. We're afraid of losing the peace and quiet we enjoy (pleasure and safety). We hate the simple inconvenience that always accompanies an angry child. We have to *deal* with their anger, which usually isn't easy or fun.

In other words, when our children are angry, we're afraid of losing the Imitation Love we get from them, a "love" we have no right to demand (Chapter 6). And then we respond with our own Protecting Behaviors:

1. We attack them with *our* anger.
2. We become offended and act like victims (pp. 51-4).
3. We avoid them, which is a form of running (p. 55).
4. We ignore them when they're angry. We just deny the fact that they're angry, which means we're using the Protecting Behavior of lying.

When we manipulate our children in any way that makes them afraid, we're attacking them. We do that a lot, using anger, intimidation, and guilt. When a child defends himself with angry words, we commonly react in a threatening way, using our voice, facial expression, and physical posture. We commonly fail to appreciate that almost anything we do can be perceived by a child as intimidating. We can crush a child with a word or a frown. We often say something like, "Don't you talk to me like that." What we mean is this: "I'm your parent and you must therefore respect me and not do anything that confuses or frightens me." And we imply there will be a punishment if they don't do as we wish. We intimidate them with our authority and make them feel guilty for not making us happy. We attack our children quite often.

Sometimes our attacks do get us some of the things we want. We can get instant attention and obedience. But the price is high. The whole reason our children attack us in the first place is that they feel alone and afraid. When we respond by threatening them with our authority, anger, and disapproval — often without words — they feel even more unloved and alone, the worst thing we can do to them. And we give them greater reason to protect themselves with anger. In short, we make things much worse when we protect ourselves.

CAN WE CHANGE?

It is never necessary to be angry at a child. That sounds impossibly idealistic to some people, but only because they haven't seen children raised without anger. When we don't feel loved ourselves and don't know another way to teach children, we can't avoid becoming afraid when they're angry. And then anger becomes natural, almost unavoidable.

Most of us have never seen an example of children being unconditionally loved and taught. How can we do what we've never seen? In the absence of such an example, we're afraid that if we don't intimidate them when they're angry and rebellious, they'll continue being angry and will inconvenience us, hurt us, or make us look bad. We also have some genuine concern that they'll hurt themselves. So we get angry and control our children, doing what we've seen everyone around us do all our lives.

In Chapters 9 and 20, I'll discuss specifically how to respond to an angry child, but the important thing to know is that everything changes for us as parents when we feel unconditionally loved ourselves. This is not a fairy tale. As I learned to unconditionally love my children, their arguments stopped. One of my daughter's high school teachers asked each student in the class how their family handled conflicts. My daughter replied, "We don't have any conflicts." The teacher didn't believe her and asked more about it. My daughter explained how powerful it was for her and her siblings to feel unconditionally loved by their parents. She said that when she felt loved, everything else seemed pretty insignificant, and there was nothing worth fighting about.

When children have what they need most, they're not empty and afraid. Anger is a reaction to emptiness and fear, and when those conditions don't exist, anger has no *purpose*. It then naturally disappears. In Chapter 5 we'll address how we can find Real Love for ourselves as parents.

ACTING LIKE A VICTIM

If I appear pathetic and helpless enough, I can attract your sympathy and accomplish two things: you might not hurt me (protecting) and you might give me what I want (getting).

Victims work with three tools:

"Look at what you — or someone — did **to** me." (protecting)
"Look at what you — or someone — should have done **for** me." (getting)
"It's not my fault." (irresponsibility)

To a victim, everything is unfair. He believes people should do things for him and should never inconvenience him. He makes other people feel responsible to make him happy, using expectations, demands, and guilt. His favorite words are "but" and "should." Children who act like victims are spoiled, irresponsible, and lazy.

In our society, people act like victims so commonly that we have come to accept it as normal. We must be able to identify this behavior, or we'll be unable to do anything about it. Following are some examples of children acting like victims.

We talk to them about a mistake and they say, "I couldn't help it." They're claiming to be victims of circumstance or of the actions of other people. They're claiming to be helpless victims who had no responsibility for their own choices. That is rarely true.

We tell them they can't buy something and they say, "But all my friends have one; it's not fair." They're claiming to be victimized by us in the hope that we'll feel obligated to eliminate this grave injustice that has been done to them and will then give them what they want.

We tell them they can't go somewhere and they counter with, "But everybody else is going."

We tell them they can't do something and they get that pathetic look on their face as they say, "please." They're telling us that if they don't get what they want, *we* are unbelievably selfish and have treated them badly.

We ask why an assigned task isn't done and they say, "There wasn't time." Victims claim that nothing is ever their fault. And if we dare to claim otherwise, we are insensitive and unkind. If we push the victim to accept responsibility for his behavior, he makes us feel guilty for hurting him, making him even more victimized.

Children who act hurt and who sulk are acting like victims. They have learned that the more wounded they appear, the less likely we are to punish them and the more likely they are to get what they want and to get away with unacceptable behavior.

Children often choose to wait till the last minute to study for a test in school. Then when they're poorly prepared and get a bad grade, they blame the teacher for giving a "hard" or "unfair" test. They falsely portray themselves as victims.

We teach our children to be victims by allowing them to manipulate us and by setting the example of victimhood ourselves.

Allowing Victimhood

One day I watched a toddler trip and fall as he ran. His outstretched hands made a loud noise on the floor, but he wasn't hurt. He looked around to see if someone was watching, and when he saw his mother, he burst into tears. She rushed over, picked him up, and made quite a fuss over him.

Minutes later, the same child fell again. As before, he looked around for a possible source of attention, but this time he saw no one. Without a sound, he got up and continued running.

We don't intend to do it, but we encourage our children to be victims when we give them sympathy and rescue them instead of satisfying their real need for acceptance and guidance. They use victimhood as a Getting Behavior, and then we tend to give them what they *want* instead of what they *need*. Pages 311-12 describe how a parent could handle the above situation in a way that a child is not encouraged to act like a victim.

Years ago, my ten-year-old daughter spent the night with a friend. She called me at 10:30 p.m. to get permission to go to a party, but I said it was too late. In the background, I heard her friend say, "Have a tantrum. Beg."

My daughter smiled and said, "That doesn't work in our family."

Children learn to act like victims — by whining and making us feel guilty — because they've seen that we're then more likely to give them what they want. My daughter's friend often did that, and because of it, her parents gave her what she wanted. When we reward that kind of behavior, we teach them to be victims.

Children also use victimhood as a Protecting Behavior. When they make mistakes and say they "couldn't help it," they make other people and things responsible for their poor choices. They do that to protect themselves from our disapproval. When we allow them to make those excuses, we encourage them to be victims. Children who are loved and taught to be responsible don't need to act like victims to protect themselves and to get what they want (Chapter 14).

Acting Like Victims Ourselves

Children learn to act like victims by watching us. When a child behaves in a way we don't like, we commonly say something like, "I'm disappointed in you," or "How could you do such a thing?" Or perhaps more often, we indicate our disappointment without words. We silently spear the child with a disgusted expression. We act like they've hurt us so they'll feel guilty and be more likely to do what we want and not do the things we disapprove of. The message we communicate to our children is this: "How could you possibly do this **to me!!**" Without realizing it, we are acting like enormous victims with our own children, making them responsible for our happiness.

In the presence of our children we whine and complain about many things: the boss, our co-workers, our spouse, the government, the neighbors, and so on. We blame other people for being monsters that treat us unfairly instead of being responsible ourselves for how we feel and behave. Our children see us do that and thereby learn to act like victims themselves — especially with us. When they don't get what they want from us, they sulk, cry, beg, and act wounded, all to create the image that we've treated them unfairly. They hope we'll then feel an obligation to give them what we've cruelly withheld — and it often works.

The Cost of Being a Victim

A spoiled, complaining child is not happy, even when he gets what he demands. He doesn't feel the happiness that only unconditional love can provide. Children who act like victims can manipulate us and others for attention and safety, but they still feel unloved and alone. In Chapter 21, we'll talk about how to respond to such children.

RUNNING

If we simply move away from a source of pain, we're less likely to be hurt. Withdrawing, avoiding people, leaving relationships, and being shy are all forms of running. So are drugs and alcohol.

Children most commonly run from their parents by simply avoiding them. How many teenagers come home from school and look for us so they can get a hug and have a conversation? Not many. They tend to stay away from us, and that's only because we don't give them the love they need. We give them disapproval and criticism instead. When we do that, they avoid us, which is the Protecting Behavior of running.

Running is an effective form of protection, but the runner is always alone. As we learn to love our children, they lose the need to run from us (Chapters 9 and 22). Children naturally want to be with the people who make them feel loved.

CLINGING

Clinging is a Getting Behavior. We see it in a young child who can't stand to be out of his mother's sight, clinging tightly to her leg. That can be healthy at an early age, but many of us encourage our children to continue clinging to us emotionally far longer than is appropriate. We enjoy being indispensable in their lives. But such children don't become independent and happy human beings. We'll talk more about clinging in Chapter 22.

*****

AGAIN, IT'S ALL ABOUT LOVE

Allow me to summarize what we've discussed thus far in the first three chapters. Without Real Love from us, our children feel empty and afraid of not being loved. And then they use Getting and Protecting Behaviors to get Imitation Love and protect themselves from more pain. We see these behaviors every day:

when they argue with us or their siblings (attacking);
when they avoid us (running);
when they worry about earning the approval of friends with their choice of clothes, hair, and behavior (lying);
when they watch television all day (running);
when they make excuses about how they "couldn't help it" (victim);
when they use drugs and alcohol (running);
when they hide their mistakes (lying);
when they complain about what they don't have (victim); and
when they get frustrated and irritated at the little things that happen around them (attacking).

With these Getting and Protecting Behaviors, they purchase praise, power, pleasure, and safety. They get a brief sense of connection to the people who give them those things, and they temporarily feel less helpless and alone. But they still don't feel unconditionally loved, and they can't be genuinely happy.

THE PRICE OF ALL GETTING AND PROTECTING

Despite the temporary relief we get from Getting and Protecting Behaviors, the overall effect is disastrous. Those behaviors actually make it impossible for us to feel loved.

It's Real Love when someone cares about *my* happiness without any concern for what *they* might get. It's Real Love when I care about someone else's happiness with no thought for my own reward. Real Love is always a gift freely given and freely received. It's a genuine caring that cannot be manipulated, traded, or forced. When we do *anything* to get people to like us (Getting Behaviors) or to hurt us less (Protecting Behaviors), what we receive is not freely offered and can only be Imitation Love.

Without Real Love, it's natural that we manipulate people to get attention, praise, and power. We briefly feel better when we get those things, but the moment we reach out in any way to get something from another person, we ruin any possibility of receiving a true gift from them.

Allow me to borrow a metaphor from *Real Love—The Truth About Finding Unconditional Love and Fulfilling Relationships*:

Imagine that you see me walking toward your house with a bushel of apples. Eager to have some for yourself, you hurry out and say to me, "I haven't had a bite to eat all day (**lie**), and nobody will give me anything (**victim**)."

Me: "But . . ."

You: (interrupting me) "And I hope you remember all the things I've done for you in the past (**attacking** me with guilt)."

I then give you the apples without you knowing that I had picked them for *you* and was bringing them to you as a gift.

Now imagine a different scene, where I suddenly appear in your doorway with a bushel of apples and say, "I picked these for you, and I hope you enjoy them." You had no expectation that I was coming, and it's clear from my behavior that I expect nothing from you in return.

Although you received the apples in both scenes, you felt very differently about them on each occasion. In the first scene, you lied, acted like a victim, and attacked me (Getting Behaviors) before I could offer you my gift. The apples still tasted good, but you could not *feel loved* because you knew that *you had manipulated me* to get them. Real Love can only be felt when it's freely offered *and* freely received. Although I offered my gift freely, you did not receive it freely. In effect, you *bought* the apples with your behavior — by acting like a victim and attacking me — just like you'd paid for them with money. Because of what you did, what I gave you could not *feel* like a gift. In the second scene, however, you were touched by my gift, which was freely given and received.

When we do *anything* to manipulate attention, approval, praise, sex, and so on, from another person, whatever they give us can't feel like a gift, and we will not feel unconditionally loved. When we receive something after manipulating someone for it, we can only feel as though we *paid* for it with our manipulation. Even when a gift *is* freely given to us, it *feels* purchased when we use Getting and Protecting Behaviors. With manipulation, we transform any possibility of Real Love into Imitation Love, like turning gold into lead. Most of us have been lying, attacking, and running — filling our lives with Imitation Love — for so long that we don't even recognize when we do those things.

And now we understand the real reason why it's so bad when our children engage in any of the Getting and Protecting Behaviors. Sure, it's inconvenient and frustrating for us when our children lie, get angry, act like victims, etc. But that's not the real disadvantage of those behaviors. When our children use Getting and Protecting Behaviors, they make it impossible to feel unconditionally loved. They walk a path that takes them away from genuine happiness. We can and must learn to respond productively when they engage in those behaviors, or we cannot help our children to be happy. We'll discuss how to respond to each behavior in Chapters 18-22.

Unintentionally, we actually motivate our children to use Getting and Protecting Behaviors. By loving our children more when they're "good," and withdrawing our approval when they're "bad," we encourage them to respond to us – and manipulate us – with getting and protecting. They do whatever it takes to *get* more of our "love" and *protect* themselves from our disapproval. And then they can't feel *unconditionally* loved — only empty, afraid, and unhappy. We don't mean to do this, but we nonetheless teach them well, and they continue this pattern with everyone else in their lives.

CHOICE

We're not helpless. We choose to use Getting and Protecting Behaviors, and we teach those behaviors to our children. Whatever we choose, we can learn to choose differently. As we learn to feel loved ourselves, we can eliminate Getting and Protecting Behaviors in our own lives and can teach our children to do the same.

Chapter Summary

Without Real Love, children can only feel empty and afraid. To fill their emptiness, they use Getting Behaviors — lying, attacking, acting like victims, and clinging — to obtain Imitation Love. To eliminate their fear, they use Protecting Behaviors: lying, attacking, acting like victims, and running. With those behaviors, they temporarily feel less alone and powerless, but they don't feel loved.

We also use Getting and Protecting Behaviors with our children, which only makes our children feel more empty and afraid.

Chapter 4

It's Not All Your Fault

It's obvious that if our children don't feel loved, *we* are responsible for that. Who else could be? We're the only people who have been with them from the beginning. And even if we could blame someone else—as I described on pp. 12-13—what good would that do? We simply must take responsibility for the emptiness, the fear, and the Getting and Protecting Behaviors in our children's lives. It's the only reasonable and effective thing to do.

However, we don't need to wallow in guilt about this. We don't intentionally withhold love from our children. I've never met a parent who got up in the morning and thought, "Today I could unconditionally love and teach my children and fill their lives with joy. But no, I think I'll be selfish, critical, and demanding instead." What an absurd notion.

WE CAN'T GIVE WHAT WE NEVER GOT

The only reason we don't unconditionally love our children is that we were not unconditionally loved ourselves. We can't give what we never got. We introduced this subject briefly on pp. 11-12.

Many of us sincerely believe that we *were* unconditionally loved as children, but the evidence rarely supports that belief.

Karen came to me in a state of utter frustration about her children. They were angry, rebellious, and no longer listened to a word she said. With tears running down her cheeks, she said she had no idea what to do with them. I explained to Karen that her children were reacting to a lack of Real Love in their lives, but I emphasized that I understood that Karen was doing the best she could. She had failed to love her children because she had never been unconditionally loved herself. Karen was astonished.

Karen: "But both my parents loved me very much."

Me: "There's no doubt in my mind that your parents loved you as well as they could. We're not here to criticize your parents, but we are here to look at what made *you* the kind of parent you are now. So let's do that, without trying to make anyone look good or bad.

"How often did your father hold you and tell you he loved you? How many times each day was he obviously delighted when you entered the room? How often did your mother sit with you and ask what was happening in your life — just to listen, not to give advice?"

Karen was speechless. Although she was raised by parents as good as any she knew, she couldn't think of a single time when any of those things had happened.

Me: "More important, what happened when you made mistakes and disappointed your parents? Did you feel just as loved then as when you were 'good' and did what they wanted?"

As Karen described the details of her childhood, it was obvious that she had been loved conditionally. Her parents were kind when Karen was obedient, but they were critical and harsh when Karen misbehaved. Karen realized that she had never been corrected and loved at the same time.

There were many other evidences in Karen's life that she had not been loved unconditionally. She often argued with her husband over little things (attacking). She withdrew from conversations and relationships that she found stressful (running). She easily became angry at other drivers in traffic (attacking). She acted like a victim when people confronted her about mistakes she made. All those Getting and Protecting Behaviors were absolute proof that Karen did not feel unconditionally loved. People who feel loved don't use those behaviors.

Does Karen sound familiar? She should. Most of us are just like her. When we don't feel unconditionally loved, we engage in the same Getting and Protecting Behaviors that she did.

BLAMING OUR PARENTS VS. UNDERSTANDING OUR PAST

"In our emotional development as children, there was nothing more important than a supply of Real Love. Without it, we were guaranteed to become empty, frightened, and unhappy adults — and deficient parents. While it's useful to *understand* that our parents were responsible for loving us as children, and are therefore responsible for a great deal of how we function now, it's very unproductive to *blame* them if we're unhappy now. *Understanding* is a simple assessment of how things are, while *blaming* is an angry attitude that can only be harmful to us and to others." (*Real Love—The Truth About Finding Unconditional Love and Fulfilling Relationships*)

Although our parents had an enormous impact on our lives, *we* must take responsibility for the choices we make now. Continued resentment and anger will not help us make wise decisions in the present. In addition, blaming our parents is especially inappropriate when we understand that *they gave us the best they had*. Our parents loved us as well as they could. If they failed to give us the Real Love we needed, it was only because they didn't have it to give. If *they* weren't unconditionally loved, they couldn't possibly have given us the Real Love we required.

CHOICES

Years ago, I asked my oldest son, Jonathan, to clean the garage. He was about ten years old at the time. When he hadn't done it after two requests, I angrily confronted him and yelled at him. "How many times have I told you about that garage?" I ranted. And I physically leaned over him and intimidated him as I delivered my hateful lecture, watching him cower and shrink within himself as the emotional beating continued.

If I had hit Jonathan with my fists, I couldn't have injured him much worse. As I've said before, we must take responsibility for what we've done as parents – not for the purpose of feeling guilty – but so we can make different decisions and can now help our children. What I said and did to Jonathan on this occasion was terribly hurtful, and this episode was only one of many like it. And yet, with what I knew then, I could not have chosen to behave much differently with him. I could not have chosen to be loving with Jonathan because at that time I didn't feel unconditionally loved myself. We simply cannot give what we don't have ourselves.

As I learned how to find Real Love for myself (Chapter 5), my life changed dramatically. Years after that experience with Jonathan, I asked my youngest son, Benjamin, to clean off the driveway. Busy with the scholastic and social affairs of high school, he ignored two such requests. One day when he came home from school, I got up from my desk and met him in the kitchen. I threw my arms around him and told him how glad I was to see him. We talked about what he had learned at school that day and discussed his plans for the rest of the evening. After several minutes, I told him that I needed him to make cleaning off the driveway his first priority, and I asked him if he needed any help getting that done. He broke into a huge smile and said: "No, Dad, I don't need any help. I've been putting that job off for several days. I was hoping you wouldn't have to remind me about it again. I'll go and do it right now."

Do you remember how you felt on pp. 9-10 when you planted the bushes all wrong and I came to help you fix them up without caring about your mistake? That's how Benjamin felt when I reminded him of the job he hadn't done. He could *feel* that I was not angry at him. He *knew* that I loved him.

We can't make choices we've never seen. When we feel empty and afraid, we choose the only reactions we know — usually Getting and Protecting Behaviors. That's what I did with Jonathan. When our children behave badly or inconvenience us, we often don't know *how* to unconditionally love and teach them. Most of us have never seen anyone do that.

The purpose of this book is to provide additional choices that are far more effective than the ones we've used all our lives. We can all learn to love and teach our children instead of protecting ourselves and making them feel alone and unhappy. That's what I eventually learned to do with Benjamin.

Chapter Summary

Every time we're disappointed or angry with our children, we communicate our own lack of Real Love, and that causes emptiness and fear in children. We don't give Real Love because we didn't get it ourselves and therefore have none to give.

Chapter 5

Finding Love for Ourselves
Before We Try to Give It to Our Children

When we unconditionally accept and teach our children, they learn, grow, and become happy despite all the other mistakes we make with them. With Real Love, being a great parent is simple. Without it, nothing else we do really matters.

GETTING REAL LOVE

We all *want* to love our children, but if we've never been given Real Love ourselves, we *can't* give it to them, no matter how much we wish to. We can't give what we don't have .

Parenting is not a technique. We can't raise responsible and happy children by learning clever words or psychological methods. *We must find Real Love for ourselves* before we can give our children what they need most. I can't emphasize this too strongly. Fortunately, we can all learn to find Real Love.

There are four steps to finding unconditional love:

(1) the desire to change;
(2) faith;
(3) telling the truth about ourselves; and
(4) giving up the Getting and Protecting Behaviors.

1. THE DESIRE TO CHANGE

Although we *say* we want to be better parents, most of us demonstrate with our behavior that what we really want is to change our *children* and make them more grateful, obedient, successful, and convenient. That's a selfish and short-sighted desire. Our children can't be all those things until they feel more loved — and that is *our* responsibility. We must find Real Love for ourselves and then share it with them. It's our desire to change *ourselves* that starts that process.

George's parents praised him when he was good, but they were disappointed and critical toward him when he was bad. Naturally, he learned to do the things that earned him praise and approval, and he continued to do those things all his life. As an adult, he worked hard at his job, made a good living, and received the respect and admiration of those around him. But he was not genuinely happy. Every bit of attention or affection he received was purchased with his good behavior, and though he wasn't consciously aware of that, he still didn't feel loved unconditionally. Because of the lack of Real Love in his own life, he was unable to unconditionally love his wife or children. He couldn't give what he didn't have.

George was pleased with his children when they did what he wanted, but he was disappointed and impatient when they were irresponsible or otherwise inconvenient. And he tried to make them successful like himself. There's nothing wrong with achievement, but without Real Love, it's worthless, and George's children were becoming miserable as he criticized them and pushed them toward success. George's son Dan especially resented being controlled and criticized. He increasingly avoided his father and began to get in trouble at school and elsewhere.

George tried everything he could think of to change Dan's behavior, but it only got worse, along with their relationship. George came to see me and explained some of Dan's problems.

George: "What am I supposed to do with this kid?"

Me: "Your son is not the problem."

George: "Then what is?"

Me: "You are."

George: "What?!"

Me: "He's just a boy. You're the father. It's always our responsibility as parents to raise our children, and when things go badly, the problem lies with us, not them. If you're willing to accept that responsibility and make changes in yourself, you may be able to start helping your son. But if you're not willing to change *you*, there won't be anything you can do to help him."

I explained that both he and his son were unhappy because they didn't feel unconditionally loved. There was no blaming in any of this, but George had the sole responsibility of starting the process of changing, not his son.

George was committed to do whatever was necessary to help his son. He had a real desire to change. And he subsequently proved that by taking the other three steps toward finding Real Love and changing his life (below).

We all want our children to be happy and responsible. But do we want that enough to change our own lives? Until we want to change *ourselves* — and not our children — our desire to be better parents is empty talk, and there is little we can do to help our children.

2. FAITH

When we only trust what we know for certain, we stay just like we are. Faith is the act of consciously choosing to experience what we don't know. That exposes us to possible danger, but it also creates the opportunity to learn and grow. Only with faith can we find Real Love and genuine happiness.

Review the story of the Wart King on pp. 39-41 and re-read the section about Truth → Seen → Accepted → Loved on pp. 41-2. The Wart King exercised faith when he left the bag off his head as he continued to talk with the Wise Man. He chose to expose himself to an experience that was uncertain. Although he had been hurt many times in the past under similar conditions, he chose to trust the Wise Man to give him a different experience. Similarly, our lives cannot change until we have faith that we can find Real Love as we tell the truth about ourselves.

3. TELLING THE TRUTH ABOUT OURSELVES

Like the Wart King, we hide ourselves — we lie — because we learned at an early age that people often found us unacceptable when they learned the truth about our flaws and mistakes. They criticized us, laughed at us, punished us, and avoided us. When we lied, we briefly felt safer — but then we always felt unloved and alone.

Truth → Seen → Accepted → Loved. The Wart King took the bag off his head and exposed the **truth** about himself to the Wise Man. Only then could he be truly **seen** and feel **accepted** and **loved** by the Wise Man.

It works the same for each of us. When you tell me the truth about you, including your flaws and mistakes, that can be frightening because you create the opportunity for me to dislike you. But you also create the opportunity for me to see you, to know who you really are. Only then can you feel like I genuinely accept and love *you*. If you lie to protect yourself, you make all that impossible — you're hidden and I can't see you. You can never feel that I love *you* when all I see is your lies.

George made a decision to take the bag off his head. He took a leap of faith (step 2, above). As we talked about Real Love and about George's life, he learned some important things, and he *talked* about them.

George: "I can't believe this. I came here thinking that my son was the problem, but that's not true. He's just been reacting to my not loving him. I'm embarrassed."

This was big moment for George. He had always worked very hard to look good to everyone around him, which involved hiding his mistakes. But here he admitted that *he* was the problem in his relationship with his son. He went on and talked about his feeling of embarrassment, which is as close as most men will come to saying, "I am afraid." George was saying that he was afraid of being seen as a failure as a father and as a human being. That took real courage.

Me: "There's nothing for you to feel guilty or ashamed about. You did the best you could. You didn't feel loved yourself and couldn't have done any better with what you had at the time. You're right that you didn't love your son unconditionally, but what matters now is that you had the courage to tell the truth about that – very few men can do that. Now that you see the truth, you can *do something* about it and help your son. That's what really matters, isn't it?"

George didn't need me to throw my arms around him and tell him I loved him. He just needed to feel accepted. He only needed to hear that he wasn't disgusting for having made a mistake. The whole reason we lie and hide our mistakes is that we live in terror that people will be revolted and horrified by us when they learn about our flaws. We must tell the truth about ourselves and find people who will show us that they won't be.

Truth → Seen → Accepted → Loved

Each time we tell the truth about ourselves, we create the opportunity for that miraculous healing process to happen.

Me: "What else have you learned about yourself?"

George: "I haven't loved my other children, either — or my wife. When they haven't done what I wanted, or when they've been inconvenient or gotten in my way, I've been critical and angry and really hurt their feelings. I feel bad about that. And when you were talking about Imitation Love a few minutes ago, I realized that I've filled my whole life with that — money, power, the praise of other people, sex. My life's a mess, isn't it?"

Me: "How do you feel right now?

George: "I feel stupid, like I've wasted my life. But I feel relieved, too, like I finally see what I've been doing wrong all these years. And I'm amazed that you see all this about me and you don't seem to think any less of me. I don't think anyone has ever talked to me about a mistake of mine without being disappointed or saying something critical. I know I've never had a conversation like this."

It is no exaggeration to say that George's entire life began to gradually change after that single conversation. A year later, George and I talked over dinner.

George: "Do you remember when I first talked to you about my problems with Dan?"

Me: "Sure."

George: "I really hated it when you told me that *I* was the problem."

Me: "I understand. I didn't like it much when I saw that I was the whole problem in my own family, either."

George: "I didn't like seeing the truth about myself. I had always managed to hide that from everyone — even from myself. I was really afraid that day to keep talking to you. I almost got up and left."

Me: (laughing) "I think I understand that feeling."

George: "But I'm glad I didn't. And you know how that feels, too. Look at my life now. I used to be angry all the time. I yelled at people in traffic. I was a terror at work. My children avoided me. I didn't even know how much my wife avoided me — she never dared to talk to me about it. My marriage is happier now than I ever thought it could be. Dan doesn't walk into the next room when he sees me. In fact, we talk a lot. My whole life is different."

I did not change George's life. I'm not indispensable. Unconditional love changed his life as he told the truth about himself to me and later to many other people. Real Love has a powerful effect. As George began to feel accepted for who he really was, he gradually lost the emptiness and fear that had always caused him to react badly to his son's behavior — and to other people. He began to see and accept his son for the first time. Before feeling loved himself, he could only see what his son should or should not do to make *him* happy.

I have seen this happen hundreds of times. When we follow the steps to find Real Love, the results are predictable. We can all find unconditional love. As we take the bags off our heads and allow people to see who we really are, we create the opportunity for them to accept and love us. And then we find the love and happiness we have searched for all our lives. It starts with such a simple act: telling the truth.

Tell the Truth to Whom—Wise Men and Women

To feel loved, we must find people capable of seeing and accepting us — especially with our imperfections — people who won't run away in disgust when they see who we really are and won't manipulate us for what they want. We don't need someone who is perfectly loving, just someone capable of seeing us clearly and accepting us for moments at a time. That's what the Wise Man did for the Wart King.

People who don't feel loved are *empty* and *afraid*. That makes them blind to us, because they can't see us as we really are. They can only see what we can do **for** them or **to** them. A wise man (or woman) is someone who feels loved enough — even temporarily — that he's not blinded by his own emptiness and fears. He can then see people clearly instead of only seeing what he wants from them and what they could do to hurt him. We'll be referring to wise men frequently in this book. A wise man is anyone who is capable of accepting and loving us when he (or she) sees the truth about us.

Where do we find them?

Fortunately, we can all find these loving men and women who will change our lives. We don't need to go to the top of a mountain, as the Wart King did. We don't need to attend expensive seminars run by impressive institutes and special motivational speakers. We rarely need professional therapy. Wise men and women are all around us, and to find them we only need to tell the truth about ourselves. Wise men are irresistibly attracted to the truth. *Tell the truth and they will find us.*

What do we say to find these people? What words do we use? It's not complicated, but it is different from what we're used to. We talk to people all the time, but we tend to talk about nothing. We talk about the weather, shopping, cars, money, and events — things that don't really matter very much. Sometimes we talk about our feelings, but we don't do it in a truthful and useful way. For example, we might say that we're angry, but then we blame that on someone else, which helps no one. We need to learn to tell the truth about ourselves in a way that will change our lives.

I suggest that you make a commitment to try something different in the near future with a friend that you trust. Take a chance and allow that friend to see who you really are, as George did with me in our conversations above. The reward can be astonishing. Say the kind of straight-forward things that George did. Following are a few examples of some additional things you could say:

"My son has had a terrible attitude about a lot of things for a long time: school, his chores around the house, the family. And I've really been leaning on him to change all that — restricting him, getting mad at him, stuff like that. Now I'm beginning to see that his attitude is *my* fault. All he ever wanted was for me to love him no matter what, and I haven't done that. When he screws up, I get irritated at him, and then he can see that I *don't* love him unconditionally. I didn't understand until now how much that has hurt him. I thought I was a much better father than I really have been."

"My wife did something last night that I didn't like, and I got angry, as usual. But I've been thinking about that lately. We've been growing farther apart for years, and I always blamed it on her. Now I don't think she's the problem. I haven't been a very loving husband. I've been selfish and critical — much more concerned about what I wanted than what would make her happy. I've never admitted that before. I feel embarrassed talking about it now."

"For all these years, I've been working to accumulate all the *things* I could: money, house, cars, job, the usual. But I'm starting to think I've missed something. I haven't paid as much attention to people as I should have."

"I've been reading a book (*Real Love—The Truth About Finding Unconditional Love and Fulfilling Relationships* or *The Truth About Parenting*) that says that when people get angry, they're just protecting themselves. I've been thinking about that, because I've always blamed everybody else for making me angry, and that has never made me happy or helped my relationships. I may have a lot to learn about relationships."

If you say something like that to a friend and they look at you like you're crazy, you haven't lost a thing, have you? Simply change the subject to the weather or whatever's comfortable, and you will still have the same relationship you had with them before you said anything.

But don't stop there. Keep trying that same conversation with other friends, and eventually, you *will* find someone who doesn't give you a blank, confused stare. You *will* find someone — likely several people — who will say something like, "Wow! That was honest." You will find someone who is attracted to the truth and who will accept you as you are. And they will share the truth about themselves with you. That's how you find a wise man. They're everywhere, and most of them don't even know who they are. When you finally get that warm feeling of unconditional acceptance from one person, you won't care one bit how many puzzled expressions you got before that. Real Love is worth everything we invest to find it. Everything.

In short, to find a wise man, we simply tell the truth about ourselves and wait for those people who can see us and accept us while we're being truthful. It's that easy. It's also more life-changing than we can imagine until we experience it. You can read much more about how to tell the truth, and the effect of doing that, in *Real Love—The Truth About Finding Unconditional Love and Fulfilling Relationships.*

Don't look for someone capable of seeing you clearly all the time. That would require a person who always feels loved, and you won't find many people like that. But you can find someone who feels loved enough to see you and accept you with one or two of the flaws you describe. Then you'll find other people who can do the same, and as you tell a little of the truth about yourself on many occasions, you'll eventually feel entirely seen and loved.

Not only do we *find* wise men by telling the truth. We actually *create* them. We all want to be accepting and loving. Many of us simply don't get the chance to do that because we never hear people tell the truth about themselves. As we tell the truth about ourselves, some people will *discover* their ability to accept us as we are, an ability they didn't know they had. As we all practice telling the truth together, we *learn* to see and accept each other. *We* become wise men and women ourselves, and then we become capable of truly loving our children.

The Risk of Telling the Truth

Although the potential benefits of telling the truth about ourselves are so great — feeling loved and being genuinely happy — we are still very afraid to start doing it. We keep lying because we're afraid of the risk that people might not like us if they learn the truth about us. But let's examine the real risk involved.

If you lie to me, you can *never* feel genuinely accepted by me. There is a *zero percent* chance of you feeling Real Love, and you'll always be alone. It can't get worse than that. If you tell the truth about yourself, it is possible that I won't accept you, but now you've created *some* possibility of me accepting you and you feeling loved. That possibility can't be less than the zero% chance you have with lying, so you literally *can't lose* by telling the truth. On close examination, lying is stupid and telling the truth isn't risky at all.

We temporarily avoid criticism when we lie, but ironically, we hear the criticism in our heads all the same. We're certain that we *would* have been criticized if we had told the truth, so we feel the criticism as though it had actually happened — and then we feel unloved and alone. Telling the truth is the only way to be happy.

4. GIVING UP THE GETTING AND PROTECTING BEHAVIORS

As long as we're using Getting and Protecting Behaviors, we make it impossible to feel Real Love (pp. 56-8). Those behaviors, and the Imitation Love that we get from them, are a huge distraction that keep us from feeling Real Love. For that reason alone, we have to make efforts to abandon those behaviors.

George wanted to change his life (Step 1 in the process of finding Real Love), and he exercised the faith (Step 2) to tell the truth about himself (Step 3) and expose himself to the opportunities to be seen, accepted, and loved. However, those early feelings of being loved were often overwhelmed by the effects of a lifetime of not feeling loved. He noticed that particularly on the occasions when he used Getting and Protecting Behaviors. One evening George called me on the phone.

George: "I feel terrible. I thought I was learning something about being more loving with Dan, but I just yelled at him and made him feel awful. As soon as I got angry, I knew I should stop, but I just couldn't."

Me: "Always keep it simple. The only person you can change is you, and the only thing that will change you is Real Love. You know the four steps involved. (1) I know you have the desire, or you wouldn't be working at this, and you wouldn't have called. (2) You have amazing faith, which you've shown by (3) telling the truth about yourself to many people. That takes great courage.

George: "So what's the problem?"

Me: "The fourth step. The Getting and Protecting Behaviors are very distracting and make you feel like you're going backward. In your case the distracting behavior is attacking, which includes anger, criticizing, and controlling. You've always done those things because in the absence of Real Love, they've made you feel better. You do them without thinking. When you get angry, and when you criticize and control people, you get Imitation Love in the form of power, praise, and safety.

"But while you're doing those things, you can't feel loved or loving. You've been feeling more loved and loving lately as you've told the truth about yourself, but those good feelings just disappear when you get angry, don't they?"

George: "Yes, so what do I do when I get angry? Pretend I'm not?"

Me: "Of course not. That wouldn't work. But the moment you're angry, you *can* do something different than you've always done. You can shut your mouth. Immediately quit talking to the person you're angry at and call someone who accepts and loves you instead. Talk to someone who loves you until you don't feel angry. Then finish your conversation with the person you were angry at."

The very next day George did exactly what I suggested. The moment he felt irritated with Dan, he told his son they would finish their conversation later. He then called me. We talked about the mistakes he was making with Dan, and we talked about the many mistakes I've made with my children.

Me: "When you called, you were angry at Dan and quite unhappy. How do you feel now?"

George: "I don't feel angry anymore, and now I get the point you were trying to make yesterday. When I get angry, everything goes badly, for me and for my children. When I feel that way, I need to stop talking to them and talk to someone who can help me feel different."

George made a decision to give up his usual Getting and Protecting Behavior in his conversation with Dan. Instead of attacking his son to selfishly get a sense of importance, power, and safety for himself, he called me to experience a moment of unconditional acceptance instead. It was a far healthier thing to do. Eventually, George learned to do that with several friends, and he quit getting angry at Dan or any of his children. By doing that, he gave them an incalculable gift and exchanged his former fits of temper for a profound and lasting peace.

The Interaction of Self-Control and Finding Real Love

In the above section, I suggested that we would feel more loved if we simply exercised more *self-control* and stopped using our Getting and Protecting Behaviors. Those behaviors are distracting and destructive. They make it very difficult for us to find and feel Real Love. On the other hand, I have said many times that in the absence of Real Love, we are empty and afraid, and in that condition, we *will* use Getting and Protecting Behaviors. So how can I now suggest that we simply *stop* them?

Don't we have to find Real Love *before* we can stop using our Getting and Protecting Behaviors? No, not entirely. We can engage in both efforts at the same time, and both efforts complement each other. The more we can exercise our self-control and restrain our natural tendency to use Getting and Protecting Behaviors, the less distracted we will be in the process of feeling unconditionally loved and loving. When we can avoid lying, and being angry, and acting like victims, it's much easier to feel loved and loving. And the more we tell the truth about ourselves and find Real Love, the less need we have to use Getting and Protecting Behaviors.

Changing our lives is not a matter of just sitting back and feeling more loved. Nor is it a matter of gripping life by the horns and taking charge. We need to do all we can of both.

THE EFFECT OF A PARENT GETTING REAL LOVE

If a mother — or father — has been unconditionally loved, she has the most important and fulfilling thing in life. She's not empty or afraid and therefore has no need to get Imitation Love or protect herself. Without the blinding effect of need and fear she sees her child clearly and cares about him. She naturally reaches out to her child and weaves a powerful connection between them. Her child feels included and senses that he's a valued part of a greater whole. He feels loved and not alone.

As George felt loved, he found that (1) he wasn't afraid and didn't need to protect himself all the time, and (2) he didn't need to manipulate people to change their behavior to make him happy. George no longer needed to control or criticize Dan. He accepted him and cared about his happiness (Real Love). Instead of trying to change him, he loved him and taught him. He had faith that Dan would learn from his own choices (Chapter 8) and be happy without George's interference and control. As George practiced loving Dan, he naturally became better at it and had even more love to give him.

As Dan felt his father's acceptance, he no longer needed to work for his father's "love," nor did he need to protect himself from his father's expectations and criticism. They developed a loving and delightful relationship.

MY OWN EXPERIENCE

For many years, I was held up as an example of what a father should be. I spent a lot of time with my children, and they were high achievers and well-mannered. The truth is, I was a terrible father. I was kind to my children when they were successful, obedient, quiet, and cooperative. I provided them a beautiful home, excellent education, transportation, entertainment, great family vacations, the most fashionable clothing, etc. All that was absolutely worthless because when they were loud, disobedient, irresponsible, and otherwise inconvenient, I was harsh, critical, and unloving. On those occasions, it was quite clear that my love for them was conditional. I proved that every time I was disappointed and angry when they didn't do what I wanted.

As a result, they became increasingly empty, afraid, and unhappy. They naturally reacted by using all the Getting and Protecting Behaviors. They were angry and argued with each other. Their grades were affected. They began to associate with friends who encouraged them to participate in drinking, drugs, and sex. And they understandably avoided me whenever possible. It was obvious they were miserable.

I wanted to be a better father. And I tried to do be, but nothing worked because I felt unloved and empty myself and couldn't give my children the one thing they needed most. We can't give what we don't have. I became more alone and frustrated, as a father and as a human being. I became a drug addict for several years, and during that time, I was even more critical of my children. As I sat in the woods behind my house with a gun to my head, I realized I needed help.

I finally entered a treatment facility, and accepted the responsibility for everything wrong in my life and in the lives of my children. That was the most difficult thing I'd ever done, but it gave me the freedom to change. I eventually learned to tell the truth about myself and found people to love me unconditionally. In the beginning, those moments of acceptance were brief and infrequent, but I persisted in taking the steps described in this chapter, and my life began to change. The more loved I felt, the more love I was able to give my children. As I learned to unconditionally love them consistently, their lives changed. They no longer had a need to get Imitation Love or protect themselves. Their self-destructive behaviors stopped.

When people feel loved, there's nothing to argue about or be afraid of. My family is now more loving and happy than I would ever have thought possible. And it all started when I accepted the responsibility for not loving them. Being wrong is a small price to pay for lasting happiness. And the steps to finding Real Love are so simple.

REAL LOVE—THE TRUTH ABOUT FINDING UNCONDITIONAL LOVE AND FULFILLING RELATIONSHIPS

This chapter is intended to be a brief introduction to finding Real Love. I strongly recommend that every parent read *Real Love— The Truth About Finding Real Love and Fulfilling Relationships* for much more about the process of receiving and giving Real Love.

Chapter Summary

If we haven't received Real Love for ourselves, we can't give it to our children, no matter how much they need it and how much we want to give it to them.

We become better parents only as we find Real Love. There are four steps we can take toward finding love:

Having the desire to change ourselves

Exercising the faith that we can change and that telling the truth about ourselves will make a difference in our lives

Telling the truth about ourselves, after which we're seen, accepted, and loved

Giving up the Getting and Protecting Behaviors

Chapter 6

Expecting Love From Our Children

"Does anyone love you unconditionally" I have asked many adults that question, and one common answer is this: "Yes, my *children* do." That belief is almost always inaccurate. In addition, it's inappropriate and often dangerous. Our children are not responsible for loving us, and with rare exceptions, they're quite incapable of doing that.

WE DON'T HAVE THE RIGHT TO GIVE OUR CHILDREN THE RESPONSIBILITY TO LOVE US

It's not intentional, but most of us place considerable responsibility on our children to make us feel good. Every time we're disappointed in them or angry at them, we're loudly declaring that they are responsible for making us happy — and we're mostly unaware of how often we do that.

Our happiness is not determined by the behavior of our children. Our happiness is a result of how much unconditional love we've received over a lifetime of experiences with parents, teachers, friends, and spouses — and by how loving *we* are. As I described on pp. 11-12, most of us were not unconditionally loved, and without that, we become unhappy as adults and parents. But now it is not our children's responsibility to give us the Real Love we need. Children need to *be loved* by us. They need to be filled up with the unconditional love they require to be happy. Children become whole only when love is initially a one-way flow, from us to them. That can't happen while we're demanding something from them in return.

Again, we don't intend to place the burden of our happiness on our children, but when we're not filled with Real Love, we do whatever it takes to decrease the pain of our own emptiness. We use all the Getting and Protecting Behaviors (Chapter 3) to manipulate people — including our children — for Imitation Love, unaware of the damage we cause as we do that.

Our Children *Can't* Love Us Unconditionally

We want to believe that our children love us unconditionally, but if they haven't received Real Love from us — as very few of them have — how can they give it to anyone else? In most cases, when we expect love from our children, we're asking them to give us what they never got from us. Their task is impossible, and the burden is crushing.

In addition, we need to remember that love can only be unconditional when it is freely given (pp. 56-8). The giver of unconditional love can't be empty or afraid. When people are empty or afraid, they can only manipulate other people to get what they want or protect themselves from being hurt. Such people certainly can't give Real Love. Almost without exception, our children are both empty and afraid. They badly need us to love them and are scared to death of losing our love. Those are *normal* conditions for a child, and for those reasons, they can't give us Real Love.

We love our children more when they're good — when they do what we want. They can feel that our approval is not unconditional, but it feels better than nothing, so they do their best — in the beginning, at least — to earn more of it by giving us what we want: gratitude, obedience, affection, etc. We feel good when we get those things, and understandably, we believe that our children are "loving" us. But they're not giving us those things unconditionally; they need our approval and love far too much to give us anything without expecting something in return. They give us what we want so we'll give them the "love" they desperately need. They also give us respect and gratitude because they're afraid of the painful disapproval that we give them when they're *not* respectful and grateful.

What our children give us is full of unconscious expectations and fears. That is not Real Love. All this trading of Imitation Love is not intentional or malicious. We and our children are just doing our best to survive in the absence of Real Love.

Failure to See the Expectations We Have of our Children

We have great expectations — even demands — that our children will love us and make us happier. That is quite understandable. When we feel unloved and empty, we have natural expectations that the people around us will soothe our pain and fill our emptiness. Without meaning to do it, we heap some of those expectations on our children.

Although we have these expectations every day, we don't see them. We express them in subtle ways. For example, we don't say to a child directly, "I need you to love me." Instead, we say, "Give Mommy (or Daddy) a kiss." But that child then feels an obligation to give us affection so we won't be disappointed. He can't feel unconditionally loved as long as he senses that we have any expectations for him to make us happy — even if our expectations are unconscious.

How can we know if we have selfish expectations of our children? Easy — disappointment. Disappointment means that *we* didn't get something that *we* wanted. It's selfish. But we get disappointed and angry about the behavior of our children so often that we accept those feelings as normal. We justify our disappointment, saying that it's acceptable when a child makes certain kinds of mistakes, or is disobedient, or is disrespectful, etc. When our children behave badly, it *is* our responsibility to correct them, but disappointment and anger are never a part of loving and effective teaching.

When we have expectations of our children, we clearly communicate that they have an obligation to do something for us in order to *earn* our "love." Certainly, that's not unconditional love, and our children then feel empty and afraid. We reveal our expectations for their "love" when we demand respect, obedience, gratitude, and affection from them. We don't do it intentionally, but when we're empty ourselves, we forget that it's *our* responsibility to love and teach our children. We do not have the right to expect them to love *us*.

I'm not saying that children shouldn't be respectful and obedient — far from it. They need those qualities to be happy. But they acquire those characteristics far better when we just love and teach them. Children don't learn real respect — and certainly don't feel Real Love — when we expect and demand it from them. We'll talk more about how to love and teach children in Chapters 9-16.

GETTING IMITATION LOVE FROM OUR CHILDREN

We expect our children to make us happy, and we "love" them more when they do — that's Imitation Love. In return, they give *us* Imitation Love — praise, power, pleasure, safety, and conditional approval.

Praise

From the time our children are very young, they hear these words from us when we give them a gift, even something small like an ice cream cone: "Now what do you say?" In effect, we force them to be grateful for everything they get from us. Teaching children to be grateful is important, but the problem is that we don't teach them to be grateful **for** what they have. Instead, we require them to be grateful **to us**. The difference is enormous.

When children are grateful **for** what they have, they're more aware of the gifts and the joy in their lives. That kind of gratitude magnifies the enjoyment of every experience and opportunity. With it, children feel more loved, hopeful, and happy.

But we don't teach children to be grateful in that healthy way. We teach them to be grateful **to us**, and our reasons are mostly selfish. When children thank us for what we give them, we tend to feel gracious, generous, and important. We expect their gratitude and receive it as a form of praise (Imitation Love). We like that feeling and manipulate them for even more of it. We prove that our motivation for encouraging their gratitude is selfish every time we become disappointed on the occasions when they're *not* grateful. The things we give them are therefore not real gifts. We're actually *buying* their gratitude and trying to make them feel obligated to us. Our expectations show that we care about *our* happiness, not theirs. That places a great burden on our children and isolates them from us.

If you doubt that you expect gratitude for the things — and the time — you give your children, imagine this scene: you've spent a great deal of time, effort, and money to buy a special birthday present for one of your children. When he opens the gift, he throws it on the floor, breaks it, and stomps off into the next room. Be honest – do you feel irritated? That's natural, but it also means you expected a reward for your gift. You wanted something for yourself — gratitude, affection, something – and you became irritated because you didn't get it. Having expectations when we give people something is so common that we can hardly imagine living otherwise. But it's not unconditional love — it's Imitation Love, and it's selfish. Most of us have harmful expectations of our children every day.

How would it be different if you felt unconditionally loved? What if you had taken the steps to find Real Love as described in Chapter 5 — how would you respond to a child who behaved as described above? Your concern would be for *his* happiness, the definition of Real Love. You wouldn't care about the broken gift, which means nothing at all, nor would you care about the time and effort that you spent getting the gift. What matters is the happiness of your child. You would know that when a child behaves like that, he simply feels unloved. You would accept complete responsibility for that, but you would also not feel guilty about it. You would find your child and indicate your acceptance and love for him, completely unconcerned about the birthday gift. It's an amazing thing to see the effect of Real Love between a parent and child. I have seen it many times.

But don't children need to learn gratitude? Of course they do. However, they will not learn genuine gratitude as we demand it from them. They learn it as we love them unconditionally and teach them. We'll talk more about how to teach gratitude on pp. 157-9.

Power

Children are in a position to be controlled much more easily than adults, and we unconsciously use that to feel important. A man without Real Love must get a sense of importance somewhere. If he can't get it at work or from his wife, he can usually find it by commanding the respect of his children as he uses his authority as a parent. Despite her best efforts, a mother may not receive the love she wants from her husband and others. But she can manipulate the affection of her children rather easily. When we control the behavior of our children in any way that benefits us, not them, we're getting Imitation Love from them in the form of power.

We don't intentionally use power over our children, but we still do it. In the absence of Real Love, the sensation of control feels better than being completely helpless and alone. We hate to admit we do this because it makes us look bad, but on the occasions when our children rebel and resist our authority, we're uniformly disappointed or angry. That reaction proves how much we hate losing our control over them. And then we intimidate and otherwise manipulate them to regain our control. Until we see that we do this, we'll continue to use our children instead of loving them.

John talked about the behavior of his son Parker with a wise friend. Remember, a wise man is anyone who is capable of loving us unconditionally when they have seen the truth about us.

John: "He's becoming more disrespectful all the time. I don't know what to do. If I don't say anything to him about it, how can he learn respect? But when I do say something, he gets mad, and then I get mad, and it turns into an argument, and then we both feel bad. I don't see another solution."

Wise man: "You seem angry about it."

John: "Sure I am. It's wrong for him to talk to me like he does."

Wise man: *"Before you react with anger,* how do you feel when he doesn't respect you?"

John had a hard time describing the feeling, but his friend helped him see that when Parker was rude and disrespectful, John felt:

(1) unappreciated;
(2) afraid that he was a failure as a father;
(3) unloved;
(4) empty and alone; and
(5) helpless.

Wise man: "When you feel unloved and afraid yourself, you
naturally want the people around you to love you,
including your son. When he doesn't, you protect
yourself from the unpleasant feeling of being unloved
and helpless to do anything about it. You also don't
like the feeling that you might not be a good father.
So you get angry and insist that he respect you. When
you're angry, you don't feel as helpless. And when
you make him respect you — even if it's just for a
moment — you don't feel like such a failure as a
father."

John: "Well, I *am* his father. Don't I deserve to be respected?
Isn't that's how it's supposed to be?"

Wise man: "You only want respect because you don't feel
loved. Without Real Love, respect becomes a kind
of Imitation Love that makes you feel important.
Because you're empty and afraid, you're blind to
what your son needs. You can only see what *you*
want. In that condition, you *can't* unconditionally
love him — and he feels that when you get angry.
That adds to *his* emptiness and fear, and then he gets
even more angry to protect himself.

"If you felt unconditionally loved, you'd be happy
and full. You wouldn't need him to behave in a
certain way to make *you* happy, and you wouldn't
be hurt when he was disrespectful. You'd see that his
disrespect is just a way of attacking you to protect
himself. It's a Protecting Behavior he uses when
he's afraid. He only does that when he doesn't feel
loved. That doesn't make it right, but it does make it
understandable. When you feel loved, you'll be able
to love him when he's angry instead of being hurt or
angry yourself."

Without Real Love, we're already in pain, and naturally, we want to prevent anything from adding to that discomfort. When children are disobedient or disrespectful, that is more than enough to threaten us, and we respond with anger to protect ourselves. Anger makes us feel strong, or at least less powerless. We command attention and respect from our children because then we feel less helpless and alone. In addition, when we're angry, our children often stop doing what was inconveniencing and annoying us.

John learned to tell the truth about himself, and he began to feel unconditionally accepted by wise men and women, as George did in Chapter 5. As John felt loved and happy, he no longer had a need to demand respect from his son. Compared to Real Love, Imitation Love soon loses its appeal. As John's anger disappeared, it became obvious that his previous anger came from his own emptiness and was not caused by his son.

Obviously, children *do* need to be obedient and respectful. Children with those qualities are much happier than those without them. But it's critical that we examine our motivation as we teach them these principles. How do we do that? From moment to moment, how can we tell whether our motivation is selfish or loving? How can we know if we are teaching our children to be respectful for *their* benefit? Easy — if we're interested only in the happiness of *our children*, we don't get *disappointed* or *angry* on the occasions when they're disrespectful.

What a disrespectful child needs is to be loved and guided. We can't offer that when we're disappointed and angry, since those are reactions to not getting what *we* selfishly want. We first need to get Real Love for ourselves (Chapter 5). We'll talk about responding to an angry, disrespectful child in Chapter 20.

THE EFFECT OF SELFISH MOTIVATION

Children are a great deal more perceptive and sensitive than we realize. When we demand respect and obedience for our own convenience and pleasure, they feel that. They know we're not loving them, and then they feel used and separated from us.

Frank was angry when his son Tyler arrived home long past the hour they agreed upon. Tyler tried to make the excuse that it wasn't his fault, that other people had delayed him — which was only partially true — but Frank only became more critical and angry. Finally, Tyler gritted his teeth and turned to walk away.

Frank: "Don't you turn your back on me, young man! You stand there and listen to me when I'm talking to you."

Frank was feeling unloved and empty. In that condition, he could only protect himself and get Imitation Love. In this case, he used his position of authority to get a feeling of power over his son.

Anger has terrible effects on our children:

1. When we're angry, they feel unloved and alone, as we discussed above and in Chapter 3. This effect alone is deadly.

2. Our children can't learn anything when we're angry at them. Imagine that you're assigned to memorize a sonnet by Shakespeare. Would you be able to do that better if I slapped your face and held a gun to your head while you read the poem? Ridiculous. But that's what it's like for our children when we're angry as we talk to them. They're too distracted by fear to learn anything we're trying to teach them.

Frank wanted Tyler to listen as he taught a lesson about being responsible, but as soon as Tyler saw that his father was angry, the lesson was over. It's true that Tyler needed to listen to his father, but Frank's anger clearly stated that he was not primarily interested in Tyler's happiness. He wanted obedience and respect for *himself*. He wanted Imitation Love. Tyler immediately felt that and knew he wasn't being loved, a feeling that always provokes fear in a child. He reacted to his fear with Protecting Behaviors: attacking (anger, shrugging his shoulders) and running (walking away). He couldn't hear a word his father said.

3. When we get angry, we teach our children to lie. When Frank told Tyler to not turn away, he was really saying this: "Don't you be angry. When you're afraid, don't do the natural thing that I do and that everyone else does, which is to protect ourselves. Be happy and loving instead, even though I've never shown you how to do that. In other words, don't be yourself — instead, **lie** about how you feel and make me happy." No child can be happy when he hears that message.

TEACHING CHILDREN RESPECT WITHOUT MANIPULATING FOR POWER

If Frank had been filled with Real Love himself, how would this interaction have happened?

1. He would still have questioned Tyler about the time he got home. Teaching responsibility was still his job as a parent.
2. *Frank would not have been angry.* People with Real Love are happy and have everything they could possibly want. Small inconveniences are no longer painful to such people, and they have no need to protect themselves with anger. Feeling loved, Frank would simply have pointed out Tyler's lack of responsibility, or he would have given Tyler a chance to acknowledge the mistake himself. Loving parents don't ignore irresponsibility or disobedience, but while they teach their children what is right, there is no disappointment or anger. Anger is never loving.
3. Without Frank's anger, it's unlikely that Tyler would have felt afraid. He would then have had no need to protect himself with anger and running.

This kind of interaction with a child is not impossibly idealistic. Parents all over the country have learned to unconditionally love their children like this. Children learn far better this way than they do with impatience and anger. Children also learn to tell the truth about themselves instead of lying, attacking, etc., and that creates an environment where they can be seen, accepted, and loved. In Chapter 14, we'll discuss several examples of parents responding to irresponsible behavior.

It's important for children to respect their parents. However, real respect is a natural result of being genuinely loved, not a product of demanding it.

PARENTS GETTING POWER BY ACTING LIKE VICTIMS

Another way for us to get power over our children is to act like victims.

Janet went outside and told her son Joel that he couldn't continue playing with his friends until his jobs around the house were completed. Joel stomped into the house with a scowl on his face, muttering how stupid and unfair it was. Janet looked hurt, and tears came to her eyes.

Janet: "Joel, it hurts me when you talk like that."

Joel felt guilty when he saw that he had hurt his mother's feelings, and he immediately stopped complaining.

Because she didn't feel unconditionally loved, Janet felt helpless and afraid when Joel became angry at her. She naturally protected herself and attempted to get Imitation Love from her son. She chose the Getting and Protecting Behavior she was most familiar with — she acted like a victim. By doing that, she succeeded in stopping Joel from attacking her with his anger. She also got a sense of power (Imitation Love) from controlling his behavior.

Janet didn't do this intentionally. She reacted automatically, having learned this from childhood. When she was a child, Janet's parents did not allow her to show any sign of anger, so she learned to hide her anger and never used that as a way of getting what she wanted. Prevented from using attacking as a Getting and Protecting Behavior, she learned to protect herself and manipulate people by acting like a victim — crying, looking injured, etc. When she did that, her parents and other people felt sorry for her and stopped their displays of disapproval. As an adult, she continued to use victimhood as a Getting and Protecting Behavior, as she did here with Joel. We all choose the Getting and Protecting Behaviors that work best for us.

Janet's original goal – at least partly – was to teach Joel about responsibility. He needed to finish his jobs around the house before he played with his friends. But the moment she acted like a victim, the focus was completely on *her* and the lesson on responsibility was completely lost. She did succeed in manipulating Joel – he stopped complaining – but he only learned to behave in a way that made his mother happy. He learned nothing about real responsibility. When we use Getting and Protecting Behaviors with our children, we teach them nothing useful. We only *use* our children in a selfish way.

If Janet had felt loved herself, how would the above interaction have gone? In the first place, it probably wouldn't have happened. Parents who feel unconditionally loved naturally accept their children and teach them to be responsible. It's likely that Joel would have done his jobs around the house before going out to play. However, if he had not, Janet would have spoken plainly to him about his responsibility, with no irritation or acting like a victim. She would not have needed her son to withhold his anger to make her happy. Under those conditions, children can usually hear what they're being taught. But Joel might still have been irritated – children tend to prefer playing over working, after all – and Janet would then have simply restated his responsibility. We'll discuss teaching children about responsibility in Chapter 14.

SAFETY

If we can't have Real Love, we'll take Imitation Love instead. If we can't have praise, power, and pleasure, we can at least minimize the pain we experience from criticism and inconvenience. That's what safety is — minimizing pain — and we often manipulate our children to get it.

Ray didn't feel unconditionally loved, so he tried to find happiness in the praise and power he got from doing a good job at work. When things didn't go well there, he temporarily lost his source of Imitation Love, and that left him completely empty and miserable. In that condition, he felt threatened by anything that demanded his attention or disturbed him in any way. So when Ray came home from a bad day on the job, he minimized his emptiness and pain by speaking harshly to his children, knowing that they would then be quiet and stay out of his way. When Ray couldn't get Imitation Love at work in the form of praise and power, he got it at home in the form of power and safety.

When we already feel unloved and alone, we're eager to minimize any further discomfort (safety). So we often require our children to be quiet and cooperative. I can't begin to imagine how many times a day children hear the words, "Be quiet."

Another way we achieve safety with children is to always be right. When we insist on being right with our children — exercising our power over them — we don't have to experience the discomfort of being wrong and looking foolish (Chapter 23). Many of us have never admitted to our children that we were wrong about something specific. We forget — or have never understood — that it's our job to love and teach our children, not to use them to feel safe and comfortable.

MANIPULATING OUR CHILDREN FOR IMITATION LOVE WITH ANGER

I have spoken in this chapter about how we manipulate our children — mostly unintentionally — for Imitation Love in its various forms: praise, power, and safety. The most common and effective way we do this is to communicate anger to our children. They will do almost anything — use all of the Protecting Behaviors — to avoid any expression of our disapproval: a sigh, a frown, a raised eyebrow, a change in our tone of voice, or heaven forbid, an unkind word. To our children, disappointment and anger are different only in degree, and both are devastating. I repeat: although we are usually unaware of it, we selfishly use our anger to get our children to behave as we want.

In our defense, when we don't feel unconditionally loved ourselves, we're empty and afraid. In that condition, how can we possibly avoid becoming disappointed and angry at our children when they don't do what we want? We can't. On p. 48, I said this:

"We must understand that our children get angry only because they don't feel loved. They get angry to protect themselves and to get Imitation Love in the form of praise and power. They discover at an early age that when they're angry, they don't feel as empty and helpless, two feelings they hate. When they're angry, they can also get people to do things for them and to stop hurting them."

We get angry for exactly the same reasons our children do. We get angry at our children because *we* don't feel unconditionally loved, either. But that condition existed long before our children came along. *Our children did not cause it.* It's critical that we understand that. Our anger is a reaction to the emptiness and pain that began in our childhood when we didn't feel loved. Our children had nothing to do with that. Our children are *never* to blame for the anger that we feel toward them. When we accept that, parenting immediately becomes much easier — for us and for them.

NO ONE EVER MAKES ME ANGRY, AND ANGER — IT'S A CHOICE

We blame other people for our anger so often that we've convinced ourselves that we're *right*. With rare exceptions, when we get angry, we're angry *at* someone else. Anger and blaming walk hand in hand. When we feel irritated, we immediately look around for the person who made us feel that way. Blaming causes even more unhappiness: for our children, our spouses, our friends, and for ourselves. But we keep right on justifying our right to blame people for our anger. Because anger is so destructive, and because blaming others only makes the continuation of anger a certainty, I want to offer several proofs that other people are never the cause of our anger. These will also stand as proof that our children never make us angry.

Proof 1:
The self-evident proof.
We always have a choice.

As human beings, we have a position unique in the universe. Although there is certainly much that is beautiful and awe-inspiring – the stars, planets, mountains, trees, birds, fish, oceans, sub-molecular intricacies, and so on – we alone have the ability to determine our own course. The behavior of everything else is determined by gravity, the Big Bang, instinct, the weather, training, and DNA, but we human beings can actually comprehend our position, ponder it, and decide to change our course. In fact, we're quite jealous of that ability and will defend to the death our right to exercise it. We have fought many wars against those who would claim to tell any of us what we can or cannot do.

As proud as we are of our ability to make our own decisions about everything else, why is it that we are so quick to claim that other people can *make us* angry? We seem to give up our right to determine how we feel quite easily. "You makes me so mad" is a common expression, and if we don't say it out loud, we certainly think it or imply it with our behavior. We claim that we can make our own decisions about everything else, but not about how we feel. Why is that?

Because we claim the ability to make choices only when it *suits* us. We *like* being responsible for choosing what we eat, and what we wear, and where we live, and whom we'll marry. Because we like the consequences – the rewards – of those choices. But we don't like being held responsible for our anger. We'd rather blame that choice on someone else.

Rain *makes* the ground wet. The sun *makes* the grass warm. The ground and the grass have no choice in the matter. But we human beings are not dirt and grass. We do have choices – about many things, including about how we feel. When people treat us badly, we make decisions about how we will respond. In the absence of Real Love, our ability to respond *is certainly impaired* – sometimes severely – but we can still choose to limit our Getting and Protecting Behaviors (including anger) to some degree. I talked about that on p. 80-1. The more we understand about the behavior of other people, and the more loved we feel, the more able we become to make wise and loving choices. Self-control and Real Love enjoy a powerful synergy.

Proof 2:
It's *your* emptiness and fear — determined by the amount of Real Love you have —
That leads to anger, *not* what someone else does to you.
(Two dollars vs. twenty million)

Imagine that you're hungry and only have two dollars left in the world. Putting the money on a table, you get ready to go out and buy something to eat. Suddenly, I burst into the room, grab the two dollars, and run away before you can stop me.

How would you feel? Almost certainly, you'd be angry, and you'd say that *I caused* your anger. Most people would. But now imagine a different scene. You've just eaten a full meal and you're sitting at a table loaded with delicious food. In addition, you have twenty million dollars in the bank. Suddenly, I burst into the room and grab two dollars that are sitting on the table and run away before you can stop me.

How would you feel this time? With a full stomach and twenty million dollars, you probably wouldn't even care if I took two dollars. The loss of two dollars is nothing when you have so much.

We've just proven that I didn't "make you angry" in the first scene. We know that because on both occasions, *I* did exactly the same thing — but *you* chose to react differently the second time. If **I** *made* you angry the first time, you could not have been anything but angry the second time — but you were. The real difference between the two events was not *me*, but how much money and food *you* had.

That's how it is in every experience we have with other people. Our reaction is determined by how unconditionally loved *we* feel, not by what the other person does. When people inconvenience us, disappoint us, or attack us, each of these events contributes to us feeling a little more empty and afraid — like they're taking two dollars from us, as in the example above. Without sufficient Real Love, we feel unbearably empty, and the loss of two dollars is a major injury — as in the first scene between you and me. On the other hand, if we feel unconditionally loved, it's like having twenty million dollars all the time, and the little inconvenient things people do become relatively unimportant. With Real Love, we have everything that matters. Without it, we become afraid and protect ourselves with anger. Our anger is caused by the lack of Real Love, *not* by what someone else does.

The primary purpose of this illustration is to show that other people don't make us angry. I obviously did not focus on the fact that anger is a choice. Remember that self-control and Real Love work together toward the elimination of Getting and Protecting Behaviors.

Proof 3:
When two people respond differently to the same person,
You can't claim that person *makes* you angry.

I went with some friends on a canoe trip down a stretch of river that included some challenging white-water rapids. My friend Gene was less experienced than the rest of the group, but I took him in my canoe and assured him that all would be well. During our passage through one of the more difficult rapids, two of the men in another canoe were goofing around and intentionally bumped their canoe into mine. Gene was startled, lost his balance, and fell out of the canoe. Of course, that tipped the canoe over and threw me into the water, too.

Gene had already been anxious about this outing. He had never canoed a river this rugged. And now he found himself dashing between large rocks while gasping for air in the cold, churning water. This had become an understandably terrifying experience. I hurried to make sure that Gene was all right, and when he reached the calmer waters, he was fine physically, but he was furious at the two men who had bumped into our canoe. I was glad he didn't have a gun. Clearly, he blamed them for his anger.

This incident proved that other people don't *make* us angry. The exact same thing happened to Gene and myself. We were both bumped by the other canoe, dumped into the cold water, and forced to swim through the rapids down the river. But our reactions were strikingly different: Gene was enraged at the men who had run into us, and I found the whole incident rather humorous and invigorating.

What was the difference? Gene was *unprepared* for what happened, in at least two ways. First, he was physically unprepared. When he was bumped by the other canoe, he had no experience — through no fault of his — and didn't know what to do. He lost his balance and fell into the water. He was also emotionally unprepared. He had never been unconditionally loved in his life. When he became frightened, he immediately reached for the Protecting Behavior he had always used: anger. It was the only thing he could do.

Because I was physically prepared for canoeing, being bumped by the other men was not overwhelming to me. However, I was still thrown in the water because of Gene's reaction. Because of that inconvenience, I could then have reacted with anger to all three men, but I had been prepared emotionally by years of being unconditionally loved (Chapter 5). I didn't feel empty or afraid, and had no need to use any of the Getting and Protecting Behaviors. I was not a better man than Gene, just better prepared to react to that incident — which did *not* make me angry. I still do get angry on occasions when I forget that I'm loved — foolish on my part.

We see examples all around us of people reacting differently to the same events. In World War II, millions of people were imprisoned and killed in concentrations camps, by the Germans and by the Japanese. We have many oral and written accounts from survivors of those camps, and we have learned that many of those people understandably became very angry and bitter because of the unspeakably hateful treatment they received at the hands of their captors. But some of those inmates chose to not become angry. They forgave their tormentors and even learned to love them. They saw the terrible effects of anger and hate, and they refused to give in to them. Victor Frankl spoke of such people in *Man's Search for Meaning*. So did Corrie ten Boom.

Some people get angry when people do terrible things to them, and other people do not. Clearly, the problem is *not* the people who do the terrible things, is it? If that were so, then *everyone* would become angry when they were treated badly, and that does not happen. In fact, if you get angry when I do something, and we can find even one person in the world who does not get angry when I do that same thing, then I did not *make* you angry. Apparently, some people *choose* to become angry and others do not. Anger is a choice.

Proof 4:
When *Imitation Love* makes your anger go away,
You can't claim someone else caused your anger.

I was having lunch with my friend Larry, and he mentioned an incident with his son Jordan. Larry had clearly told Jordan to never use Larry's expensive video camera. But Jordan ignored his warning, and while Larry was out of the house, Jordan used the camera, dropped it, and caused serious damage to it. Larry was furious at his son. During the conversation, he used this phrase, "Sometimes, that kid makes me so mad."

Me: "If I gave you a million dollars in cash right now — and a new car — would you be less irritated with him?"

Larry: (laughing) "Yes, I guess I would."

Me: "Then Jordan didn't make you angry."

Larry: "I don't understand."

Me: "If a million dollars would make your anger go away, then obviously the real cause of your anger is the lack of a million dollars, not Jordan — right?"

A common greeting in our society is to ask people, "How are you?" or something like that. A frequent reply to that query is "Fine" or "Good." What we almost always mean by that response is that *things* are going well. We mean that our supply of Imitation Love is adequate for the moment, and *that* is what keeps us from being angry. But if we're running low on praise, power, pleasure, and safety, watch out! That's when we become irritable. People who would ordinarily not bother us suddenly become enormously irritating when we don't have enough Imitation Love.

Once again, it isn't *people* who make us angry. Anger is our reaction to the emptiness and fear that always accompany the absence of Real Love. When we have sufficient Imitation Love, we can often temporarily ignore the emptiness of not feeling loved. When we run out of Imitation Love and get angry, a new supply of Imitation Love usually makes our anger go away.

Proof 5:
When Real love makes your anger go away,
Then it's obvious that the lack of it was the real cause.

Remember the story of George on pp. 68-80. George was initially irritated with his son Dan's behavior. He was certain that his anger was caused by Dan. That seemed to make sense. After all, if Dan had behaved responsibly, George would not have been annoyed. Therefore, Dan *caused* George's feelings of impatience and irritation — right? No. As George learned to tell the truth about his own inability to love his son, he experienced the unconditional acceptance of other adults. As he felt loved himself, he no longer felt empty and afraid, feelings that had dominated his entire life. He then had no need to protect himself, or to demand Dan's respect, and his anger disappeared.

As George felt unconditionally loved, he lost his need for anger, which is a Getting and Protecting Behavior. He quit being angry *even though Dan's behavior remained the same* for quite some time. And thus he proved that Dan had never been the cause for his anger. If Dan had really been the cause, George would have continued to be angry.

I have observed the effect of Real Love on the lives of hundreds of people. George's story isn't the least bit unusual. People certainly don't lose their anger all at once as they feel unconditionally loved, but it does go away .

Proof 6:
Real happiness doesn't easily evaporate.

I defined real happiness on p. 16-17. It doesn't come and go with changing circumstances. It comes from feeling loved and from loving other people, and that feeling stays with us through struggle and hardship. Genuine happiness does not mean being entertained. *Being* happy is quite different from being *made* happy for a moment, as a dog is *made* happy for a few seconds when he gets a piece of meat or gets his belly scratched. You can *make* a dog happy when you give him what he wants in the moment, and you can *take* happiness from him by kicking him or snatching a bone from his mouth.

Genuine happiness doesn't work like that. People who feel unconditionally loved don't lose their happiness when *things* change. If you are truly loved and happy, nothing that someone else does will take your happiness away from you. They will not be able to *make* you angry because genuine happiness is within you. It is not dependent on every piece of meat that is handed to you from minute to minute, like a dog.

In summary, if you think someone is *making* you angry, you're only learning that you were not genuinely happy in the first place. When you do become angry, don't think of yourself as defective. Don't feel guilty about it. You just need more Real Love in your life.

The Freedom That Comes From Being Responsible For Our Own Anger

It's understandable that we believe that other people cause our anger. When we get angry, there is always someone conveniently close by — even if we have to find them in our own minds — and we can sure make it look like they did something wrong. But just because they happen to be there when we're angry doesn't mean they *cause* our anger, any more than someone causes a train wreck just because they happen to *see* it.

We blame people because it's better than taking the responsibility ourselves, and we learned to do it from birth. But when I blame you for my anger, I'm stuck. I'll be angry forever unless *you* change. That's unfortunate for two reasons: it's very impractical to have my happiness chained to your decisions, and it's simply untrue that my anger is caused by you. When I realize that my anger is a reaction to the emptiness and fear caused by a lack of Real Love in my life, I can now do something about it. I can tell the truth about myself and get the unconditional love I need. I can quit being angry at my children and instead be a loving parent to them. An infinitely better choice.

WHY WE HAVE CHILDREN

Without Real Love, we try to fill that huge emptiness with any praise, power, and pleasure we can find. We lie, attack, act like victims, and cling to earn the attention of others — but it's exhausting, and the Imitation Love we get is unpredictable. Because children are so dependent on us, we can use them more easily and consistently as a source of Imitation Love than we can do with other people. Adults resist our manipulations and require more from us in return. And we feel safer around children: they don't ask us why we don't get a better job; they don't tell us to be more responsible; they don't suggest that we lose some weight; they don't make us feel unattractive; they don't intimidate us in as many ways as adults do.

We don't like seeing this, but a significant part of the motivation for many of us to have children is that we feel alone, and we hope a child will love us and make us happier. That's understandable, but if we don't have enough Real Love ourselves, we will *use* our children to make *us* feel better.

Alexis and Chris lived together for two years. Both came to the relationship without experiencing Real Love, and each expected the other to make them happy. Naturally, the result was disappointment and bitterness. As their relationship was failing, Alexis thought a baby might bring them together again. Without telling Chris, she stopped using her contraceptive and became pregnant. But soon after that, Chris left the relationship completely and moved away.

Alexis: "Well, at least when the baby comes, I won't have to be alone."

What a fate! Before his birth, this child was given the responsibility to make his mother feel loved. That's a burden no child can carry and be happy — but *that's the job most children are given*, and it destroys them.

REAL LOVE FROM A CHILD

Is it ever possible for a child to unconditionally love his parents? Yes, but only after that child has been unconditionally loved himself for a long time. Very few children have been loved in that way. And no loving parent would expect such love from a child. When it comes, it's just a delightful bonus for a parent who is already loved, loving, and happy.

Chapter Summary

Parents are responsible for loving their children. Without being consciously aware of it, we inappropriately burden our children with the responsibility to love us. We do this when we manipulate them for gratitude, praise, respect, obedience, affection, and safety.

Chapter 7

The Family Meeting and
The Rules of Seeing

Imagine a large corporation where there are no meetings for training, planning, or coordination between departments. People do what they want and report to no one. However, when mistakes are made, supervisors punish the employees involved. Such an organization wouldn't last long — but that's just how most families function. Families are far more valuable than any corporation, but the planning, education, and communication in families are usually greatly inferior to those found in an average business.

PURPOSES OF FAMILY MEETINGS

With experience and insight, we learn to be stronger and happier. We learn much faster when we share our experiences with those who are learning the same things and with those who have already learned them. Family meetings give us these opportunities to share and learn.

We talked on p. 16 about the primary responsibilities of parents. The goals of family meetings are naturally similar:

1. To create opportunities for parents to see and love their children (Chapter 9)

2. To teach children how to love others (Chapter 13)
3. To teach children responsibility (Chapter 14)

When family meetings accomplish these purposes, they considerably accelerate the growth of family members. Meetings are worthless if we only use them to schedule, report, and organize *things*. We'll discuss examples of family meetings throughout the book, and will more thoroughly describe their potential structure and content in Chapter 17.

FREQUENCY

When my family first started having meetings, we had them every day. We had that much to learn. Years later, we still had them every day. It was the most important activity we did as a family. These meetings don't have to take a lot of time, sometimes only a few minutes.

THE RULES OF SEEING

Truth → Seen → Accepted → Loved (pp. 41-3). Family meetings are wonderful opportunities for children to learn to tell the truth about themselves, and to be seen and accepted by their parents and siblings. Most of us have hidden who we are — lied — for so long that we really don't know how to be truthful about ourselves. In the beginning, it can be uncomfortable and confusing, like learning another language. The Rules of Seeing make it far easier for our children to tell the truth and for us to see them. Family meetings are a great place to teach and use these guidelines.

The First Rule of Seeing: One Speaker

When two or more people compete to speak, no one is completely heard or seen. Therefore, during any truly productive interaction, there can only be *one speaker* at a time. When the speaker has been completely heard, someone else may then become the speaker. A speaker is anyone who communicates something, even without words. A child may speak by frowning or by throwing a coat on the floor.

Samantha had the responsibility of keeping the kitchen clean; her brother Aaron took care of the family room. In a family meeting, Samantha spoke.

Samantha: "You keep making a mess of the kitchen, and then I have to clean it up. I'm tired of it."

Aaron: "And you leave stuff in the family room, so you have no right to talk."

We all know where the conversation went from there. She accused him and he blamed her. Neither of them heard the other, and both felt more angry and alone. This happens in countless conversations every day, and those involved are utterly bewildered by what's happening or how to prevent it. It's all unavoidable when two people try to be seen at the same time. Let's try this interaction again with the help of a wise man (a parent) and the First Rule.

Samantha: "You keep making a mess of the kitchen, and then I have to clean it up. I'm tired of it."

Aaron: "And you leave stuff in the family room, so you have no right to talk."

Wise man: "Aaron, let's listen to Samantha before we hear what's bothering you. We can really listen to only one person at a time.

Aaron: "But she . . ."

Wise man: "I'm not saying Samantha is without fault here; I've seen the messes she makes all over the house. And you *will* have a chance to speak about that. But you two have already proven with years of experience that conversations are worthless when you both talk at the same time — haven't you? So would you be willing to try something different?"

Aaron: "But she does leave stuff in my room."

Wise man: "I know, and we will talk about that, but not right now. It simply doesn't work when both of you try to be heard at the same time."

Aaron: "All right — I'll wait till she's done."

Wise man: "Not quite. You can't bring it up until tomorrow. If you plan on talking about her immediately after she talks about you, you won't really be listening to her. You'll be thinking about what *you're* going to say. And then she'll feel like you're just attacking her in return for what she said."

So Aaron listened. He'd never done that before — he'd always defended himself when he felt threatened. That gave him moments of relative safety, but it also left him feeling anxious and alone. And it made Samantha feel unloved and angry. This time, though, Samantha said everything she wanted without being interrupted and attacked. As he listened, she felt like he saw her, and to his surprise, Aaron felt happier than he ever had when he attacked her. None of that could have happened while they both insisted on being seen at the same time.

The Second Rule of Seeing: Whoever Speaks First Is the Speaker.

This rule eliminates arguments about whose turn it is to speak and be heard. In the interaction above, Samantha spoke first, so she was the speaker. Aaron wasn't forbidden to speak; his turn was just briefly delayed.

The Third Rule of Seeing: the Speaker Describes Himself.

Virtually every time a person speaks, he's saying something important about *himself* — even when he thinks and says that the subject is other people or things.

When Samantha confronted Aaron, the important issue was not what *he* did, even though her words were about him. Going over the details about who did what would only have been distracting, confusing, and irritating to everyone. The real message Samantha was trying to communicate was that *she* felt unloved, frightened, and alone. When people are angry, they're always empty and afraid. They're trying to defend themselves and to find someone to love them. People open their mouths so *they* will be seen and heard. The most important thing we can do is hear what the speaker is saying about himself.

While Samantha talked, her father sat next to her and listened — not sympathizing or taking sides, but accepting her and occasionally asking questions. He helped her see that Aaron leaving things in the kitchen took only seconds for her to clean up — that wasn't what really mattered to her. Her real pain came from interpreting the messes in the kitchen as one of many indications that Aaron didn't care about her. In fact, she often thought she wasn't loved by anyone.

As she felt the acceptance and love of her father, her fear and anger toward her brother evaporated. And Aaron saw the effect on Samantha of being accepted and loved. He'd never seen her calm down so quickly. Arguing with her had never done that. In addition, as he listened to her, he found himself caring about her happiness (Real Love).

The most important subject to a child who is needy and fearful is *himself*. A wise parent knows that a child who is angry, lying, acting like a victim, or running is really describing his emptiness and fear. As a parent sees and accepts his children, they finally get what they really need — Real Love — and that eliminates their emptiness and fear. Such children no longer have a need to use Getting and Protecting Behaviors.

The Fourth Rule of Seeing: If You Can't Be a Wise Man, Get One.

If you feel nervous, irritated, or impatient as you talk to your children, it means you're
not feeling loved. Blinded by emptiness and fear, you can't see them clearly. *Stop talking*. Without Real Love, you won't do them any good. See if your spouse is feeling less afraid and angry than you are and can function as a wise man. Or talk to someone who can accept you, as George did on pp. 68-73.

When you're empty and afraid, you're blind to your feelings and to your Getting and Protecting Behaviors. That makes a productive conversation with your child impossible. A wise man helps you see what you're really feeling and doing. As he accepts and loves you, you can often feel safe enough to stop protecting yourself, and then you can see and accept your child. You can then go back and have a loving conversation with your child that would otherwise have been impossible. Our children need our love more than anything else we have to offer.

*****

The Rules of Seeing are useful not only in family meetings. They make all interactions with our children more productive, and I'll demonstrate their use in many kinds of situations throughout the book. The Rules also facilitate our communication with spouses, friends, co-workers, etc.

Chapter Summary

Family meetings have these goals:
1. To create opportunities for parents to see and love their children

2. To teach children how to love other people
3. To teach children responsibility

The Rules of Seeing greatly facilitate children being seen and accepted. The Rules are as follows:
1. One speaker
2. Whoever speaks first is the speaker.
3. The speaker describes himself.
4. If you can't be a wise man, get one.

Chapter 8

The Law of Choice

Nothing is more essential to our growth and happiness than the right to make our own choices. Without that ability, we become mindless objects in the hands of whoever makes our choices for us, no different than a piece of furniture or lump of clay. We cannot learn and grow unless we make our own decisions, including those which are wrong. Our children are no exception — anything that interferes with their right to choose has the potential of destroying their happiness.

This is the Law of Choice: *everyone has the right to choose what they say and do.* We must understand this before we can effectively teach our children, and they must understand it before they can be happy and develop loving relationships.

We jealously protect our own right to choose, but we do not as vigorously defend that right for others. In fact, we frequently interfere with the choices of others when those choices inconvenience us. With our behavior, we demonstrate that we believe the Law of Choice goes like this: "**I** always have the right to choose what I say and do, and . . ."

"Other people have the same right as long as they do what I want."

"Others have that right unless they get in my way or hurt me."
"Everyone else has that right unless they happen to be my son
   or daughter."

I am not saying we should never tell our children what to do.
There are many occasions when that's exactly what they need,
especially when they're young. But we're wise to remember
that when we control our children, we risk violating the Law of
Choice, and the potential price for that is very high.

UNDERSTANDING   CHOICE   AS   WE   TEACH
CHILDREN

Children are an *occasional* exception to the Law of Choice.
Sometimes we do need to control our children's choices. For
example, a parent would be foolish to allow a two-year-old
child to decide for himself whether he plays in the middle of the
highway, or drinks cleaning solvent, or plays with explosives.
However, we can abuse these "exceptions." Most of us control
our children far too much and far too long. Despite the potential
dangers of making their own choices, children must learn to
choose for themselves as early as possible — that's how they
learn and grow.

As children make their own decisions, they unavoidably
make many mistakes and experience the sensations of failure,
the disappointment and anger of others, loneliness, and
embarrassment. That's how they learn the consequences of
making unwise decisions. It's also how they learn about the needs,
fears, and the Getting and Protecting Behaviors of themselves
and other people. It is not a wise goal for a parent to protect a
child from all these inconveniences and discomforts. Eventually,
children must function independently. To prepare them for that,
we have to allow them to increasingly choose their own way,
even at the price of painful mistakes.

We can help our children avoid some of the discomfort of
life without losing the useful learning experiences. We can do

that by limiting *some* of their choices until they understand the consequences of making them. However, we're justified in making their choices only when the consequences are *unnecessarily* damaging, as in the case of allowing a young child to play on the highway.

HOW WE VIOLATE THEIR CHOICE

Without thinking, most of us control our children every day. We tell them what they can and cannot do about so many things. And we often disguise the ways we control them as we offer "advice" about what they should wear, how to comb their hair, what friends they should have, how to sit in a chair, what they should do in their spare time, what they should do for a career, how they should raise their children, and so on. We hide our controlling by saying that we're only offering "suggestions." We may even "mean well," but it's still a desire to change who they are, and the effect on them is much more harmful than we appreciate.

WHY WE VIOLATE THEIR CHOICE

Our children don't need to be controlled. They only need us to *teach* them and *love* them. With years of experience, we've already proven that controlling them doesn't make *them* genuinely happy, but we still do it because it protects *us* and brings *us* various kinds of Imitation Love, as we discussed in Chapter 6. Following are some of the excuses we use to control the choices of our children:

"I was just trying to help."

We sincerely believe that our children can't do the right thing without our interference. Because we have no faith in the power of simply loving and teaching them, we often give them "help" they don't need. The truth is, we often help them so that *we* will look good — and we're mostly unaware that we do that.

Eric was cutting a long wood pole to support a birdhouse. His father, my friend Ron, saw him and went out to help. He took the saw from Eric's hand and showed him a better way to use it. Ron's father saw them both working and also came to help. He took the saw from Ron's hand and showed him an even better way to cut the pole. Ron's grandfather came out, took the saw, and finished the cut.

As Ron told me this story, he was amazed in hindsight at the selfish mistakes they had made. Each father was "just trying to help," but each had failed to see that cutting a piece of wood correctly was far less important than allowing his son to make his own choice. As Ron took the saw from his son's hand, he could see the disappointment on his face, but he took the saw anyway. And Ron felt the same disappointment when his father took the saw from *his* hand. Ron later realized that what his son really wanted was his complete acceptance, not his interference. By comparison, cutting the wood correctly was meaningless. Three generations of fathers missed an important opportunity to be wise men who saw, accepted, and loved their sons.

We use many variations on "I was just trying to help" to justify our efforts to control the behavior of our children:

"He doesn't know how."
"He's too young."
"I'm his mother."

"But he's making a mistake, and I don't want to see him hurt."

We feel especially justified in interfering with our children's lives when we're protecting them. We forget that children learn from making mistakes. They *must* make mistakes. When we protect our children all the time, we may save them from a little pain, but we cheat them of valuable opportunities to learn from their mistakes.

One reason we rescue our children is that *we* then look strong and wise. We look like good parents on those occasions, and we enjoy being thanked for "saving" them.

We have another selfish reason for controlling our children's mistakes. When we don't, they can often cause us enormous inconvenience and make us look bad. Watch a parent who is yelling at his child for playing badly during a Little League baseball game. The parent is not primarily interested in helping his child. He's trying to avoid the embarrassment he feels as he imagines that other parents are laughing at *him*, the parent of a failure. Many parents push their children to get good grades for the same reason. We don't like our children to embarrass us.

THE SELFISHNESS OF CONTROLLING

Parents who are having trouble with a child commonly ask me, "How do I *get* him to ..." Wise parents don't "get" children to do anything. They teach them and love them. We can't see our children clearly and accept them while we're thinking about how to get them to do what *we* want.

Instead of justifying the times we control our children, we need to realize the selfishness of it. We enjoy controlling people — it makes us feel temporarily safe, important, and strong. As parents, we have many opportunities to tell our children what they "should" do. Be careful. If we don't accept and love them as they are, we won't see them clearly and will steer them in a direction that benefits us, not them.

THE COST OF VIOLATING THE LAW OF CHOICE

When we control our children's choices too much, we do prevent some of their mistakes, but the consequences are serious:

Dependent and Weak

Children gain experience and wisdom only as they make their own choices. If we make their decisions for them, they can't learn or grow, just as an athlete can't become strong without doing his own training. We cripple our children as we control their behavior.

Unloved and Unhappy

You can only feel my love if I love who you really are — an independent person making your own decisions. If I control you in any way, you can't sense that I love *you.* You can only conclude that I'm trying to change you into something else because you're defective. You can only believe that I love something that I'm trying to make you become.

Children can only feel truly loved when they make their own mistakes and then feel accepted and loved *with* those mistakes. That's the love that counts, the love that powerfully connects them to us and others. If we love them only when they do what we want, that's not Real Love, and then they feel unloved and alone. They can't feel unconditionally loved when we're trying to control their behavior.

Rebellion

It's ironic that we're mystified by the rebellion of our children — because in large part, we're the cause of it. When we control them, they sense that their inalienable right to make choices is being taken from them, and that's a frightening thing. To protect themselves, they rebel, which gives them a sense of power that feels much better than the helplessness and loneliness of being controlled and unloved.

*****

Don't throw up your hands in despair. I'm not saying that children shouldn't be corrected or guided (Chapter 11). That *is* our job as parents. I am saying that the Law of Choice is very important, and we need to remember that fact every time we interfere with a child's right to choose.

HOW CAN WE KNOW WHETHER WE'RE CONTROLLING OR HELPING?

When we tell our children what to do solely for *their* benefit — which we must do on many occasions — that's called teaching. When we limit their choices for our own convenience, we're controlling and using them.

It's easy to *say* we're doing something for the benefit of our children, but how can we *know* whether we're controlling them or teaching them? Easy — *disappointment and anger*. If we're disappointed or angry when our children don't listen to our guidance, it means there's something we want for ourselves — praise, power, gratitude, etc. Disappointment and anger tell us that we're controlling our children, not helping them. It means we're selfish and not concerned primarily for *their* happiness (Real Love).

EXAMPLES OF ALLOWING OUR CHILDREN TO MAKE THEIR OWN DECISIONS

As children get older, we can allow them to make more decisions. I'll discuss here just two examples of decisions that parents and children share. As I talk about suggested ages, remember that some children are prepared to make these choices at *very different ages*. These are *very loose guidelines*, intended only to illustrate that children can make progressively more decisions with greater age and experience.

Schoolwork

Age 8. Few children this age understand the importance of study and preparation. If they were allowed to make their own choice about when to do their homework, television and everything else would come first. They would establish a pattern of irresponsibility that would greatly interfere with their happiness for decades. The cost of allowing them to make that choice at age eight is *unnecessarily high* (pp. 120-1). This is an appropriate place for parents to make a child's choice or strongly influence it with consequences (Chapter 11 and 14). Rules need to be established about when homework is done relative to other activities.

Age 13. Joseph wanted to spend the evening with a friend. Although I knew that he had not completed his English homework, I allowed him to go, anticipating that he'd learn something from this experience. I would not have allowed this to happen when he was eight. After school the next day, I asked how he did on the English assignment.

Joseph: "I didn't get it finished, so I got a zero."

Me: "How do you feel about that?"

Joseph: "I hate it. I wish I hadn't gone to my friend's house last night."

Joseph learned that being irresponsible is expensive, and he subsequently made better decisions about his homework. He learned this wisdom because I allowed him to make his own choice and mistake. The price he paid, getting a lower grade in a class, was insignificant compared to the value of the wisdom which he later applied to many other decisions in his life. If I had made the choice for him, he would only have learned this: "I have to do my homework because Dad makes me." That is not a useful lesson in life.

Cleaning Their Room

Age 6. Most parents nag and punish children for having a messy room without understanding the *purpose* of a child cleaning his bedroom. Contrary to the prevailing parental belief, no child dies from a filthy room, and the neighbors do not circulate rumors about our child's pig sty and ruin our reputation. The real reason for children to clean their room is to learn responsibility (Chapter 14). They need to understand that we all have responsibilities, and that there are consequences for choosing to ignore them (Chapter 11). It is not appropriate to allow a six-year-old child to choose whether he keeps his room clean.

Age 13. When a child gets old enough, he needs to be allowed to keep his room as he wishes. We can't make their choices forever. If it bothers you to see a messy room, shut the door.

*****

We'll discuss more about teaching responsibility and using consequences in Chapters 11 and 14. We'll also discuss in Chapter 15 how to teach children the Law of Choice and how that affects their relationships with other people.

Chapter Summary

We all have the right to choose what we say and do. That is the Law of Choice.

We have the responsibility to help our children learn to make choices. Occasionally, when the consequences of a mistake are unnecessarily high, we need to make choices for them.

We tend to control the choices of our children for our own convenience. That makes children dependent, weak, unloved, and unhappy.

Disappointment and anger tell us whether we are telling our children what to do for their benefit or theirs.

$$\textit{Chapter 9}$$

Learning to Love our Children

In Chapters 1-5 we discussed the need that our children have for Real Love, and how they behave when that need is not filled. We then talked about how you can get the Real Love that *you* will need before you can unconditionally love your children. In Chapter 6 you learned that it's inappropriate to expect your children to love you, and in Chapter 8 you were cautioned about violating your children's right to make their own choices. In Chapter 7 you learned about some tools for communication.

Now we're ready to talk about how to actually love your children. We *learn* how to love our children, just as we learn anything else: we need to be taught; we make mistakes; and with instruction and practice, we get better at it. Delightfully, loving our children is something we can all learn to do.

LOVED → SEEING → ACCEPTING → LOVING

We talked about the process of *being loved*: Truth → Seen → Accepted → Loved in chapter 3. In this chapter, we'll discuss the process of *loving others*: Loved → Seeing → Accepting → Loving.

Loved → Seeing

What keeps us from loving our children all the time? How can we be so filled with love and understanding toward them on some occasions, and then experience moments when we want to strangle them? What happens? On the occasions when our children are difficult to love, we simply don't *see* them clearly. It's easy to accept and love them when they're "good," but when they're disobedient, angry, and so on, we don't *see* – either we forget or we never knew – that those are all Getting and Protecting Behaviors they use only because they're empty and afraid. We do not see that what they need right then is our love, not our anger and controlling.

Every time our children misbehave, they're crying out for help, and *we can't see that if we are empty and afraid ourselves.* In that condition, we can only be concerned about ourselves. We can only protect ourselves and fill our own needs. How tragic that is for our children.

Truth → Seen → Accepted → Loved. Our children must feel *seen* by us before they can feel accepted and loved. And we can't learn to see them by reading a book. Seeing them is not an intellectual exercise. When we *can't* see them, the problem is not a lack of technique. Our blindness is caused by emptiness and fear, and only unconditional love can give us sight. As we take the steps to find Real Love for ourselves (Chapter 5), we can eliminate the blinding distraction of our own emptiness and fear and begin to see our children clearly. Only then can we begin to truly understand that they're not being angry and rebellious to hurt *us*. Only then can we stop reacting to the inconvenience that their Getting and Protecting Behaviors cause *us* and begin to accept and love *them*. When our children feel our unconditional concern for their happiness, everything changes.

Loved → Seeing → Accepting → Loving. Seeing, accepting, and loving our children is a natural result of feeling loved ourselves.

Kate, 14, came home from school, threw an envelope on the kitchen table, and stomped off to her room. The envelope contained Kate's grades, which were poor, and several teachers' comments that Kate's attitude was awful. Her mother, Patricia, went to Kate's room and confronted her.

Patricia: "How could you do this?"

Kate: (angrily) "I hate school. My teachers are stupid and unfair."

Patricia: "We're going to see some changes around here, young lady. You are restricted to the house. Your friends are not coming over here, and you can't use the phone. And I'm going to check your homework every day."

They were both angry, and their conversation went downhill from there, with shouting, blaming, and crying.

Patricia had been empty and afraid her whole life. In that condition, she saw everything that went wrong as a threat to her happiness. When Kate came home with bad grades, Patricia resented having another problem to take care of. She was also afraid she'd look like a bad mother. Patricia was drowning in her own needs and fears, and anything Kate did could only make Patricia more empty and afraid. Patricia couldn't see that her daughter was drowning, too. Instead, Patricia protected herself with anger, which made Kate feel even more afraid and angry. Two drowning people can only drag each other under the water.

Over the years, Patricia had experienced countless arguments like that with Kate and with Kate's older brother. When the frustration was finally more than she could stand, she met with a wise friend and asked for advice. Patricia was looking for ways to control Kate's behavior, but her wise friend suggested that Patricia was the real problem, not her daughter. Patricia didn't like hearing that, but she also realized that the way she'd been doing things wasn't working, and she wanted to change her life and help her daughter. She listened to her friend and tried the things she recommended. She read *Real Love—The Truth About Finding Unconditional Love and Fulfilling Relationships,* and she learned to tell the truth about herself. With time and experience, she began to feel unconditionally accepted and loved. As her emptiness and fear faded, her vision became less distorted, and she was able to see herself and her children more clearly.

Patricia saw that she had always accepted Kate conditionally. When Kate was cooperative and easy to love, Patricia was accepting and kind, but when Kate was inconvenient and "bad," Patricia communicated her lack of acceptance with words, facial expressions, tone of voice, etc. Patricia realized **that** was the cause of Kate's anger, not school or "stupid teachers." Kate's anger was a reaction to the emptiness and fear that resulted from the lack of Real love in her life — a problem that *her mother* was responsible for. Patricia had the courage to see that *she* was the principal cause of Kate's anger. Most important, Patricia saw that what Kate needed now was to be loved, not criticized and controlled. As Patricia felt more loved by wise friends, she was able to share her love with Kate.

The next school term, Kate came home with bad grades again and the same bad attitude. Patricia went to Kate's room.

Patricia: "All your life I've been disappointed and angry when you did anything I didn't like. I was wrong to do that, and it hurt you. I did that because I didn't feel loved myself. I didn't know how to love you. I could only see what **I** wanted, not what *you* needed.

"I can't change the past, but I can start loving you now. I'm not worried about your grades. They mean nothing compared to you knowing that I love you."

Kate couldn't believe what she was hearing. Her anger began to disappear. Over the following weeks, she saw even more evidence that her mother was seeing and loving her. As Kate felt her mother's love, their arguments had no purpose. And as a bonus, without any pushing from Patricia, Kate's grades began to improve.

THE RULES OF SEEING—AGAIN

We can accelerate the process of seeing our children when we remember the Rules of Seeing (pp. 112-16):

Rule 1 — One speaker
Rule 2 — Whoever speaks first is the speaker
Rule 3 — The speaker describes himself
Rule 4 — If you can't be a wise man, get one

It's impossible for two people to be heard at the same time (Rule 1). When parents are empty and afraid, they tend to use their position of authority to forcibly take the position of speaker and be heard. That leaves their children unheard, unseen, and alone.

Ryan, 8, came home from school with a frown on his face. His brother said something unkind, and Ryan snapped at him. His father, Charles, heard this and spoke harshly to Ryan.

Charles: "Don't talk to your brother like that. Now, go do your homework."

Charles was not intentionally unkind or insensitive, but he had never been unconditionally loved himself and was therefore entirely blinded by his own emptiness and fear. He didn't see that when Ryan came into the house frowning and snapping, he was communicating something, with and without words. Ryan was therefore the *speaker* (Rule 2). He was trying to say something about himself (Rule 3), even though he didn't realize *what* he was trying to say — that he needed someone to see him and love him. How many of us have the insight and courage to say that we need to be loved?

Charles knew something was wrong with the way he treated his children. That was obvious from their unhappiness. But he didn't know what to do about it. He eventually asked for help from a wise friend, and without realizing it, he was following Rule 4. As he told the truth about himself and took the steps toward feeling loved (Chapter 5), he was preparing *himself* to be a wise man, much like Patricia did (pp. 131-2). He began to share his love with his children.

One day, Charles saw Ryan snap at his brother again.

Charles: "You look unhappy. What's wrong?"

Ryan: "Nothing."

Children say "nothing" when we ask them personal questions for two reasons: (1) they usually don't understand what's really bothering them, and (2) they have plenty of experience to support their conclusion that we won't actually listen and accept them if they do tell us what's wrong.

Remembering Rules 1 and 2, Charles decided to listen to what Ryan was really trying to say instead of interrupting and talking about how Ryan had treated his brother – a different subject entirely. Charles remembered Rule 3 and knew that Ryan was trying to say something about *himself* — especially about his needs and fears. Charles got up from his chair and put his arms around his son. Ryan resisted that for a moment, but he relaxed as he felt the acceptance of his father.

Charles: "What matters to me is that you're happy, and that frown on your face tells me you're not. You don't have to tell me anything, but I'd love to listen to you."

As Ryan felt seen and accepted, it was easier for him to tell his father what was really bothering him. And Charles *helped him put into words* the frustrations he was feeling. Ryan felt like nobody listened to him or cared about him. His brother was always taking things from his room without asking, and then losing them. His mother always seemed to be yelling at him about something. And his father — Charles — never spent any time with him. Ryan felt alone, afraid, and angry. Charles later said that he'd never done anything more important in his life than listen to his son on that occasion. It was the first of many such conversations.

Without help, Ryan would never have talked about all those things. Without understanding the Rules of Seeing, Charles would never have understood the real reason that Ryan was snapping at his brother. Seeing our children has a miraculous effect.

Talking to an unhappy child is not a matter of learning a particular technique. You may not take the some approach that Charles did above. Sometimes you only have to express your acceptance or affection to an angry child in order to make a big difference. When they feel seen and loved, their Getting and Protecting Behaviors melt away. In Chapters 13 and 15 we'll talk about some other specific ways you can interact with an angry child.

THE REWARDS OF SEEING

Loved → Seeing → Accepting → Loving

When we feel **loved** ourselves, we see our children without the distortion of our own needs and fears, and then we see that all their "ugly" behaviors — attacking, disobedience, accusing, manipulating, selfishness, anger, sulking, and so on — are reactions to emptiness and fear. They're not trying to annoy us or hurt us; they're trying to fill their emptiness and protect themselves. **Seeing** them clearly, we can then **accept** them effortlessly and completely. That's always accompanied by an increased interest in their happiness, which is what Real **Love** is. Again: Loved → Seeing → Accepting → Loving. This process is simple and consistent.

Seeing clearly yields enormous benefits to *us*, too:

No More Hurt Feelings or Anger

When we finally see that our children do inconsiderate and hurtful things only when they are empty and afraid, we understand how foolish it is for us to feel hurt or angry because of their behavior. Would you be angry if a drowning man splashed you with water as you helped him into a boat? Of course not. Such behavior is normal for a drowning man. And selfish, hurtful behaviors are normal for children who feel unloved, empty, and afraid. When we remember that — when we see our children clearly — we are not hurt by our children, nor do we feel angry at them. That clear vision, however, is not possible until we feel loved ourselves.

No More Guilt

Our own anger and unkind behaviors toward our children are also reactions to emptiness and fear. When we see that, feeling guilty becomes foolish.

As Wayne told the truth about himself, he felt the love of wise men and women who saw and accepted him. Freed from the blinding effects of emptiness and fear, he saw for the first time that he had not been loving toward his children. And then he felt a terrible guilt about it.

Wayne: "I did so many things to hurt my children. How can I ever be forgiven?"

Wise man: "What did you do?"

Wayne: "Whenever they got in my way, I was angry and criticized them. I only thought of myself and failed to give them the love they needed. I hurt them a lot."

Wise man: "Were *you* feeling unconditionally loved at the time?"

Wayne: "Hardly."

Wise man: "You can't give love to anyone when you don't have it yourself. That doesn't change the pain that your children experienced, but you gave them all the love you had. You were empty and alone, so you could not have loved them unconditionally. Feeling guilty about that is a waste of time, energy, and happiness. All you can do now is tell the truth about your mistakes and feel the acceptance of loving people. As you feel loved, you'll be able to share that with your children."

Some guilt is useful. It motivates us to see our mistakes and learn from them. But prolonged guilt is an unnecessary and destructive burden that actually interferes with our ability to see and love our children.

ACCEPTING

When we're empty and afraid, we can only see what our children might do *for* us or *to* us. When they don't give us what we want, or when they inconvenience us, we naturally *can't* accept them. With sufficient Real Love, our emptiness and fear go away, and then we can see our children clearly. We see that they don't have an obligation to make us happy, so there's no reason to feel critical toward them. When we truly see our children, we effortlessly accept them, and we're not disappointed or angry with them. Most of us have never seen acceptance like that.

Accepting a Child Does Not Mean Approving of Bad Behavior

Accepting children does not mean approving of their selfish and irresponsible behaviors. We need to correct those, but we can do that *while* unconditionally loving our children. Most of us have rarely seen correction and real acceptance at the same time. Almost every time we've heard disapproval of our behavior — as children and as adults — it's been accompanied by the frowns and disappointment that make us feel unloved and alone.

Many of us *say* to our children that we love them when we scold and punish them. We say, "I love you, but I'm angry at your behavior." Although unintentional, *that is a lie* we use to justify our anger. When we genuinely accept our children, we do not feel disappointment or anger as we describe their mistakes. Disappointment and anger are selfish reactions to not getting something *we* wanted. When we learn to love our children unconditionally, we lose those feelings.

One of my younger sons recently came to tell me that he had wrecked my car. In the past, I would have angrily and self-righteously told him how foolish and irresponsible he was. I would have made him feel terrible. I had done exactly that with his oldest brother eight years earlier. During those eight years, I had learned how to feel loved myself and how to love my children. However, that did not mean approving of his irresponsible behavior. I asked him what he learned from his experience.

He said, "I learned that I can't talk to the person next to me, listen to three people in the back seat, eat a sandwich, listen to the radio, and still drive a car safely."

I didn't need to tell him that he'd made a mistake. He knew that. And my anger would only have distracted him and made it much harder for him to have learned anything I was trying to teach him. The most important thing for children to know at all times is that we love them. If they don't feel that, their emptiness and fear will drive them to use Getting and Protecting Behaviors, and they will be incapable of hearing or learning anything. My son needed to know that I accepted and loved him *while* he was careless and inconvenient to me. Loving doesn't mean ignoring bad behavior. But children learn every lesson far better while being loved than they do while feeling unloved and alone.

There were still consequences for my son's behavior. He had to pay for the increased insurance costs that resulted from the accident, and he received some defensive driving lessons from me. He learned an important lesson the same way I learned most of mine — by making a mistake. I accepted that — and him. The effect of accepting children while they make mistakes is powerful.

Although it's best to allow children to tell the truth about their own mistakes, they don't always do that without help. Sometimes we do need to point out their errors. We'll talk about that much more in subsequent chapters.

I'M SORRY AND I FORGIVE YOU

We spend a great deal of time and energy expecting or demanding that our children apologize for their mistakes. And then we consider whether we'll generously dispense forgiveness or withhold it to punish them.

If we truly accept a child, why would he ever have to apologize to us? As children learn, they must make mistakes that inconvenience people, including some that inconvenience *us*. When we insist on hearing an apology, we're saying they have no right to make mistakes that affect *us* — as though somehow we're more important than everyone else in the world. How self-centered we are.

Apologies rarely mean very much. When children apologize, they usually mean something like this: "I hate it that I got caught, and I hope that if I apologize, you won't be as angry at me." Children generally apologize to look good and to get out of trouble. It's much more productive for children to simply *see* their mistakes clearly. When we truly accept our children, we don't make them beg us for forgiveness. We have faith that when they see their mistakes, they will learn from them and be less likely to repeat them. I am not saying there is no place for a sincere and selfless apology, especially in a world where that is a well-entrenched custom. However, on the whole, children do not need to apologize to *us*, their parents. They need to see their mistakes, admit them, and learn from them as we unconditionally accept them.

LOVING

Loved → Seeing → Accepting → Loving. When we finally get Real Love for ourselves, we can give it to our children. Let me compare loving our children to sharing a bucket of water with them. When our bucket is empty – when we don't feel loved – we simply don't have anything to give them. Even when we want to love and help them, we *can't*. There's nothing in the bucket to pour out. But when we do what it takes to start filling our own bucket, we can share what we have with our children. The more we have, the more we have to give. When our bucket fills to overflowing, loving them becomes effortless.

In the beginning, you won't have a lot of love in your bucket, and on many occasions your children will do things that will completely empty your bucket. When that happens, you'll feel relatively helpless as a parent. So do something about it. Go through the steps described in Chapter 5. Tell the truth about yourself as often as possible and get as much Real Love as you can. Your children need all the love you can find. So do you.

Your first attempts at unconditionally loving your children — when you're inexperienced and don't have a lot of Real Love yourself — may feel awkward and stumbling. At times you may have difficulty knowing whether you're giving Real Love or Imitation. Real Love has consistent characteristics that help us to identify it.

Freely Given

We talked about this on pp. 56-8. Real Love is given freely, with no expectations, manipulations, disappointment, or anger. When we're disappointed or annoyed with our children, we are not giving them Real Love. We don't need to feel guilty on those occasions, but we do need to be truthful about them so we can get the love we need (and that our children need).

Effortless

Once we have sufficient Real Love, it naturally and effortlessly flows from us. If we're "trying" to love our children, we're usually not giving them Real Love. When loving is stressful, it's a sign that we're working to get something for ourselves, or we're protecting ourselves. Although Real Love benefits enormously from conscious effort, unconditional loving is not exhausting.

In the beginning, loving *will* seem like work. That's understandable. It's not something were accustomed to doing. As we feel more loved ourselves, it will become easier and more natural for us.

Self-rewarding

I compared loving our children to sharing a bucket of water with them. After we get our own bucket filled, we can share with them. However, love differs from water in a miraculous way. Unlike water, when our bucket gets sufficiently full of Real Love, what we share is immediately and effortlessly replaced. In fact, the more we give, the more we have. When we truly love our children unconditionally, the effect is energizing and joyful to *us* as well as them. As delightful as it is to be loved, loving others produces a happiness that is far greater.

MAKING A CONSCIOUS DECISION TO LOVE

There is only one way for you to experience the miracle of love multiplying in your bucket as you share it with your children. You have to actually *do it*. It would be convenient if we could wait until we felt perfectly loved ourselves before we had to interact the first time with our children, but it doesn't work like that. Our children need us sooner than that. As I said earlier, "Changing our lives is not a matter of just sitting back and feeling more loved." We need to make a conscious decision to love our children. As we do that, our children will feel more loved, and the Real Love and happiness in our own lives will also grow.

Be aware that you are simultaneously doing two things. First, you are filling up your own bucket with Real Love. That will give you the love you need to give your children. Second, you are making the conscious decision to pour the water out of that bucket and give it to your children even when you don't have a lot to give. As you do that, you will find that you'll have more Real love than you started with. The economics of Real Love really is delightful.

When I suggest that we make a conscious decision to love our children, what exactly do I mean? What does that look like? Does that mean we have to give children whatever they want and spoil them?

Real Love means caring about the genuine happiness of our children, and that involves loving them and teaching them. We'll be discussing many examples of loving them throughout the book, but let's go over a few here. There are many things you can do to show your child that you care about his happiness.

"I love you"

Many of us — especially men — are reluctant to speak these words, except on special occasions. Our children need to hear us say, "I love you" as often as possible: when they get up in the morning, when they leave for school, when they go to bed at night – and for no reason at all. However, these words are not a substitute for Real Love. "I love you" means very little if it is obviously contradicted by our behavior, by our disappointment and anger. We'll talk more about that shortly.

Talking

In the thirteenth century, Frederick II, Emperor of the Holy Roman Empire, wanted to find out which was the oldest of all the human languages, so he organized an experiment which would be impossible today. It is described by Salimbene di Adam in a book by Provence and Lipton (1962). Frederick ordered a group of infants to be raised by foster mothers and nurses in a unique and horrifying way. The children were to be fed and bathed, but they were never to hear a spoken word. The Emperor hoped to learn whether the infants would begin speaking in Hebrew, or Greek, or Latin, or Arabic; or perhaps they would speak the language of their birth parents. But the quotation from Salimbene, who lived at the time, states that Frederick "laboured in vain, because the children *all died*. For they could not live without the petting and joyful faces and loving words of their foster mothers."

Our children *need* us to speak to them — often and lovingly. They need to hear our words as much as they need to be fed and sheltered. When a child passes through our peripheral vision, we need to stop what we're doing and say something to him. They *feel* our words as we reach out to them. When we speak to them without criticism, they feel our concern for their happiness (Real Love).

Don't force these light verbal contacts. Don't push them to share information that they don't want to give. Speaking to them with expectations is worse than not speaking at all. Simply speak their name as they pass through the room. Children — and all people — love to hear their name spoken. Have frequent family meetings. Those provide many opportunities for talking to your children. Talk to them about their friends. About school. The rest of the book will provide examples of things to talk to them about. As you speak to your children consistently, they will become accustomed to it. They will yearn for it, like food or water. They will seek out your company because you fill up their bucket.

Touching

At the beginning of the twentieth century, one of the great orphanages in Germany conducted a statistical study of the children in their care. They discovered that nearly *three-fourths* of their infants under one year of age died despite the benefit of excellent hygiene and nutrition. At about the same time, more than a dozen large orphanages in the United States reported death rates as high as *90%* for their infants, who had also received good nutrition and medical treatment.

After reading descriptions of these institutions, I'm convinced that these children died because they were deprived of one physical requirement: touch. The infants spent their days lying in individuals cribs and were not handled by the busy staff except to be washed or fed. Compared to "normal" children outside the orphanages, these "institution" babies were given more food, lived in a cleaner environment, and had access to finer medical care. They were not deprived of human speech, as the children of Frederick II had been. But still they became physically and mentally ill, and they *died*.

And then the standard practice for the care of orphaned infants began to change. Experiments were conducted in foster care, where babies were placed in homes. The children were fed no better, nor were they kept any cleaner than in the institutions. But they were physically *handled* a great deal more than they ever were in the orphanages, and they stopped dying in those horrific numbers that had previously been reported. All that tragedy had occurred because those babies were simply *not picked up and held* when they cried. They were not stroked and petted on demand, as infants usually are in most homes. It had never occurred to the administrators of those institutions that the babies needed to be held as much as they needed to be fed and washed. *So do our children.*

When our children are not afraid of being used or hurt by us, they love to be touched. We all do. We feel a delightful sense of connection to people when they touch us, as though something were traveling from their soul to ours. Our children need that.

We have so many opportunities to touch our children. Use those opportunities and see what happens. Instead of talking to your children from across the room, sit quite close. As you talk, occasionally reach out and touch their hand. When your child watches television, don't just pass through the room or sit in another chair or at the other end of the couch. Sit next to him. We sometimes act like we're afraid of our children. That's because we *are* afraid. Reach out and put your hand on your child's knee and give it a gentle squeeze. Or put your arm around his (or her) shoulder. Don't do anything that makes him uncomfortable. That's foolish. But don't avoid contact because *you're* uncomfortable.

Touch your children as you pass by them in the house. Touch them on the cheek as you experience a tender moment. Hug them when you feel affectionate. If you don't usually do that, you have to start some time. When you first see a child after he comes home from school, or when he gets up in the morning, that should be a cause for celebration, should it not? Who else in your life is more important? Why do we wait to throw our arms around them until we've been apart for months or years? Or until they're graduating or getting married? In our home, I often run across the room and hug my children when I haven't seen them for just a few hours. We get a kick out of that. Keep making physical contact with your children, and they will come to love it. Children love to be touched when we genuinely love them.

Looking

Studies have shown that most of us become uncomfortable when people look directly into our eyes for more than a few seconds at a time. We're uncomfortable because we're certain that the person looking at us will find something wrong with us. It always boils down to a lack of unconditional love. When we're confident that we're loved, direct eye contact can be an extraordinarily loving gesture. We need people to look at us, talk to us, and touch us, and we're not getting nearly enough of any of those. Neither are our children.

Most of us have a tendency to not look at our children. When they pass through the room, we're vaguely aware of their presence. We may nod at them, speak to them, or look in their direction, but we rarely look directly into their eyes. Our children need us to look at them. It nourishes them. We need to experiment with that. They won't be comfortable with you looking at them for prolonged periods of time in the beginning. It's just too strange. But you'll discover something that is acceptable to them, and eventually, they will enjoy you looking at them. It's an intimate way of making contact with them, much like a hug.

Time

I don't have to ask a man (or woman) what's important in his life. I only have to *watch* him for a day, or a week. We invest our *time* in the things that are important to us. Many parents have told me that their children are the most important thing in their lives, and then as I talk to them, it becomes clear that they devote little or no time to their children.

We *make* time for the things that are important to us — *and our children know that.* When we're always busy with other things — no matter how brilliant our excuses are, and how terribly important we make those other things out to be — our children can only conclude one thing from our behavior: "You don't love me." And they're quite right, are they not? Certainly we love them less than the other things we're doing. And a child doesn't care what all those other things are. A child only knows whether he's being unconditionally loved in sufficient quantity or not. Yes or no. Our excuses are quite irrelevant to him.

A father recently said to me, "I wish I had more time with my children." He said this after he had described the Getting and Protecting Behaviors of his children which proved that they were quite unhappy.

Me: "You can spend all the time you want with your children."

Father: "My job doesn't allow me to be home as often as I want."

Me: "You sound so helpless. Do you want to be a good employee or a good father? Do you want a happy boss or happy children?"

Father: "You don't understand."

Me: "I understand completely. You've chosen to please your employer and use him as an excuse to neglect your children."

Father: "If I told my boss that I had to spend more time at home, I might lose my job."

Me: "Then lose it and get one that will allow you to be a good father. Decide whether you're going to be a loving father or not. Your children are dying without your love. No one in the world can help them but you. Are you willing to do what it takes to love them?"

We rarely have to get fired to spend more time with our children. But we do have to consciously make decisions to be with them. What do we do in our time with them? Talk, play games, work, attend athletic events, even sit and read in the same room (preferably next to them). When we spend our time with them, they can feel our concern for their happiness, which is the definition of Real Love.

Forgiving, the absence of anger

This evidence of our love is so important I will address it in a separate section below.

*****

We choose the way we see our children — and everything else. We can choose to be angry and selfish — or we can choose to be loving. We can't choose to change from selfish to loving overnight, but we can decide to start taking the steps to finding Real Love for ourselves (Chapter 5). And then we can begin to see, accept, and love our children. It doesn't happen by accident. We choose to love.

WE CAN CHOOSE NEVER TO BE ANGRY

If I could only give one piece of advice to every parent, young and old, it would be this: **Never express disappointment or anger to a child**. Why, of all the things I could say, would I choose that? Because despite doing twenty things *right* with a child, if we express anger toward a child even *once*, that child will feel unloved. The effect of disappointment and anger is more devastating and profound than we can imagine. We simply must eliminate it from our lives.

Choosing to eliminate anger from our lives might be the single most loving thing we can ever do for our children.

How do we do that? Remember that anger is a Getting and Protecting Behavior, and those behaviors are eliminated by the presence of Real Love. In the long term, we will eliminate anger from our lives as we find Real Love, and we learned how to do that in Chapter 5. Feeling loved and not being angry in the first place with our children is by far the best approach. However, that takes time.

In the beginning, you can't start off with a full bucket of Real Love, and there will be occasions when your children do things that will lead to you feeling empty and afraid. They'll inconvenience you, disobey you, etc. When you do become angry, is there something you can do to prevent the terrible injuries that always result when your children are assaulted by that hot stream of irritation that boils out of you?

There's a lot you can do. I suggest four steps. These are found in *Real Love—The Truth About Finding Unconditional Love and Fulfilling Relationships*.

1. Be quiet.
2. Be wrong.
3. Get loved.
4. Be loving.

1. Be quiet.

When you're angry, your child can only hear four words from you: "I don't love you." Period. The thing they want most in all the world is to be loved by you, and the instant you get angry, the only thing they feel is the withdrawal of your love. I am not exaggerating one bit. When you're angry, you might as well beat them on the head with a board.

When you're angry, your children immediately become empty and afraid. In that condition, they can only use Getting and Protecting Behaviors. They can't listen to what you're trying to teach them. Consider the foolishness of continuing to speak. Consider the damage you're doing to your children. And then be quiet. Whatever you have to say can wait until you're more loving. Your child won't hear you until you're more loving anyway. Or you could get your spouse to talk to your child. Remember the Fourth Rule of Seeing? If you can't be a wise man, get one. Perhaps your spouse won't be angry and can handle the situation better than you can. Never afflict your child with disappointment or anger.

2. Be wrong.

You will find it much easier to take the first step (Be quiet) if you simultaneously take this second one. Say this to yourself: "If I'm disappointed or angry, I'm wrong."

This is not a difficult conclusion. On pp. 60-4, we proved at great length that other people don't make us angry. Anger is a choice. Remember that? In this case, we are choosing between two things, anger or love. Let's examine those choices.

A. Anger. Anger is a Getting and Protecting Behavior which selfishly serves *us*. It absolutely destroys the happiness of our children and creates an emptiness and fear which they will likely carry with them for the rest of their lives.

B. Love. Love is what they need more than anything else. It's what we can selflessly give them when we care about *their* happiness.

On p. 16, I said, "The entire goal of life is to be happy .... Since happiness is the central goal of life, a behavior is right when it contributes to genuine happiness — in other words, when it leads to being unconditionally loved and to loving others. Any behavior which interferes with feeling loved and loving others is therefore *wrong*."

Being disappointed and angry at our children would therefore qualify — in every imaginable way — as *wrong*. Certainly we can try to justify our anger by pointing out that our children's behavior is also wrong, and certainly it often is. But what they need most to be happy is to be *loved and taught*. Do we want to fulfill our primary responsibilities as parents or not? In subsequent chapters, we'll be discussing many examples of how to love and teach our children. But their behavior *never* justifies our anger. Nor is it *benefitted* by our anger. Our anger is wrong *and* ineffective.

When we're angry, we're unloving, blind, ineffective, selfish, and controlling. Could we be any more wrong? It's very helpful to see that we're wrong because it's *being right* that helps fuel the fire of our anger. It's difficult to continue being angry when we see that we're wrong.

3. Get loved.

We only get angry at our children because we're empty and afraid — because we don't feel loved. When we get the Real Love we need — when we have that one thing that matters most in all the world — the things that our children do are no longer threatening to us. We don't become more empty or afraid and have no *need* to get angry.

In Step 2, I suggested that you admit to *yourself* that you're wrong when you're angry. It makes an even bigger difference if you can admit that to someone else. When you get angry at your children, talk to someone capable of seeing and accepting you — a wise man (Chapter 5). When you do that, you create the opportunity for someone to love you while you're making a mistake. That is a powerful feeling indeed. *That* is the Real Love that will greatly reduce or eliminate your emptiness and fear. Without those feelings, anger will gently slip away.

On pp. 68-73, George learned how to respond differently to his anger. For years his anger had made him unhappy, hurt his son, and destroyed their relationship. But on this occasion, he learned something. When he felt himself become irritated at his son, he stopped talking – he took Step 1 (Be quiet). He realized that being angry was the wrong thing to do (Step 2). And then he took the additional step of calling someone who could see and love him. As he told the truth about himself, he felt accepted and his anger vanished.

Sometimes we don't actually have to make contact with a wise man to eliminate our anger. On some occasions it's enough for us to just *remember* that we're loved. When we feel stressed, sometimes we can lean back in a chair, close our eyes, and picture ourselves resting on a beautiful, warm, sandy beach, with a gentle breeze blowing, and the sound of a quiet surf lapping a few feet away. We can relax as we picture that without actually *being* on that beach. As we remember feeling unconditionally loved, the sensation can be even far more powerful.

Of course, you can only *remember* that you're loved if you've previously taken the steps to find Real Love and have actually felt the acceptance and love of wise men and women. Once you've done that, you can carry the memory with you everywhere you go. Your anger is a sign that you are not feeling loved. As you're learning to find Real Love for yourself, it's only natural that there will be situations with your children – especially with them – where your half-filled bucket gets drained faster than you anticipated and you'll be angry before you realize it. At those times, make a conscious effort to *remember* the Real Love you've been given – even before you make an attempt to contact someone to get more love.

Remembering that you're loved can also prevent anger from starting. As you feel loved consistently, you'll find that you rarely get angry at your children when they do the things that used to irritate you. Real Love eliminates your fear and your *need* to get angry.

4. Be loving (Do something loving).

As I said on pp. 141-2, "There is only one way for you to experience the miracle of love multiplying in your bucket as you share it with your children. You have to actually *do it*." Loving our children is mostly a conscious decision — a decision to care about their happiness over our own. If you want to eliminate your own anger, make a decision to do something loving for them — or toward them.

Like what? This isn't hard. What would you like done for you in a situation where someone was angry at you?

Years ago, my son Mike called me at home to say that he'd been in an automobile accident. After learning that he was all right physically, I drove to the scene, which was not far from our home. It didn't take long to determine that he had been driving much too fast on the wet road, and without the excuse of any other driver on the street to cause the accident, he had driven off the road, through three people's yards, and wrapped my car around a power pole. All on a straight stretch of road. I was already irritated when I asked him what happened, and when he told me that it was the street's fault, I was really angry. Of course, I felt justified because the insurance rates for a sixteen-year-old driver were already high enough. I could only imagine what they would be after this.

I knew that it was wrong to be angry at my son (Step 2 above). I already had years of evidence that anger had caused great damage to my children, and I had begun to learn to love them unconditionally. I knew that I needed to shut my mouth (Step 1). But I needed something more. I was about to open my mouth and say something unkind, and I knew that wouldn't help. So instead I gave Mike what I thought he needed most. I put my arms around him, told him I loved him, and said that we'd figure out all the details after we cleaned up the mess.

After we took care of the accident, he understood completely that he was in the wrong. He didn't need to be beaten over the head with that. He learned from his mistake. What he needed was to feel loved while he made his mistake.

In the moment that you're angry, there are many things you can do to indicate your love for your children. Hug them or otherwise touch them. Speak softly to them. Look them directly in the eye. Tell them you love them. If they appear hurt or afraid, ask them how they feel, even though they may not know or may not tell you.

It's best to take steps 1-4 *before* your children realize you're angry, but we all need to understand that we express our anger much sooner and much louder than we think. Our children pick up the slightest hints of our disapproval in our posture, facial expression, tone of voice, choice of words, and physical avoidance of them.

When you've expressed your disappointment or anger, remember how hurtful that is to your children. Remember that it's your job to heal those wounds. Have the courage to tell your children that you were wrong. Have the courage to say – at the time or later – "My anger has nothing to do with you. It is not your fault. I'm simply not being loving enough, and that's my problem, not yours." There's one example of me doing that with my son Benjamin on p. 185.

Don't stop with an explanation or an apology. It's Real Love that heals wounds. We should always be loving our children, but after an expression of anger, we really need to pour it on. We need to do those things we discussed on pp. 143-8, and more.

*****

As we simply eliminate the destructive forces of disappointment and anger from our lives, our children feel a great acceptance from us. When we go beyond that and actively show them our acceptance and affection, their happiness grows exponentially.

REAL LOVE IS NOT ALL OR NOTHING

The more loved we feel and the more we practice seeing and accepting our children, the more loving we become. We *will* make mistakes, and at times, we'll be empty and afraid instead of loving. There's no need to feel guilty about that. We just need to keep telling the truth and taking the steps toward feeling loved and loving (Chapters 5 and 9) — as we do that, our ability to love will grow.

As we're learning to love, we'll be confused at times about why we're doing something for our children: "Is this really for them, or is it for me?" For an individual act, we may have some selfish expectation for gratitude or praise mixed in with our genuine concern for their happiness. Don't worry about it. We're all learning. As we honestly acknowledge the selfish part of our motivation, and as we practice loving, Real Love will become an increasingly greater portion of our motivation.

THE EFFECT OF LOVING OUR CHILDREN

All the problems with our children result from them not feeling unconditionally loved. The solution is obvious: love them. Sometimes other things need to be done, also, like imposing consequences (Chapter 11). However, if Real Love is left out of any solution, it won't work.

As we see, accept, and love our children, they're filled with what they need most. They no longer feel empty or afraid. They have no reason to get Imitation Love or protect themselves. They feel safe telling the truth about themselves, making it possible for them to feel even more seen and loved (Chapter 12). Without the blinding effects of emptiness and fear, they can see other people clearly, and can learn to be accepting and loving themselves

(Chapter 13). They also learn to be responsible (Chapter 14). And finally, as we love our children, *we* are always happy. Real Love changes everything.

Chapter Summary

Loved → Seeing → Accepting → Loving. As we get Real Love in our own lives, we eliminate the need and fear that blind us. We can then see our children clearly, which is followed naturally by our accepting and loving them. With Real Love, children become happy and loving.

As we see clearly, we lose our own anger, hurt feelings, and guilt.

Real Love is freely given, effortless, and self-rewarding.

Our capacity to love our children grows much faster if we do more than just wait to feel loved. We need to make conscious decisions to share the love we have with them and to eliminate anger from our lives.

Chapter 10

Faith

In Chapter 5, we talked about the necessity of having faith as we tell the truth about ourselves in the process of feeling seen, accepted and loved. To be wise and loving parents, we must now take our faith a step further for the benefit of our children. We need faith (1) in the power of truth, (2) in the power of Real Love, and (3) in our children.

FAITH IN THE POWER OF TRUTH AND LOVE

Many times I shook my head in frustration as I wondered, "What is it going to take to make this child understand this? What is wrong with him?" I was utterly baffled that a child could so stubbornly resist learning such a simple principle as going to bed on time, or brushing his teeth, or doing his homework consistently. Could learning be that complicated? I know that millions of other parents have wondered the same thing.

Learning is not complicated. Learning is simple *when the teacher doesn't get in the way*. That had been the problem all along. I thought I was teaching my children, but I kept getting in the way.

Our children only need two things as they learn and grow. They need to be taught the truth — the difference between right and wrong — and they need to be unconditionally loved while they're learning. *With enough love and guidance, children tend to do the right thing and be happy.* Children do not need to be manipulated, controlled, and punished to do the right thing.

It's clear that most of us do not believe that. We control the behavior of our children every chance we get. And then we justify that approach with every mistake they make, certain that if we didn't control them, they would undoubtedly make even more mistakes. We can't imagine that if we controlled them *less*, they would actually learn *better* and make fewer mistakes. It takes *faith* to release our tight grip on them and allow truth and love to change them instead of us.

Are we not a bit arrogant to think that *we* can control our children's lives with better effect than the power of truth and love? And yet we do that regularly. And it's understandable that we do that. Where have most of us ever seen an example of someone teaching and loving a child without controlling him? How would we ever have developed faith in raising a child that way?

In the face of uncertainty, we don't do what's right or most effective — we do what we're most familiar with. As parents, we do what we saw our own parents do. That's why we keep hanging on to the controlling and anger we've always used to get our children to do what we want. We're understandably skeptical of raising children in a way we've never seen.

Making a leap of faith to the way of teaching and loving is much easier when we remember that all the bad things our children do — being disobedient, selfish, angry, etc. — are just Getting and Protecting Behaviors they use when they feel unloved, empty, and afraid (3:1). When children feel unconditionally loved, they lose the *need* for those behaviors and stop using them. It's our responsibility to give them that love. They can't feel loved while we are still impatient with them and controlling them. As long as they feel our lack of acceptance, their Getting and Protecting Behaviors are certain to continue. It doesn't seem like such a leap of faith to love them when we see that *not* loving them guarantees that they can't change their behavior.

When we have faith in the power of teaching and loving our children, we don't need to get excited about every little mistake our children make. We know that mistakes are part of growing, and we trust that with love and guidance, they'll learn everything they need to know. We can give up all the criticizing, controlling, and punishing that work so poorly, require so much effort, and make everyone so very miserable. The worry and frustration of parenting disappear.

FAITH IN LOVE IS A CHOICE

There's only one way to know that our children will be happier as we love them unconditionally — we must *choose* to love them *before* we have proof that it will work. That's why it's called faith. The change in our children only comes *after* we've exercised faith and given them the gift of Real Love.

Faith is much more than words. Faith means believing that something is true and then *acting* on that belief, despite our fears. We're afraid to just love and teach our children and then wait for the result. That fear could only come from a belief that our children have a basic desire or tendency to choose poorly. We think we have to control them before they'll go in the right direction. We're wrong. Our children are *not* bad. Believing that is not a trick of positive thinking — it's the truth, and it becomes obvious *after* we choose to exercise our faith, love them, and experience the results.

When we don't believe in the basic goodness of our children and in the power of the truth and love, we control them and treat them in ways that make them more empty and afraid. And then they use even more Getting and Protecting Behaviors. Without faith in the power of love, we cannot be better parents and help our children to be happy. Have we not already proven that in the world a billion times over?

FAITH IN OUR CHILDREN

It's not enough to have faith in the truth and in love. We must also have faith in our children. They need to feel our belief that they're doing their best to learn and grow as we love and teach them.

Nancy was upset at her sixteen-year-old daughter, Lindsey.

Nancy: "You told me that all my problems with her would disappear if I accepted and loved her."

Me: "They usually do. What happened?"

Nancy: "I haven't said an angry word to her for nearly a week, but her behavior hasn't changed a bit."

Me: (laughing) "You're just getting warmed up. You've hurt her a thousand times or more over the years with your disappointment and criticism, so it's understandable that she doesn't yet believe at this point that you won't keep doing that. In addition, as you're learning how to love her, you naturally make mistakes and go back to being irritated with her — as you are right now. Lindsey sees those times as evidence that you haven't changed."

Nancy: "How long do I have to keep doing this?"

Me: "*As long as it takes.* You want her to be nice to *you*, and that's not an appropriate expectation for a parent. It's your job to love *her* and have faith that your love and guidance are all that she needs. That will take time — you can't force her to hurry up and trust you."

Nancy: "But she'll take advantage of me being nice to her and will keep being disrespectful to me."

Me: "Yes, she might do that for a while. So what? You have nothing to lose. It couldn't be worse than the relationship you have now. And it's your job to love her even while she is disrespectful.

"In the meantime, you need to be loved by other people (Chapter 5). You need to have faith that *you* can change and learn to be loving. You need faith that loving Lindsey — not nagging and controlling her — will make her happy and loving. *And* you need faith in *Lindsey*, that she's doing her best as she's learning and making mistakes. If you don't do all that, you'll never have a loving relationship with her, and she won't learn anything."

Nancy: "You're saying this is all my fault?"

Me: "Sure. It's always the parent's fault. You can insist on being right if you want — and you probably are right about a few things — but is that more important than your daughter's happiness?"

Nancy: "What happens if I love her and she doesn't change?"

Wise man: "That's why it's called faith. You love her without any proof that it will produce what you want. If you keep loving her without her doing anything to earn it, she'll feel that, and she will almost certainly change — although it may happen more slowly than you'd like."

Nancy: "I'm supposed to love her even when she's being
            rude to me?"

Wise man: "Of course. Real faith means believing that she's
            doing her best to change her life *even when it appears
            that she's not*. It takes no faith to do something when
            you get an immediate reward for everything you do.
            That's easy. Until you're willing to have faith, your
            relationship with Lindsey is doomed."

While we're loving and teaching our children, they *will* "use"
us. It won't be "fair." We will give them far more than they give
us. That's the way it's *supposed* to be. Loving our children *is* a
one-way affair, from us to them.

When we have faith in our children, they feel accepted and
worthwhile. They're more likely to tell the truth, feel loved,
and abandon their Getting and Protecting Behaviors. They're
far happier and learn more quickly than children whose parents
don't trust them — parents who rely on criticism and controlling
instead.

Very few of us have faith in our children. We prove that
each time they make mistakes. Instead of unconditionally loving
them and believing that they're doing their best to learn, we nag,
criticize, control them, and withdraw our approval and affection.
Those behaviors are absolute proof that we don't have faith
that they're doing their best. Instead, we believe that our lazy,
irresponsible, and basically flawed children must be controlled
and manipulated to do what's right. Although we don't intend to
communicate that message, we say it with our behavior — and
they feel it.

Without Real Love, children feel empty, alone, and afraid,
and then they do whatever gets them Imitation Love. They lie,
attack, act like victims, cling, and run — all the things we find
irritating in a child. And we cause it by not unconditionally
loving them and having faith in them.

Faith in Our Children Is A Choice

"Trust is earned." We've all heard this old saying many times, usually spoken in an accusing way to someone whose trustworthiness is in doubt. And many of us have applied it to our children. Every time we act disappointed when they make mistakes, we teach them that they have to *earn* our faith in them. They can't feel loved when we do that, and then they use Getting and Protecting Behaviors to diminish the pain of being alone.

Everything in our lives changes when we see that faith is a *choice*. Faith is not a feeling. It's not wishing or hoping. It's faith when we *choose* to believe something is true and then *act* on that belief.

Our children are most likely to make the right choices and be happy if we simply love them and teach them. That's all we need to do. We prove that we have faith in that when we don't control them, and when we don't get disappointed or irritated at them when they make mistakes. It's real faith when we continue to love and teach them — trusting that they're doing their best — *as they make their mistakes.*

Kylie was always in trouble, at school and at home. Her parents tried criticizing, controlling, yelling, and punishing, but none of that worked. With the help of wise friends, they took the steps necessary to get Real Love for themselves (Chapter 5). With that, they were gradually able to accept and love their daughter.

Even though she was beginning to feel the love of her parents, Kylie still made mistakes. One night, she came home several hours past the time she had agreed to be in the house. Her father, Jack, was furious and talked to his wife, Marsha.

Jack: "She's never going to change. All this loving and teaching isn't doing any good. I'm going to put a stop to this behavior right now."

Fortunately, Marsha was feeling more loved at that moment than Jack.

Marsha: "Have you noticed how much happier she is than she was a month ago? She smiles more. She doesn't slam doors as often. She speaks to us when she comes in the room. She still has lots to learn, but she's not going to learn it while we yell at her and make her feel bad. We already proved that in the past. All we can do is continue to love and teach her. I believe she really is doing the best she can. Trust her and it will be all right."

Jack: "(Pause) I'm not so sure."

Marsha: "Have a little faith. You stay here, and I'll talk to her about being late."

The moment we choose to not trust our children, they don't feel loved, and then they're certain to use the very Getting and Protecting Behaviors we're trying to eliminate — the behaviors that are hurting them and making them unhappy. Marsha had faith in the process of loving her daughter, and she trusted that Kylie was doing her best. It made an enormous difference in their relationship.

NOTHING TO LOSE

We're afraid to have faith in something new. We're afraid it won't work. And we worry, as Nancy did (pp. 160-2), that our children will take advantage of us. *So what?!* That won't kill us. It can't be worse than the anger and unhappiness we have now as a result of controlling them. Nothing will change until *we* do something different. We have nothing to lose by having faith that our children only need to be loved and taught. Why keep repeating what we're doing, however well-intended, when it doesn't work?

Chapter Summary

Children do not need to be controlled. They only need to be taught and loved while they're learning. We show faith in that when we continue to teach and love them while they make their mistakes.

When we have faith in the truth, in Real Love, and in our children, our children feel much more loved and learn more quickly.

Chapter 11

Correcting a Child

As children make choices, they learn what makes them happy and sad, loved and despised, entertained and bored. Because of their inexperience, they often make unwise choices that result in unhappiness for themselves and inconvenience for others. Those mistakes are unavoidable. It is then our responsibility to correct them, to an extent that varies according to their age (Chapter 8).

THE PURPOSE OF CORRECTION

Our purpose as parents is to teach children to feel loved, to love others, and to be responsible. That is the formula for happiness. Correction has the same purposes, and is intended only to make our children happier. When we forget that, we correct our children in harmful ways and for selfish reasons.

WHAT CORRECTION IS NOT

The word "correction" has many negative connotations. We send convicts to "correctional" facilities. We "correct" an irritating problem or terrible mistake. Correction implies that something is defective and unacceptable. Unfortunately, when we correct our children, we usually *do* think they're defective, and *they feel that*. Let's discuss two of the unproductive ways we correct our children.

Correcting Them for Our Own Convenience

Children require a great deal of time and attention. Although we don't like to admit it, we often find that inconvenient, and on many occasions, we correct their behavior solely for the selfish purpose of reducing the inconvenience to ourselves. For example, when children make a lot of noise, why do we tell them to be quiet? Because we think it would make *them* happier? No, because *we* don't like the noise, and because we're *bigger* than they are and can *make* them stop. There's nothing selfless about that.

We often correct our children's behavior for selfish reasons, and they can see that. They're not stupid. They see in our frowns and tone of voice that we don't care about *their* happiness. They see that we often think of them as an inconvenience that must be moved out of our way. When we correct them for those reasons, we hurt them.

Stopping Them From Doing the Wrong Thing

On p. 133, Charles stopped Ryan from speaking angrily to his brother. He felt justified in doing that because Ryan's behavior was wrong. Charles achieved a moment of peace for himself, but he failed to accomplish the far more important goals of helping his son to feel loved and teaching him to be loving. Instead, he taught Ryan this: "Ryan, I don't like it — and I don't like you very much — when you're angry at your brother." Ryan learned that something was wrong with him when he was angry. When we correct children with disappointment or irritation, they hear that they're unacceptable, and then they feel alone and afraid. They react by attacking, being victims, and running, which makes them even more empty and alone.

We often make the mistake of stopping arguments between children, reasoning that what they're doing is wrong. We forget that when they're arguing, they're describing their emptiness and fear (the Third Rule of Seeing, Chapter 7). An angry child needs to be seen, accepted, and loved — as Charles did with Ryan in their second encounter (p. 134). He may need correction, too, but never with disappointment or anger. When we love children, we eliminate the emptiness and fear that caused their anger in the first place. We treat the real problem, not just the symptoms.

We tend to respond poorly to the Getting and Protecting Behaviors of our children. Chapters 18-22 discuss how to approach each of them more productively.

HOW TO CORRECT

Correcting children effectively can be very simple. We need to:

1. Love them.
2. Teach them (tell them the truth).
3. Have faith.
4. Sometimes impose consequences.

1. Love Them

In Chapter 9, we discussed how we can learn to see, accept, and love our children. This is not a technique. It's not a collection of words to memorize and use at the right times. Just as we can't physically feed our children without having food to give them, we can't unconditionally love our children unless we feel loved ourselves and therefore have love to give them (Chapter 5). Real Love is not something we can fake, and without it, all the other steps of correcting a child are worthless.

It's tempting to believe the lie we often tell ourselves — that anger is sometimes necessary to get children to do the right thing. We use that lie because we're familiar with anger and because it often gets immediate results. But while we're disappointed or angry, our children don't hear any principle we're trying to teach. They only hear that we don't love them.

2. Teach them (tell them the truth)

We can't be happy without knowing the difference between
right and wrong (1:6), industrious and lazy, loving and selfish.
The best way to teach this to our children is to consistently tell
them when we see these qualities in *their* behavior — and we
can do this from a very early age. We need to tell them when
they're selfish, angry, and lazy — but never with disappointment
or anger. We also need to tell them when they're being selfless
and loving.

Remember that the only purpose for telling a child the truth
about himself is to help him feel loved and to help him learn to
be loving and responsible. We should not tell children the truth
about their mistakes to control them or to make them feel bad.

If a child sees his own mistake and acknowledges it, we don't
need to point it out. For example, when my son wrecked the car
(Chapter 9), he did not need to be told that he'd made a mistake
and been irresponsible. He knew that and freely admitted it.
However, when a child doesn't see his mistake, he needs to hear
the truth about it.

Christopher was ten. When he got home from school, he
ran to the kitchen, pushed aside his six-year-old sister Heather,
and ate the last cookie while she howled with frustration. Their
mother came when she heard the noise.

Mother: "What's going on?"

Heather: "He ate the last cookie — and he pushed me."

Christopher: "I got there first, so it was mine."

The first step of correction cannot be skipped. Christopher
had to feel loved before he could be taught anything, and Real
Love cannot be pretended. If we feel unloved and irritated at the

moment that an event like this drops in our lap, we will be quite incapable of teaching our children anything useful. Fortunately, Christopher's mother had previously taken the steps to find Real Love (Chapter 5) and therefore felt loved. When she participated in this interaction with her children, she didn't *hide* her impatience and anger. She felt genuinely loving and was able to teach Christopher.

Mother: "Christopher, I'm not angry at you. Do you understand that?"

Christopher shrugged his shoulders and nodded. He could feel that his mother was not angry at him. Even when we're doing our best to hide it, our children can easily feel our irritation. We express it in so many ways. It's not enough to just *say* we're not angry.

Mother: "I only want to help you see what you did. When you ate the cookie, you were thinking only of yourself. That's pretty obvious, isn't it?"

Christopher: "I guess so."

Mother: "Can you remember any times when you've shared things with Heather?"

Christopher: "Yes."

Mother: "How did you feel when you did that?"

Christopher: "Good."

Mother: "Being loving always feels good. Do you feel that way right now?"

Christopher: (pause) "Well . . . no."

Mother: "That's the problem with being selfish — you
     can get some things you want, like a cookie, but
     you never feel as happy as when you're loving.
     I'm not saying you're bad, but I can tell you that
     when you're selfish, you can't be as happy as when
     you're loving toward other people. I know that I'm
     always happier when I'm loving — like when I'm
     loving you."

It's important to tell children the truth about their behavior.
They need to know when they're selfish, afraid, and angry, and to
understand how those things make them unhappy. Those lessons
give them the insight and power to avoid Getting and Protecting
Behaviors and to choose happiness all their lives. Punishing and
controlling children don't give them that ability.

Christopher's mother simply loved and taught him. Feeling
loved, she was not distracted by her own emptiness and fear. She
was then able to see her son clearly and accept him instead of
being irritated. He felt her acceptance, so he didn't feel attacked
when she told him the truth about his behavior. Feeling safe, he
didn't need to defend himself by lying, attacking, being a victim,
or running (Chapter 3). He was then able to listen to what she
taught him.

When we genuinely love our children as we teach them
the truth, they can hear us and learn instead of protecting
themselves.

But what can you do *until* you feel loved yourself? What
can you do when you're first learning the principles of parenting
and you're confronted with a difficult child — as above — and
you become angry? You can't pretend to be loving. And you still
have to be a parent and teach your children. But correction with
anger is destructive. So what do you do?

You can at least close your mouth *while* you're angry. Any
time you speak to your children while you're angry, the damage

you do far outweighs the benefit of anything you try to teach. So you need to shut up. You can wait to have a conversation about the truth until you're no longer angry. Or perhaps you can allow your spouse or someone else to talk to the difficult child, as Jack did with Marsha on pp. 163-4. When you're disappointed, impatient, or angry, do not talk to your children. You can only hurt them with anything you say, no matter how well-intentioned you might be.

3. Faith

The effect of teaching and loving is often slow. Worthwhile and lasting changes take time. We tend to use anger and punishment because they're quicker — we can make children afraid and do what we want in seconds. Because fear has a more immediate effect, it *appears* that children learn faster when we intimidate and frighten them. But the result is a deadly illusion. Controlling children with fear accomplishes none of the real goals of parenthood. Children become happy and strong only when they learn to independently choose the right thing for themselves.

Love takes longer than fear to change behavior, but if we persist in loving and teaching instead of criticizing and controlling, our children gain real strength and lasting happiness. We need to have faith in the fact that our children will make their mistakes less when they simply see them and feel loved. It takes faith for us to give up our old habits of manipulating and intimidating. It takes faith to simply teach the truth, love our children, and wait for the results. It's worth the wait.

4. Consequences

People are creatures of convenience. We tend to do the easiest thing available to us. We also tend to repeat the same behaviors we've always done unless something motivates us to change. In physics, this is called inertia: an object moving in a certain direction will stay moving in that direction unless something changes its course. The same is true with children. They don't get wiser, stronger, and happier by accident; without our help, they would keep doing the same old things forever.

Without help, most children would not choose to work hard and be responsible. Understandably, they'd choose the easy, pleasant, and irresponsible course of eating, sleeping, and entertaining themselves. They need to be loved and taught to choose the relatively uphill path that leads to growth and real happiness. However, love and guidance are not enough in some cases. That's what consequences are for — *to motivate children to consider doing the right thing when love and guidance alone are not enough.* The appropriate role of consequences is only to guide children toward making them happier in the long run.

For example, if young children were allowed to choose whether they did their homework, they would likely never do it, establishing a pattern of irresponsibility and failure that would make it difficult for them to be self-sufficient and happy as adults. It would be unkind on our part to allow that to happen to a child. To prevent that, after a child makes poor choices about his homework, loving parents impose consequences: until his homework is done, they don't allow him to play, watch television, etc. The purpose of a consequence is *not to punish*, but to motivate a child to make a wiser decision, a decision he would not make on his own.

A consequence makes a wrong choice sufficiently inconvenient or unpleasant that a child will tend to make a right choice. Eventually, a child who is sufficiently loved and taught does the right thing simply because he wants to — because it makes him happier — and then he no longer needs consequences imposed. We can't impose consequences on a child all his life.

The difference between a consequence and a punishment is not a matter of technique or the words that are said — it's *motivation.* The same action that is a consequence when imposed by a loving parent becomes a punishment when coming from an angry and unloving parent.

Consequences are imposed:

to teach a principle.
with genuine concern for the happiness and growth of the child.
with no reward of Imitation Love (power, safety) for the parent.
with no impatience.
with no anger whatever.

Punishment is given:

to make a child "pay" for what he's done.
to teach a child the "lesson" that he must not inconvenience his
    parents.
for the sake of "justice."
with impatience.
to make a parent feel powerful and "in control."
with some pleasure that the child is uncomfortable.
with anger.
with shaming.

Any time we feel irritated with a child, we can only punish him and teach him that he's unacceptable to us. He learns that his safety and happiness are far less important to us than our own convenience. He learns that he's an object to be manipulated and controlled. He then feels empty and afraid, and responds with his own special recipe of Getting and Protecting Behaviors. Punishment might temporarily change a child's behavior, but the overall effect is disastrous.

INCORRECTLY IMPOSING CONSEQUENCES

Some parenting techniques suggest that consequences are effective if they're "appropriate," meaning that they "fit" the unacceptable behavior. For example, if a child breaks a window, an appropriate consequence would be for the child to clean up the broken glass and to pay for the cost of replacing the window. An inappropriate consequence would be a spanking or restriction of television privileges, both of which are unrelated to what the child did. But teaching with consequences is much more than a technique. Even if a consequence "fits" the crime, it's still useless, even harmful, if accompanied by any disappointment or anger.

Carsten had the responsibility of cleaning off the kitchen counters, but he often failed to do that, despite being told repeatedly. One morning, when he left for school without doing his job, the mess he left behind significantly interfered with the work his mother had to do that day. She called the school and left a message for him to come home instead of staying for football practice. He came home angry.

Carsten: "Why did I have to miss practice?"

His mother had been irritated at him all day.

Mother: "You didn't clean the kitchen counters before you left for school, and I've talked to you about it a thousand times. I'm sick of it."

Carsten's mother chose a consequence that "fit" his irresponsible behavior perfectly. She required him to come home immediately after school to do a job he should have done earlier, and he missed football practice as a direct and natural result of his own choice. But again, correcting children is not a technique. Although Carsten's mother intended to teach him about responsibility, the only lesson he learned was this: my mother is angry, selfish, and doesn't love me when I inconvenience her. Because of her anger, her "appropriate" consequence became a destructive punishment and accomplished nothing except to reconfirm to Carsten that he was not loved.

LOVING CONSEQUENCES

Bob's attitude toward work was similar to Carsten's. But Bob's mother had been learning to tell the truth about herself to wise men and women who accepted and loved her (Chapter 5). And they taught her the steps to correct a child. She did her best to love Bob and accept him while he was being angry and irresponsible (Step 1). She also told him the truth about his irresponsible behavior (Step 2) and had faith in his ability to learn and grow as he was taught and loved (Step 3).

However, after being loved and taught like this for several months, Bob was still ignoring his responsibilities. He needed a more compelling reason to change, something that would motivate him to consider his choices more carefully. One day when he hadn't cleaned off the kitchen counters, she called the school and left a message for him to come home instead of staying for basketball practice. He came home irritated.

Bob: "Why did I have to miss practice?"

Feeling loved herself, Bob's mother wasn't empty or afraid, so she didn't need him to behave in a certain way to make her happy. She was not impatient with him because of the relatively minor inconvenience he had caused her in the kitchen. Nor did she feel threatened when he angrily confronted her. She put her hand on his shoulder as she spoke.

Mother: "I love you whether the counters are clean or not. I just want you to be happy, and I've learned that we can't be happy when we're not responsible. I've talked to you many times about your jobs around here, but so far that hasn't been enough. I decided that if you had to miss basketball practice every day you didn't complete your jobs, you'd probably be much more likely to pay attention and learn responsibility. What do you think?"

It was clear from the expression on Bob's face that he was not grateful for his mother's effort to teach him about responsibility. And then she hugged him. Bob found it difficult to stay angry at his mother when she was obviously not angry at him.

The goal of imposing consequences is to motivate children to choose wisely. That's very different from forcing them to make the right choice or punishing them for choosing badly. We need to impose consequences not to hurt them, but to make unwise choices seem unpleasant and inconvenient enough that they'll consider not repeating them. By imposing a little discomfort now, we help them avoid the far greater pain and lifelong consequences that result from a pattern of being irresponsible and unloving.

Simply loving and teaching Bob had been inadequate because he'd acquired considerable inertia in the wrong direction. Bob's mother understood that imposing a consequence might help Bob consider changing his direction. And it worked. The next time he prepared to leave the house, he remembered that he didn't like missing basketball practice, and he cleaned off the kitchen counters.

NATURAL CONSEQUENCES

We've discussed the importance of consequences being imposed lovingly. In addition, they need to be related in a natural way to the irresponsible behavior. Consequences need to *make sense*. For example, when a child doesn't clean his room, yelling or spanking make no sense. Those are not *natural* consequences. Yelling doesn't naturally result from a messy room or irresponsible behavior. Anger comes from the fear of an unloved parent, and a child only learns this: "When I don't clean my room, my father/ mother gets angry and says unkind and hurtful things." That's a useless lesson to a child.

One natural consequence of a messy room is to live in it. When they were young, I explained to my children that everyone in the family keeps his own room clean, and that's done before playing, eating, etc. They *could* choose to have a messy room, but the consequence of that choice was to live in it — all the time. They had to stay in their messy room until it was clean, even if that meant missing meals, playtime, and events they had planned. No child made that choice for long, which was the goal of the consequence.

Another natural consequence of a messy room in our family was to have television privileges revoked. If you didn't have time to clean your room, you obviously didn't have time to watch television. The reasoning was natural and clear to even the youngest children, and it was very motivating.

Bob (above) experienced a natural consequence. He didn't do his job when it was assigned, and the natural consequence was to complete the job immediately, despite the inconvenience to him.

CORRECTION DOES NOT INCLUDE GUILT

Amanda often neglected her responsibility for cleaning the bathroom. She was confronted about that in a family meeting.

Father: "The bathroom's been a mess for several days, and we're tired of it. We just gave you a nice stereo for your birthday last week, and you thank us by being irresponsible."

Amanda's father wanted to make Amanda listen. His remark about the gift succeeded in getting her attention, but the effect was awful. Rather than learning to be responsible, she only learned this:

1. When people give me anything, they expect something in return.
2. When I do something wrong, my father doesn't love me and makes me feel bad.

Any time we even think, "After all I've done for you," we're using guilt as a punishment.

Whenever we use guilt or shame to teach our children, they only learn that *we* are empty, afraid, and willing to hurt them to protect ourselves. We don't teach them anything about love or responsibility. We just give them more reasons to feel unloved and alone.

FORBIDDING

It's dangerous to restrict the freedom of children to choose (Chapter 8). However, there are times when we serve our children best by restricting their choices, like stopping a three-year-old from playing in the road or other circumstances when the consequences would be unnecessarily damaging to them. Be careful — we can use this as an excuse to inappropriately control children. Remember that making mistakes is part of learning. We need to examine our motivation, whether we're controlling them to help *them* learn or to get something *we* want.

When my daughter Rachel was thirteen, I didn't know how to unconditionally love her, and as a result, she was very unhappy. Naturally, she began to look elsewhere for the attention she needed, and she found it with friends who were as unhappy as she was.

They all got praise from each other for doing foolish and daring things, and a sense of power from being angry and rebellious. Several of the girls also experimented with the praise, power, and pleasure of sex. Rachel was overwhelmed by the excitement of all this Imitation Love. But she was also confused and frustrated — despite all the "fun," she was becoming more angry and unhappy.

When I began to feel loved myself, I saw that I was the cause of her unhappiness. I tried to love her, but I was still learning and often failed to unconditionally accept her. I could see that she was taking a dangerous course in her life, and I just couldn't give her Real Love quickly enough to change that. Something needed to be done before she was seriously hurt.

I sat with Rachel and told her that I would love her no matter what she ever did. I talked about my many mistakes as a father, something we had talked about before. I reaffirmed my desire to do anything to help her be genuinely happy, and explained that the things she was doing with her friends were too destructive for her to understand. I said that I was going to help her avoid a great deal of pain by forbidding her to associate with her unhappy friends. I said that I loved her enough to do this despite the risk that she'd probably be very angry at me in the beginning.

I got considerable support from people who loved me before I met with Rachel, and I felt loved and peaceful as I talked to her. She never associated with those girls again, which initially was very difficult for her. Six months later, she talked to me about it.

Rachel: "Dad, you saved my life. My old friends are all using drugs and failing in school. Two of them are pregnant. They hate their families. They're alone and unhappy. And I would have been just like them if you hadn't stopped me from being with them."

Sometimes our children's behavior is too destructive to be approached by gradual measures. On rare occasions, we have to do more than teach and love them. Also see Chapter 25 about drugs and alcohol.

Forbidding as the Exception

If we correctly teach and love our children, we won't have to forbid their behavior often. Understanding the principle of choice (Chapter 8), we allow them to make as many of their own mistakes as possible. They learn from that. As we allow them to make their own choices, they also come to believe that we have faith in them, that we love them, and that we're not trying to control them. If we allow them to make most of their choices, they'll resist us much less (if at all) when we occasionally insist on making a decision for them. An example of this is found on pp. 393-5.

THE JOY OF LOVING

As we simply accept, love, and teach our children, they learn to make correct choices. Learning, including mistakes, becomes exciting and fun for them, not the painful experience most children are accustomed to. Teaching them also becomes infinitely more enjoyable for us.

Chapter Summary

Correcting children means teaching them how to make choices that will allow them to feel more loved and be more loving. Correcting is done with unconditional acceptance and without anger or impatience.

Correcting children is not to be confused with changing them, stopping all their mistakes, or punishing them.

We effectively correct children as we love them, tell them the truth about their behavior, have faith in them, and sometimes impose consequences.

Consequences imposed without unconditional acceptance become punishments.

Chapter 12

Teaching Children to
Tell the Truth and Feel Loved

The purpose of life is to be happy. Without that, every other success is meaningless. And it's possible to be happy every minute of every day — the supply is unlimited. Our children can learn to be happy, just as they learn to swim or do algebra. We give them that ability as we teach them to feel loved, love other people, and be responsible. In this chapter, we'll discuss teaching our children how to tell the truth and feel loved. Teaching them to love other people and be responsible are the subjects of Chapters 13 and 14.

TRUTH → SEEN → ACCEPTED → LOVED

Children must tell the truth about themselves before they can feel loved and happy. When they lie, they put a bag over their head, like the Wart King did (Chapter 3). Hidden by their lies, they can't feel seen and therefore can't feel accepted or loved. If the Wart King had kept the bag on his head, he could never have felt the Real Love offered to him by the Wise Man.

We can do nothing with our children more important than teaching them to tell the truth about themselves so they can feel accepted and loved by us and by others. If we succeed in doing that, they'll be prepared to find happiness the rest of their lives.

We are the best chance our children will ever have to be seen, accepted, and loved. If they leave home without knowing how to tell the truth about themselves and without feeling loved, they'll be crippled by emptiness and fear. They will unavoidably use Getting and Protecting Behaviors with friends, spouses, and others, hoping to find happiness in praise, power, pleasure, and safety. Unfortunately, as they use Getting and Protecting Behaviors, they will attract people who will criticize, attack, manipulate, abandon, and otherwise use and hurt them.

On the other hand, if we send our children into the world feeling loved, they'll be happy and loving. They'll have no need for Getting and Protecting Behaviors. It all starts with telling the truth. We teach them to tell the truth by (1) telling the truth about ourselves, (2) loving them when they tell the truth about themselves, and (3) telling the truth about them.

1. TELLING THE TRUTH ABOUT OURSELVES

Children tend to follow our example in everything, and they frequently see us lie. Page 37 lists just a few of the many ways we lie. We lie when we say or do anything to get people to like us or to avoid criticism. We do that every day — mostly without thinking — and it's a powerful influence on our children. If we hide our warts and otherwise lie, our children will, too. When we tell the truth about ourselves, they learn to do the same.

We make many mistakes as we interact with our children, but we rarely admit them. We're afraid to tell our children we're wrong. We're afraid we'll look weak and stupid and will lose their respect. Instead, we lie and pretend to be strong, right, and in control at all times. That's what we saw our parents and other people do. But when we lie, we separate ourselves from our children, and they feel alone, even though they can't describe it in words.

We have many opportunities to tell our children the truth about ourselves. We can talk about our mistakes, past and present, and about how we feel and what we're learning. As we do that, we give them an example to follow. They also feel connected to us as we include them in our lives.

Being Wrong

It was my son Benjamin's job to mow the lawn each Saturday morning. Late Saturday afternoon, he said we didn't have any gas for the mower, so I had to stop what I was doing and get some. I was irritated at the interruption and his lack of responsibility. I said, "Benjamin, you should have started this job hours ago. Instead, you put it off and made me stop what I was doing. You do this with your jobs all the time, and I don't like it."

What I said to Benjamin was true — he did need to be more responsible. But I communicated much more than a lesson about responsibility. My frown and tone of voice clearly said this: "Benjamin, I don't like you when you inconvenience me." That part of the message was unnecessary and destructive — and he heard that the loudest.

I found him in his bedroom later that evening and said, "Earlier today, you made a simple mistake and I got angry at you. I was wrong. We've talked about that in family meetings. Being angry is a choice (Chapter 6). I could have talked to you much differently, but I didn't. My anger was not your fault."

He hugged me and responded quietly, "That's okay, Dad. I'm glad you talked to me, though. I was feeling pretty bad."

We need to talk about the times we're wrong — about many things, not just our anger. Heaven knows we make enough mistakes to talk about. When we tell the truth about being wrong, we're afraid our children will think less of us, but that's not what happens. Instead, they feel accepted, loved, and not alone.

Telling the Truth About the Past

Each time we've been disappointed, angry, or withdrawn with our children, they have correctly heard that we did not unconditionally love them. It doesn't matter that we didn't intend that message; every one of those experiences still inflicted a wound as real and painful as any physical injury. Now when we tell the truth about the times we hurt them in the past, we help those old wounds to heal.

Imagine that I swerve off the road in my car, plow through your yard, and crash into your living room. In that moment, how would you judge me? Careless, irresponsible, and probably drunk. And you'd probably feel irritated at the inconvenience I just caused you. But suppose that days later, you learn that when I drove off the road, I was already unconscious because of a ruptured blood vessel in my head. Do you judge me differently now? Do you feel different about the experience? Of course. Learning the truth changes the way you see the past and therefore changes the way you feel in the present.

That also happens for our children as we tell them the truth about our past mistakes. We need to talk about the times that we were unloved and empty ourselves, and were therefore incapable of unconditionally loving them. They can then realize that all those times we said "I don't love you" with our anger, what we really meant — and didn't know how to say — was this: "I'm attacking you to protect myself from my own emptiness and fear, *not* because there's anything wrong with you. My anger is *not* your fault." The same applies to our other Getting and Protecting Behaviors, not just our anger.

How our children feel now is a result of countless past experiences. If they feel unloved, it's because they were assaulted by disapproval many, many times, usually from us. As we tell the truth now about our past behavior, we create the possibility that they can change those past experiences in their minds. As we tell the truth about ourselves, we can help them literally change the past, which changes how they feel in the present. That is no small thing.

In her first interaction with Kate (pp. 131-2), Patricia protected herself with anger because she felt empty and afraid. As Patricia learned to feel loved by wise friends (Chapter 5), she saw that she had made many mistakes with her daughter. She then began to talk to her daughter about them. That created the opportunity for Kate to see the events of the past — and herself — differently. Many times, she had heard her mother say with her actions, "When you inconvenience me, I don't like you." That's why Kate felt empty and unloved. That's why she was always afraid and used Getting and Protecting Behaviors with people.

Patricia continued to acknowledge her mistakes far longer than was indicated on pp. 132-3. As she did that, she effectively reached back in time and changed those experiences that had made Kate feel unloved. Of course, that was possible only because Kate had faith in her mother and accepted the love being offered to her. As Kate felt loved, her emptiness and fear disappeared, along with the Getting and Protecting Behaviors that naturally accompanied those feelings. Each time Patricia told the truth about herself, Kate felt more seen, accepted, and loved.

As we discuss our mistakes from the past, our children often feel safe enough to bring up painful experiences that have been bothering them, events that we've forgotten. On those occasions, they don't need us to suffer. They just need to feel loved and to heal their old wounds, which happens naturally as we're truthful and loving.

I was working in the garden with my son Michael. As we were hauling some firewood, the cart broke, spilling logs all over the path and causing me to stumble and fall. We repaired the cart, picked up the wood, and resumed our work.

Michael: "That was easy. Do you remember how it used to be when we worked outside together?"

I laughed as I realized what he was talking about. "I think so. What do you mean?"

Michael: "If that cart had broken, and you had fallen like that five years ago, you would have exploded. You yelled at us whenever anything went wrong."

Me: "I remember. You must have hated working with me."

Michael: "Sure I did, but I never think about that anymore. I'm just grateful for how happy our family is now."

Wonderful things happen as our children talk to us about the mistakes we made with them in the past:

1. They have an opportunity to feel accepted while they're accusing us of being wrong. Confronting people about a mistake is usually an uncomfortable experience for anyone. When we accept our children while they're criticizing us, they feel very loved. They also gain a confidence that has immeasurable value as they become older.

2. They see an example of someone feeling loved and not defensive while being told about a mistake. When we're not ashamed of our mistakes and are willing to learn, we teach them how to do the same thing. What a beautiful gift for us to give a child.

If our children don't bring up things from the past, they probably don't feel safe. We may need to encourage them, saying something like, "Do you remember when I . . .?" It's usually not enough for us to vaguely mention that we made unnamed mistakes in the distant past.

The Truth About How We Feel
And What We're Learning

Julie: "I feel alone and afraid most of the time, and I don't understand why."

Wise man: "You're no different than most people. You feel alone because you don't feel like anyone sees you clearly and accepts you. That started in childhood, when the people close to you *didn't* see and love you. But the reason you feel unseen and unloved now is that you hide who you are."

Julie: "How do I hide?"

Wise man: "When do people really get to see you? How often do you tell other people that you're afraid, angry, or alone?"

Julie: "Almost never."

Wise man: "As long as you hide yourself, you can't feel seen and loved (pp. 56-8). You don't know how to be truthful about yourself because you never saw it done. You never had an example of it. How often did you hear your mother talk about how she felt and what she was learning?"

Julie: "Never."

We think that good parents should look strong all the time. It's true that our children need us to be a source of stability and strength — they don't need to know about *all* of our mistakes, flaws, fears, and fantasies. But when we consistently hide how we feel and what we're learning, they feel isolated from us. We also rob them of opportunities to see the important lessons of life firsthand. Occasionally, they need to see us make mistakes, be afraid, and protect ourselves — and then see us tell the truth and learn to feel loved and be loving. As we allow them to see us learn, they learn those critical lessons themselves.

One day, Vicki asked her mother why she looked upset.

Mother: "I went to the auto parts store to get something your father needed. The clerk asked me some questions, and when I didn't know the answers, he was condescending and rude. I was angry and said some unkind things in return."

Vicki: "I'd be mad, too, if someone talked to me like that."

Mother: "My anger was understandable, but it was still my fault. I was afraid, and I protected myself by attacking him. It was my choice to be angry."

Vicki: "Why were you afraid?"

Mother: "When I was a child and did something wrong, or when I didn't know something, people made me feel stupid. They laughed at me or criticized me, and I *hated* that feeling. So I learned to protect myself by getting angry. If I got angry, I didn't feel as helpless, and people often stopped hurting me."

"So now, as an adult, when I make mistakes and feel stupid, I still get afraid sometimes and protect myself with anger. I did that today with the man at the store. I've been angry like that with you on many occasions, too."

What a powerful learning experience for Vicki:

1. She was given an opportunity to see that sometimes her mother felt unloved and afraid — just like Vicki did.

2. She saw her mother learn from a mistake.
3. She saw that anger is a choice, not a reaction beyond our control.
4. As her mother shared the truth about herself, Vicki felt connected to her.

Lessons like that change a child's life.

In Chapter 5, we talked about the importance of telling the truth about ourselves so we can create opportunities to be unconditionally accepted. We should only do that with other adults. It is not appropriate to tell the truth about ourselves to our children so that *we* can feel accepted by them. That's not their responsibility or capability (Chapter 6). The correct reason to tell the truth about ourselves to our children is to provide them an example of truth-telling and to help *them* feel accepted. We do it for *their* benefit, not so they'll love *us*.

2. LOVING OUR CHILDREN
WHEN THEY TELL THE TRUTH ABOUT THEMSELVES

We think we can teach our children to tell the truth by simply telling them to be honest. But with our behavior — which they hear much more loudly than our words — we teach them to lie. When we learn about their mistakes, we frown, sigh with disappointment, and withdraw our approval and love from them. We don't smile and hug them. To our children, the lesson is clear: "I'll be loved less when people learn about my mistakes. I choose to lie about them." That's the lesson Kimberley learned with her mother (pp. 34-5).

Children lie to protect themselves (Chapter 3). If we love them while they make mistakes, they'll feel safe enough to tell the truth consistently, and then they can feel seen and loved. If we criticize and punish them, they won't feel loved and will learn to hide the truth from us.

Again, loving them with their mistakes does not mean we don't correct them (Chapter 11).

Steven's father had always been critical and angry, so Steven learned to lie about his flaws. He avoided his father and became increasingly angry and unhappy. His father took the steps to find Real Love for himself (Chapter 5), and gradually, he learned to see and accept his son. The more loving he became, the easier it was for Steven, age 16, to trust him.

Steven: "There are some things I haven't told you about myself because I was afraid you'd be mad. But you haven't been angry for a long time, and I don't like how I feel when I hide stuff from you."

Father: "Like what?"

Steven: "Sometimes I smoke and drink beer with my friends."

Father: (hugging Steven) "So did I at your age. You do that because it makes you feel accepted by your friends, and because getting drunk feels good for a moment. If you had felt loved by me all these years, you wouldn't need either of those feelings. You already know that drinking isn't good for you, and I trust that you'll make the right decision as you feel more loved here at home. We'll talk about this again in a week or so, okay?"

This is an example of a parent having faith in a child. In time, Steven's father felt more loved and grew in his ability to share that love with his son. As Steven felt loved, he lost his need to smoke and drink to earn the acceptance of his friends. That is a consistent pattern with children who feel loved by their parents. Children who feel unconditionally loved don't *need* Imitation Love; it simply loses its appeal compared to the profound satisfaction of Real Love.

As our children feel accepted by us no matter what they do, they also feel safe telling us the truth about themselves. The more they tell the truth, the more accepted and loved they feel.

It's especially important to love our children *when* they lie. We tend to get angry or otherwise punish them when they lie, which only makes them more afraid. Then they have even more reason to lie and protect themselves. We'll discuss better ways to deal with lying in Chapter 19.

3. TELLING OUR CHILDREN THE TRUTH ABOUT THEM

Most of us have criticized our children for a long time, and they've grown accustomed to avoiding our displeasure by lying to us. Sometimes we need to help them tell the truth about themselves. There are only two reasons to confront a child with the truth about himself:

1. To give him an opportunity to be seen, accepted, and loved.

2. To help him see more clearly what he's doing, which gives him an opportunity to make wiser choices.

We tend to forget the purpose of truth-telling, and instead we tell children about their mistakes so they'll stop inconveniencing *us*. That selfish approach leads to endless expectations, manipulation, and disappointment on our part. It's exhausting and frustrating to us, but worst of all, the result is an unloved and miserable child. When we remember the reason for telling the truth about our children, confronting them isn't difficult or frightening — it can be a loving and rewarding experience for them and for us.

Review the story of Christopher on pp. 170-2. Christopher did not see that he was being selfish with his sister. He needed to tell the truth about that for both of the reasons stated above:

1. Children feel most loved when they are seen and accepted for who they really are. Christopher needed to be seen and accepted *while* he was selfish. His mother helped him tell the truth about himself and started the process of him feeling loved.

2. Christopher couldn't begin to care about the happiness of his sister until he saw the truth about his own behavior. His mother helped him see his behavior and made it much more likely that he would choose more wisely in the future.

Telling the Truth About What

We tend to focus on the *details* of events, but those are of little use in teaching children. Christopher's mother could easily have turned their interaction into a police investigation:

"Haven't I told you before not to push your sister?"
"Don't you know you could have hurt her? You're so much bigger than she is."
She could have listened to accusations from Christopher that
        Heather had called him names after he pushed her.
She could have dealt with charges and counter-charges from
        both children about who had eaten the most cookies in
        recent weeks.
She could have gone over a list of similar offenses committed by
        Christopher in the past year.

But she wisely did none of that. She told the truth about *Christopher*, loved him, and helped him make wiser choices. Especially in the arguments between children, we tend to get lost in the details, which are not important. We need to talk about their anger, their selfishness, their inability to love each other, and their lack of responsibility. And then we need to love them and teach them.

Helping Children Tell the Truth About Themselves

As our children learn to tell *us* the truth about themselves, they can take that ability to other relationships. If only adults understood the power of the kind of honesty depicted in the following story.

Allison, fourteen, had a terrible fight with her friend Elizabeth and came to her mother in tears, asking what she should do. Allison's mother was wise.

Mother: "Tell the truth."

Allison: "I did. I told her how selfish she was."

Mother: "No, I mean tell the truth about *yourself.*"

Allison: "But it wasn't my fault. She ..."

Mother: "You already tried the conversation your way. How did that work?"

Allison: "It was awful. She ..."

Mother: "So why keep doing something that's awful? Consider doing it differently. As you talked to Elizabeth, were you accepting and loving toward her?"

Allison: "Me?! She was the one who ..."

Mother: "Again, Elizabeth may have been completely wrong, but you've proven that blaming *her* makes you both unhappy. I'm not telling you what to do, but I can see that being angry and blaming her didn't work. I suggest that you tell the truth about *you.* Remember, I accept and love you no matter what you did with Elizabeth. Were you loving when you talked to her?"

Allison: "No, I was afraid, and I protected myself by getting mad."

Allison was able to see her Protecting Behavior only because she'd been unconditionally loved many times by her mother and felt safe enough to tell the truth about herself. In addition, they had discussed those behaviors in family meetings (Chapter 7 and 17).

Mother: "(laughing) That was very honest. I couldn't do that until I was thirty years older than you are. How does it feel to say that?"

Allison: "I was afraid to admit how selfish I was, but now I'm relieved to tell the truth and see that you're not disappointed in me."

Mother: "Now go and say the same things to Elizabeth."

Allison: "I don't think I can."

Mother: "Are you happy with the way things are now between you?"

Allison: "No."

Mother: "Then you have nothing to lose. Do it differently. Telling Elizabeth the truth will be scary at first, but it won't be as painful as how you feel now. Most important, *you* will learn to be happy all the time as you practice being truthful and loving. This interaction with Elizabeth will give you a great opportunity to do that — even if she doesn't respond well to what you say. Are you willing to try it?"

Allison did talk to Elizabeth, and she took complete responsibility for how selfish, afraid, and angry she'd been in their conversation. Elizabeth was stunned. In minutes, their friendship was restored.

How can we possibly measure the value of the lesson which Allison's mother taught her? As we teach our children to tell the truth about themselves, we teach them to find happiness for the rest of their lives. I'll provide many other examples of children telling the truth about themselves in the remainder of the book. And we'll discuss teaching children how to become loving and responsible in the next two chapters.

Chapter Summary

Children must feel loved to be happy, and they can't feel loved until they tell the truth about themselves: Truth → Seen → Accepted → Loved.

We teach our children to tell the truth by:
    telling the truth about ourselves -- our mistakes, past and
        present, and what we're feeling and learning;
    loving them when they tell the truth about themselves; and
    telling them the truth about them.

Chapter 13

Teaching Children to Love

Being loved feels wonderful, but unconditionally caring about the happiness of another person is the ultimate joy. We can do nothing greater than to teach our children how to experience the joy of loving other people.

Most of us think we can teach children to be loving by simply telling them to do it. For example, we often stop an argument between two children by saying something like, "Be nice to each other." How foolish we are. Their arguing is a Protecting Behavior which they use because they're empty and afraid. In that condition, they couldn't possibly be nice — another word for loving — to each other. Telling an angry child to be nice is like telling a drowning man to stop struggling and instead help the drowning person next to him. He simply *can't* do that.

Ironically, *we* are the reason our children argue. They feel empty and unloved primarily because we have not sufficiently loved them unconditionally. Fortunately, there's a great deal we can do about that.

LEARNING TO LOVE

Teaching our children to be loving is not complicated. They learn to love other people in four steps.

Step 1.   We see, accept, and love our children with their flaws.
            We discussed this in Chapter 9. Every meaningful
            parental instruction begins with us loving our
            children.

Step 2.   Our children tell the truth about themselves (Chapter
            12). It is almost impossible for children to take the
            bags off their heads and allow us to see their flaws
            until they feel accepted by us (Step 1).

Step 3.   Our children feel seen, accepted, and loved. This
            happens as a natural consequence of Steps 1 and 2
            (Truth → Seen → Accepted → Loved, pp. 41-3 and
            Chapter 12). Filled with Real Love, a child has the
            most important thing in the world. He feels full and
            complete; his emptiness and fear then go away.

Step 4.   Our children see and love other people. When the
            blinding effects of emptiness and fear fade, a child can
            begin to see other people clearly, and he discovers that
            what he thought were unacceptable qualities in them
            were just Getting and Protecting Behaviors. He then
            accepts other people freely and easily, naturally caring
            about their happiness (Real Love). In short, without
            emptiness and fear, a child can see, accept, and love
            people. We talked about this in Chapter 9: Loved →
            Seeing → Accepting → Loving. This happens as a
            natural consequence of the other steps, and as a result
            of instruction from loving parents.

PROVIDING A MODEL

We can't teach children to be loving by just using words. They
need to see what Real Love actually looks and feels like, and
we provide that example as we unconditionally love them. We
also teach them about accepting and loving other people as
we interact with — and talk about — employers, co-workers,

store clerks, neighbors, fellow drivers on the road, friends, and relatives. If we're critical and angry toward those people, we teach our children to feel the same about other people.

An Example

Justin and Sarah were arguing. Their mother, Diane, heard the noise and came to investigate.

Diane: "You two look angry."

Notice that Diane followed the advice on p. 194 about details. She helped her children tell the truth about themselves and did not get distracted about the details of the event. She immediately focused on what was important — her children's anger, a Protecting Behavior which proved that her children felt empty and afraid.

Justin: "All I did was use her shampoo, and then she yelled at me and said I was stupid."

Sarah: "And then he hit me."

At this point, most parents take control: "You two stop arguing right now. Sarah, don't call your brother stupid. Justin, don't hit your sister." That approach does stop the argument and creates a moment of temporary peace for the parent, but the children are not happier, and they don't learn anything about seeing and loving other people.

STEP 1 — WE SEE, ACCEPT, AND LOVE OUR CHILDREN WITH THEIR FLAWS.

Diane wisely knew it would be foolish to suddenly require her children to be at step 4, seeing and loving each other. The simple fact that they were arguing proved they couldn't do that. She started at the first step, seeing and loving *them*.

Diane remembered the First and Second Rules of Seeing (Chapter 7). Justin had spoken first, so she treated him as the speaker and listened to him.

Diane: "Justin, how do you feel?"

Justin: "I'm mad."

Diane: "I've learned that people only get angry to protect themselves when they're afraid. We've talked about that in family meetings."

Justin: "I'm not afraid of her."

Diane: "When she yelled at you about using her shampoo, what did that tell you about how she feels about you?"

Diane gently helped Justin until he saw the answer to that question.

Justin: "She's saying that her stupid shampoo is more important to her than I am."

If we don't already have enough Real Love in our lives, we don't like hearing that people don't care about us — with their words or their behavior. When we hear that, we feel worthless and alone, which is painful and frightening. That's what happened with Justin. When Sarah attacked him, Justin correctly heard Sarah declare with her actions that she did not care about him. He became afraid and reacted with anger to protect himself.

Justin could not have seen what he did without his mother's assistance, and that's the purpose of a wise man—in this case, a parent. Diane knew that at the root of all Getting and Protecting Behaviors is our fear that we'll be unloved and alone.

Diane: "What Sarah did would not have bothered you if you had felt more loved by me, and that's *my* fault. I've given you many reasons to feel unloved. I've been disappointed and angry when you made mistakes. I have not loved you unconditionally, which was what you needed. I'm learning how to do that better."

Diane had the courage to tell the truth about herself. We simply can't imagine what a difference that makes to our children until we have the faith (Chapter 10) to actually do it. But more important than anything Diane said was the fact that she was obviously not irritated — no raised voice, frowning, or sign of disappointment. It was clear that she really did accept Justin.

Diane accomplished the first step of teaching Justin to love other people — she saw, accepted, and loved him. She created an environment where Justin felt safe taking the next step, telling the truth about himself.

STEP 2 — OUR CHILDREN TELL THE TRUTH ABOUT THEMSELVES.

Diane: "Do you understand that I love you?"

Justin: "I think so."

Diane: "Do you see now what you did with Sarah?"

Justin: "I should have asked her before I used her shampoo. I knew she wouldn't like it, but I didn't care. I was selfish."

Diane: "What else did you do?"

Justin: "I got angry, but only after she yelled at me."

Diane: "It doesn't really matter what *she* did. We always choose how we respond. Just talk about what *you* did."

Justin: (laughing) "Okay. I *was* pretty snotty to her. "

Diane: (also laughing) "Yes, you were. You were selfish, angry, and mean. And I still love you a lot."

Until a child tells the truth about himself and is clearly seen with his faults, he can't *feel* seen, accepted and loved. If Justin had continued to minimize or otherwise deny his behavior, he wouldn't have *felt* seen by his mother, even though she saw him clearly.

Note that Diane did not minimize the error of his behavior. She confirmed that he had indeed been selfish — she saw him clearly — and then she accepted him *while* he was selfish (repeating Step 1). That created the opportunity for him to *feel* accepted (Step 3).

STEP 3 — OUR CHILDREN FEEL SEEN, ACCEPTED, AND LOVED.

Justin was delighted as he felt his mother's love for him. He got up from his chair and threw his arms around her. Experiences like this change a child's life. They heal past wounds and bring parents and children closer together in ways that nothing else can. Money, expensive gifts, and even praising our children's accomplishments can't do this. Children need to be clearly seen and unconditionally loved while they make mistakes. The effect is miraculous.

As you practice seeing and accepting your children, you may do Step 1 poorly — perhaps many times. You may not even get to steps 2 and 3 at all. Don't give up. Keep getting loved yourself (Chapter 5), and as you do that, your ability to see and accept your children will grow.

Even when you do have genuinely accepting moments, your child will not *feel* accepted if he doesn't yet have faith that your love is real. Again, *don't give up*. Keep doing all you can to feel loved yourself, and your ability to love will grow (Chapters 5 and 9). Eventually, your child will have faith that you do love him, and he'll feel the love you offer.

After Diane took Justin through the first three steps toward learning to love others, that was as far as she felt he could go in that moment. She then turned to Sarah and had a similar discussion with her. She helped Sarah see that she had attacked Justin to defend herself, and Diane did that in a way that Sarah felt seen, accepted and loved.

STEP 4 — OUR CHILDREN SEE AND LOVE OTHER PEOPLE.

As Justin and Sarah felt loved, their fear and anger decreased (Step 3). Without the blinding effect of emptiness and fear, they saw each other more clearly. They understood that they were each simply protecting themselves, not trying to hurt each other. It then became easier — even natural — to accept each other and care about the other person's happiness (Real Love). The issue of the shampoo became insignificant after that.

Justin and Sarah would have gained none of this wisdom if Diane's goal had been to simply stop the argument instead of teaching her children to be loving.

Another Example

Bill had established a long pattern of picking on his younger brother Jay, criticizing him and making fun of him. Because their parents knew nothing about Real Love, all they could do was command Bill to stop the bullying when they saw it. That approach briefly stopped an occasional unpleasant moment, but it didn't really help anyone; both boys were steadily becoming more angry and unloving.

Eventually, Bill's parents recognized that they needed to do something different. They learned to tell the truth about themselves and feel loved (Chapter 5) by other adults, and they began to share that love with their children (Chapter 9). One important thing they did was to have daily family meetings (Chapter 7):

Jay: "Bill keeps picking on me, and I'm tired of it."

Father: "What's he been doing?"

Jay: "Every time I talk or do anything, he tells me I'm stupid and laughs at me. And he makes fun of me in front of other people."

Bill: "I only tease him a little. He's making a big deal out of nothing."

Father remembered the first two Rules of Seeing and therefore addressed Jay as the speaker. He also remembered Rule 3 and knew that Jay was really talking about himself, not Bill. Jay was trying to say that he felt unloved and afraid when he was attacked by his brother. Father helped Jay express those feelings until he felt seen and accepted.

Father then turned his attention to what *Bill* needed to learn. Father understood the principles in Chapter 12. He knew that Bill needed to tell the truth about himself in order to feel loved and learn to love his brother. He asked Jay to give a specific example of an event in the last twenty-four hours where Bill had been unkind. As Jay described it, Bill tried to argue about the details of the interaction.

Father: "The details are unimportant. During the interaction Jay described, were you kind and loving to him?"

Bill: "Well, no, but . . ."

Father: "There's nothing you'll learn in this family more important than how to love your brother. As you learn that, you'll learn how to love other people — and that will determine how happy you are the rest of your life. If you don't learn how to be loving here, with all the help we give you, it's not likely you'll learn it later — not without a lot of pain.

"I'm not telling you this to make you feel bad. You only pick on Jay because it makes you feel strong. You wouldn't feel a need to do that if you felt loved and happy, and that's *my* fault. If you felt loved by me, you wouldn't need to pick on your brother.

"What you need is to feel more loved. You need to see that you're loved even when you're being unkind to your brother (Step 1 of teaching someone to be loving). So I'm asking the whole family to point it out to you each time you're being mean to Jay. We won't make you feel bad or tell you to stop it. We'll just help you see what you're doing until you can see it yourself (Step 2). As you feel more accepted and loved (Step 3), I have faith that you'll eventually quit picking on Jay (Step 4). You just will, whether it makes sense to you or not. When you feel loved and see the right thing to do, you'll just do it. And you'll be much happier yourself as you learn to be loving instead of angry."

The traditional approach to a situation like the one above is for the father to tell the child he's wrong and to stop doing the wrong thing. That never works for long because it doesn't address the real problem — that the child feels unloved. So the disputes keep happening and nobody is any happier.

In this interaction, Bill's father wisely understood that both his sons needed to be loved, and that Bill needed to be taught how to love his brother. Father then kept the commitment he made in the family meeting. Every time Bill was angry, the family patiently helped him see his behavior. As Bill felt loved over a period of several weeks, he slowly stopped picking on Jay. They even became good friends as they saw and accepted each other.

This approach really does work. I've seen results like those with Bill again and again. With enough love and guidance, children tend to do the right thing and be happy.

WHEN WE'RE NOT LOVING, WE'RE WRONG

I want to re-emphasize that in the family meeting, Bill's father did not get lost in the details of who did what to whom. They could have argued about that for hours and still have accomplished nothing. Instead, the father wisely focused on the fact that Bill was not loving toward his brother.

Happiness is the central goal of life and therefore the most important gift we can give our children. Being loved and loving others is the greatest source of happiness, so it is critical that we help our children identify the times when they are not loving. Rather than becoming distracted by the details of the *things* they do, we need to help them see that *when we're not loving, we're wrong*. That simple but powerful rule can change the world. If we remember that one phrase, how long could we continue an argument, or carry a resentment, or hold a prejudice? How long could we be angry at anyone? The lives of my own children have been changed more than I can describe by teaching them that one principle.

It doesn't matter what other people have done to us, or said to us, or said about us. It doesn't matter how "right" our side of the argument is. It doesn't matter whether we can justify our anger in a hundred different ways. If we're not loving, we're wrong — and we're certainly unhappy. Allison learned that, on pp. 195-7. When we can understand that great truth and teach it to our children, we give them a gift beyond price.

Chapter Summary

We can effectively teach our children to love other people as we follow the these steps:

Step 1 — We see, accept, and love our children with their flaws.

Step 2 — Our children tell the truth about themselves.

Step 3 — Our children feel seen, accepted, and loved.

Step 4 — Our children see and love other people.

When we're not loving, we're wrong.

Chapter 14

Teaching Children To Be Responsible

Children need to learn two kinds of responsibility:

1. They need to learn how to be responsible for their own feelings and behavior, rather than blaming them on other people. They need to tell the truth about themselves and be accountable for their own choices instead of lying, attacking people, acting like victims, and running from relationships.

2. Children need to learn how to become dependable and self-sufficient. They need to be responsible for tasks which are assigned to them.

We spoke at length about the first kind of responsibility in Chapters 2-3 and 12-13. In this chapter, we will address the second.

THE PURPOSE OF TEACHING CHILDREN RESPONSIBILITY

We all know that children should be responsible. But with our behavior, we confuse them about the *purpose* of becoming responsible. When our children act irresponsibly, we almost always respond with impatience and irritation. When we do that, we often claim to be teaching them about responsibility, but our selfish reaction makes it obvious that we're primarily interested in *our* convenience and not *their* happiness and well-being at all. They can only conclude that we teach them to be responsible to make *us* happy. Under those conditions, it's no wonder that so many of our children resent being taught responsibility.

The real reason to teach our children responsibility is that responsible children are happier. Children who are truthful, accountable, industrious, and independent are far happier than those who are not.

TEACHING RESPONSIBILITY

Children learn to be responsible in the same way they learn to hit a baseball or to play the piano — with practice. We must start giving them things to do at an early age. Most of us are reluctant to give our children serious responsibilities because we dislike dealing with their resistance when we push them to do something they don't want to do. We're also afraid of losing their affection when we confront them about tasks they fail to complete. We protect *ourselves* by not giving our children anything to do, and without the learning experiences that come with completing those assignments, our children are then crippled as adults.

Household Chores

In past generations, most children were raised on a farm or in a family-owned business where everyone had a part to play in the physical survival of the family. Those children *had* to be responsible — or they didn't eat. Few families today are structured in that way, but there are still many jobs that have to be done in every household each day that *can* be assigned to children to teach them responsibility: dishes have to be washed, rooms cleaned, babies tended, clothes washed, etc. We must not neglect the assignment of these labors.

As parents, we need to remember that it is not the completion of the *task* that is important. Rarely does anything terrible happen if a floor is swept poorly or a closet is left untidy. Children need to do these things because they become stronger and happier when they're responsible.

Children need responsibility for much more than just their own bedroom and the messes they personally create elsewhere. They need to understand that everyone makes a contribution to the operation of the entire household. That's a natural consequence of being a member of a healthy family. They don't help out as a favor to *us*.

One of the primary responsibilities of parents is to teach children to love other people, and household chores provide a great occasion to do that. Whenever we do something without reward for another human being, we create the possibility of feeling a moment of unconditional love for that person. That's what happens as children fulfill their duties for the family — they can learn to care about the people they serve. The child who washes the dishes for the family is doing something for people who can't directly pay him back. So is the child who does the laundry, and the child who takes out the garbage, etc. As our children serve each other, especially with our love and guidance, they're learning how to love each other.

Regular Chores

In our family, all the children — as they become old enough — are given one or more major assignments that benefit the whole family: the laundry, the kitchen, the bathrooms, the garbage, mowing the lawn, etc. It's important that each job is assigned to a child for at least several months at a time. If that isn't done, every time a job needs to be done in the house, a parent has to find a child and ask him to do it: "Please clean the kitchen," "Go vacuum the living room," etc. And then there's that confusing and irritating business of figuring out who didn't do this task or that. When the process of assignment and follow-up is done in that piecemeal fashion, it almost always becomes tiresome and stressful — for both parent and child. Long-term assignments eliminate most of that effort and conflict. With this approach, a child also feels more responsible for a job and feels like he's making a real contribution to the family.

Let's take the example of the child who cleans the kitchen in our family. That's a big job, and it's all his. If the family makes an unusually big mess in the kitchen, the job is still his. That reduces the endless arguments between children about who made a particular mess and who should clean it up. If one child consistently makes an unnecessary mess in the kitchen, the "kitchen person" can bring that up in a family meeting. We then talk to the "messy child" about how his behavior affects other people — after that, he's more likely to be considerate.

Children learn many things as they fulfill their responsibilities:

Sheryl, 8, had the job of cleaning up the living room. Her sister Megan, 10, often made a mess of that room. Sheryl had asked her on many occasions to take her stuff out of the room with her, but Megan had not listened. They were both becoming quite angry with each other over the issue, and Megan brought it up at a family meeting.

Megan: "Sheryl keeps yelling at me that I have to help her clean up the living room, but that's *her* room. So I don't have to pick up my stuff, do I?"

Sheryl: "But that's *her stuff*! She leaves *her* clothes and books on the floor! I don't make a mess in the rooms *she* cleans in the house. That's not fair!"

Mother: (speaking to Megan) "No, you don't *have* to clean up the living room. That room belongs to Sheryl, so any mess there should be cleaned up by her."

Megan: "See! I told you!"

Mother: "But Megan, you need to learn something here, too. When you leave your things in the living room, what are you saying to Sheryl with your behavior?"

They had talked before in family meetings about how behavior communicates ideas just like words do, so Megan understood what her mother was saying.

Megan: "That I don't care about her."

Mother: "Yes, and look how you feel when you're angry and unloving. You can't be happy like that. It will still be Sheryl's *responsibility* to pick up your things in the living room, but it's just as important that *you* learn to be *loving*. I suggest that you start thinking about being loving toward your sister. You could learn that by not leaving your stuff in the living room. Do you understand what I'm saying?"

Megan: "So do I have to pick up my stuff in the living room?"

Mother: (laughing) "No, you don't *have* to. I won't *make* you. I'm suggesting that you'll learn something about loving your sister if you'll do it, though. Picking up your stuff isn't something you *have* to do. It's just the *right* thing to do. It's the loving thing. We're always happier when we're loving. We'll talk about how you're doing in a family meeting some time next week."

Special Assignments, Written

Some jobs come up sporadically and are not included in regular assignments. A hose broke and needs to be repaired. Raccoons are getting into the garbage, and a live trap needs to be set. The gutters need cleaning. These assignments are written and often explained in detail at family meetings. At the top of the note is the name of the person responsible, along with the date it was written. We often write a date on the note for completion of the task. That keeps assignments clear and makes accountability much easier. These notes are tacked to a bulletin board, and each person brings his notes to every family meeting. When someone wants to watch television, use the car, attend an event, etc., he must show that his notes and regular chores are all done before he participates in leisure activities. Such accountability contributes considerably toward the learning of responsibility.

Age-Dependent Responsibilities

Children need to be given increasing responsibilities as they get older. It is not my intent to describe here all the responsibilities appropriate for each age group, only to give some general ideas. The suggested ages are very flexible. For example, when I suggest that a two-year-old can clean his room, I'm obviously not saying that he can mop the floors and scrub the walls. But every toddler who can pick up a toy to play with can also learn to put it away. Some children can do the described activities much earlier than I have proposed.

Infants

An infant's primary role is to be loved. He has no responsibilities.

Ages 1-5

Increasingly, children need to see the consequences of their behavior and be responsible for them. We can start teaching that at a very young age.

When he ate in his high chair, Marcus, age two, enjoyed throwing food on the floor. It was fun to see the food splatter and to see his mother hurry to clean it up. She told him to stop it, but he paid little attention.

His mother finally decided he was old enough to learn some responsibility. The next time he threw food on the floor, she told him to get down from his chair and showed him how to clean up the mess. At his age, it took Marcus quite some time and effort to finish the job. She didn't frown at him or raise her voice, but she did insist that he clean up the mess before he continued his meal. She did this each time he threw food, and of course, he soon quit doing it. Throwing food wasn't nearly as fun when he had to clean it up.

This is an obvious example of a natural consequence (Chapter 11). With consequences, children usually choose to stop a selfish behavior they would otherwise continue.

Children this age need to start keeping their own bedroom clean. Parents who do that job for them prevent them from learning responsibility. On the other hand, some parents make cleaning a bedroom a very unpleasant experience. Remember that the purpose of a clean bedroom is to teach your child responsibility, not to make the *room* worthy of a military inspection or to please *yourself* in some way.

As young children learn to speak, they need to be increasingly responsible for clearly expressing what they need, rather than whining or crying. If a child whines at an age when he is capable of speaking, a natural consequence would be to do without what he wants. With that approach, a child's verbal ability usually increases rapidly.

Ages 5-10

These children need to be responsible for their schoolwork and for increasing tasks at home. For example, a six-year-old can be assigned the job of sweeping the floor or cleaning off the table after meals. These responsibilities should steadily increase. Children become stronger and happier as they become capable of doing more things.

At this age, children need to spend more time on their own. That experience increases their sense of responsibility and independence. For more about leaving children at home by themselves, see p. 403.

Ages 11-14

Children this age are capable of doing more things that benefit the entire family. They can assist with the laundry, mowing the law, taking out the garbage, etc.

They need to be responsible for coordinating their activities with the family. We required our children to arrange transportation at least a day before an event. When they failed to do that, and their last-minute requirement for transportation inconvenienced others, the natural consequence was to miss the activity.

They need to be nagged less about schoolwork and be allowed to experience the natural consequences of their choices. See an example of this on p. 126.

Ages 14-18

These children will soon move away from the family and be entirely independent. It would be unkind of us to send them away unprepared. They need to take more responsibility for cooking meals, cleaning their own clothes, maintaining a checking or savings account, etc. They also need to be responsible for some of their own expenses.

Adult Children

See Chapter 26.

RESPONDING TO IRRESPONSIBLE BEHAVIOR

Holly often neglected her responsibility for keeping the kitchen clean. Despite being nagged and punished, her behavior remained unchanged.

In a situation like this, most of us continue nagging and criticizing. It's what we've seen all our lives, so it's all we know. We do it even when it's not working. In fact, the less it works, the more we do it. We somehow believe that if we just nag longer and criticize louder, it might work better.

We think we're teaching children to be responsible when we criticize and punish them, but all they really learn is to do what we want to avoid our disapproval and anger. That lesson does not produce a happy child or adult. Our children learn responsibility much better as we love them and teach them.

Love Them

Holly's parents wisely recognized that what they'd always done with her when she misbehaved — criticizing and punishing — wasn't working. And they made a conscious decision to look at themselves as the cause — and solution — of the problem. They took the steps toward feeling loved (Chapter 5). As they felt increasingly loved themselves, they were able to accept and love Holly instead of being angry and nagging her.

As Holly began to feel accepted as part of a loving family, she discovered that she didn't want to do anything that would inconvenience or hurt these people who loved her and made her happy. Because she genuinely wanted to make a positive contribution to her loving family, she started cleaning the kitchen and doing other helpful things around the house. All the nagging in the world never had that result.

When children are intimidated and frightened, the best they can learn is a rigid sense of duty and obligation. They only learn genuine responsibility as they're unconditionally accepted. We need to have faith in them, trusting that they'll learn responsibility as we love and teach them — without our criticism and disapproval.

Loving our children and having faith in them are the most important steps in teaching them to be responsible. But there are other things we can do to actively teach them responsibility, and we'll discuss those in the following sections. None of them is effective without Real Love.

Teach Them

Even though Holly was beginning to be more responsible as she felt loved, there were still times when she didn't do her jobs. It takes time to learn to do anything well.

Holly didn't clean the kitchen before she went to school, so it was a mess all day and an inconvenience for her mother, Ellen. In the past, Ellen would have been angry and punished her daughter, but because of the unconditional love Ellen had received from her husband and other people, the messy kitchen was only a minor inconvenience to her. So she was not disappointed or angry with Holly as she spoke to her.

Ellen: "You didn't clean the kitchen last night or this morning before you went to school."

Holly: "Sorry. I forgot."

Ellen: "Let's talk about 'sorry' and 'I forgot.' You're not genuinely sorry about neglecting the kitchen, or you wouldn't keep doing it. And you *forgot* to do the kitchen only because you didn't really *want* to do it."

Holly: "No, I really meant to do it. I just forgot."

Ellen: (laughing) "Do you forget your birthday or what time school gets out?"

Holly: (pause) "No. I think I see what you mean."

Ellen:	"We don't forget the things we really want to do. You didn't *want* to do the kitchen, and chose to not do it as soon as you could have. Instead, you did everything else you wanted to do first, and the thought of doing the kitchen just slowly went away. That's how you 'forgot.' Do you see that?"
Holly:	"I do now."
Ellen:	"In effect, you *chose* to forget."

Holly was able to listen to her mother because Ellen was not angry. Ellen was only interested in teaching Holly something that would enable her to choose more wisely in the future.

Understand Choice and Responsibility

Irresponsible children consistently claim to be victims, saying, "I couldn't help it." They want to shift responsibility for their behavior to anyone or anything but themselves. They need our help to see that they're not victims and always have a choice.

Children often need to be loved and taught many times before they learn the desired lesson. On another occasion, Holly didn't do her job again, and Ellen spoke to her about it one evening.

Ellen:	"You didn't clean the kitchen again before school this morning."
Holly:	"I couldn't help it. I started it, but I didn't have time to finish before we had to leave for school."
Ellen:	"What time did you get up this morning?"
Holly:	"7:00."
Ellen:	"Who made you get up at that time?

Holly: "Nobody."

Ellen: "So you *chose* to get up at that time?"

Holly: "Yes."

Ellen: "Then you could have gotten up earlier — at 6:00 or 6:30 — and cleaned the kitchen?"

Holly: "But I was up late last night!"

Ellen: "And who *made* you do that?"

Holly: "Okay, I get the point."

Ellen explained that when Holly *chose* to get up at 7:00, she knew she would not have time to clean the kitchen. In other words, she effectively *chose not to do her assigned job*. She could have chosen to get up at 6:30, but she didn't. Because her mother explained this without accusation or irritation, Holly saw that her negligence was a choice, not something she "couldn't help."

Irresponsibility and the Effect on Other People

Because Holly was listening and learning, Ellen decided to teach her an additional principle.

Ellen: "When you don't clean the kitchen, how does that affect me?"

A surprised look came over Holly's face as she struggled with an answer.

Ellen: "Clearly, you haven't thought much about that, have you?"

Holly: "No."

Ellen: "I have two choices when you leave the kitchen a mess. Either I have to work around your mess all day — which is not convenient — or I can stop what I'm doing and clean up your mess. Either way, it doesn't work out well for me. Do you remember how you felt yesterday when somebody moved one of your school books from the living room?"

Holly: (animated) "Yes. I had to look all over the house for it, and I was mad."

Ellen: "Exactly. You don't like it when other people make *your* life harder, do you?"

Holly: "No."

Ellen: "But you don't hesitate to inconvenience other people — not just me, but the other members of the family. Have you noticed that?"

Holly: "Now I'm embarrassed. I guess I do that a lot."

Ellen: "Oh, don't be embarrassed. That doesn't help anything. And remember that I still love you. You just need to see that you do this and learn from it."

Because Ellen was unconditionally accepting — gently describing Holly's behavior, not angrily blaming her — Holly didn't feel afraid and didn't need to defend herself. She was able to listen to the lesson she was being taught. It's important to note that Ellen's goal was to help Holly be responsible and care about other people, *not* to feel guilty. Ellen was not acting like a victim.

ACCOUNTABILITY

Connected irrevocably to the Law of Choice (Chapter 8) is the Law of Responsibility: "I'm always responsible for the choices

I make." Without responsibility, the freedom to make our own choices is nothing more than an excuse to be selfish.

Gary's father spoke to him at a family meeting.

Father: "Last night you ate dinner in the living room while you watched television. Do you remember what happened after that?"

Gary: "No."

Father: "You left the plate in the living room, and you spilled food on the floor without cleaning it up. With your behavior, what were you telling everyone else?"

Gary shrugged his shoulders. His father helped him see that he was saying this: "I expect other people to be responsible for the choices I make."

Father: "*You* chose to take your plate into the living room. All the consequences of making that choice then became *your* responsibility. Can you see how it wouldn't make sense for anyone else to be responsible for your choices?"

Gary: "I didn't think of it like that."

Gary assumed someone else would choose to take care of his mess. When we're lazy and irresponsible, we hope — and often demand — that other people will choose to serve us. When our children are lazy, it's unproductive to make them feel ashamed. They only learn to be afraid and angry that way. We only need to consistently point out their lazy behavior and unconditionally love them while we teach them. When we do that, they can feel safe enough to tell the truth about themselves — as Gary did — and can learn to be more responsible and happy.

Children need to be given many opportunities to account for their behavior. They need frequent evaluation and guidance. We need to point out when they do well and when they do poorly. That's how they learn. We'll discuss accountability more in Chapter 17.

CONSEQUENCES

On some occasions, consequences are required to teach children the Law of Responsibility. When they choose to neglect a task assigned to them, consequences teach them the cost of their choice. Review the nature and purpose of consequences in Chapter 11.

One summer, on a Monday, I told my son Joseph to mow, weed, and fertilize an area of the yard by the following Monday night. The week passed, and when the deadline arrived, I could see that he had done little or nothing on his assignment.

Joseph: "I haven't had enough time, but I'll get it done this week."

Despite being instructed and loved for some time, Joseph chose to be irresponsible on this occasion. He needed additional motivation to consider making the right choice.

Me: "You've had all week to do this, and I've watched you do many other things instead of this job. *You* chose to put this off, and now you get to deal with the consequences. In this case, you'll *literally* live with the consequences. Until you get the job done, you'll stay out there in the yard and live with it."

Joseph: "You're kidding."

Me: "Do I look like I'm kidding?"

Joseph: "You don't mean I'm supposed to sleep out there?"

Me: "Yes, I do."

Joseph slept outside in a tent that night. When I got home from work on Tuesday, he had made little progress in his assignment. Naturally, I was curious about that.

Joseph: "I can't do the job this week. The lawnmower needs a new spark plug, and I found out that the repair shop is closed this week. The owner is on vacation. But he'll be back next week, and I'll get the mower fixed and finish the job then."

Me: "*You* made the choice to put the job off all last week, when it would have been easy to fix the mower. Now you get to live with the consequences of that choice. I wonder how long you'll be camping on the lawn."

Joseph: "But band camp starts at school Thursday morning! I can't miss that."

Me: "I'm sorry you didn't think of that a week ago. Aren't you?"

Joseph: "How do I get the mower fixed with the repair shop closed?"

Me: "I don't know, but I'll bet you can figure it out."

Suddenly, Joseph was motivated. After several phone calls, he found a place in another city to get a spark plug for the mower. He worked constantly, sleeping and eating in the tent pitched next to his work site, and he finished the job just before band camp started Thursday morning.

Understandably, Joseph was initially irritated when he had to move outside, but he began to see that all those consequences were a direct result of *his* choices. He only saw that because:

1. I didn't change the deadline. I also refused to rescue him from the consequences of his own choices. If I had said, "Okay, you can have another week," he wouldn't have learned a thing.

2. He felt accepted. During our discussion, I did not feel angry at him, which was only possible because *I* felt loved. In addition, we had many experiences before this one where I had accepted him when he made mistakes. If I had been angry at him while I imposed consequences in this situation, he could only have felt attacked and would have protected himself with anger, acting like a victim, etc.

Joseph learned some valuable lessons from the natural consequences imposed in this interaction. Children often have no reason to change their behavior until they're required to live with the consequences of their choices. Parents need to provide those learning experiences.

POSITIVE FEEDBACK FOR RESPONSIBLE BEHAVIOR

Paula came home from school with excellent grades. She had studied harder than usual that semester and was excited about presenting her report to her father.

As a parent, how would you respond to this? You might say, "Oh Paula, I'm so proud of you!" Although that seems like a positive thing to say, most children who are praised like that feel an unbearable pressure to keep succeeding so their parents will *stay* proud of them. They're afraid that if they fail, they'll disappoint their parents and will no longer be loved by them. Their fear is justified. On the many occasions when our children disappoint us, they *do* see the many evidences of our disappointment and irritation. We don't mean to do it, but we're *not* "so proud!" of our children when they fail to bring home those successes that we praise them for. And that conditional love exacts a terrible price from our children.

We convey a similar message with words like, "You're such a good girl!" and "That makes me very happy." We intend to be positive with such phrases, but the effect is awful on the occasions when our children perform poorly and we withhold our praise. In Chapter 2, we discussed the potential dangers of praising children. Praise is a cornerstone of conditional love. So when children *are* responsible and do a great job, what *do* we say?

Paula's father, Richard, was wise.

Richard: "It looks like all that studying paid off. Are you pleased with your grades?"

Paula: (smiling) "Yes."

Richard: "Then I am, too. It feels good to work hard and do well, doesn't it?"

Paula: "Yes."

Richard: "Try to remember how you feel right now. It always feels good to work hard and be prepared like you've been this semester as you've studied."

There is nothing in life more valuable than Real Love. Because Paula already felt unconditionally loved by her father, she didn't *need* his praise. That is a hard thing to imagine for people who haven't felt unconditional love. Richard simply loved and taught Paula, which is what all children need. He taught Paula that the reward for making responsible choices is *feeling* good. It simply feels good to be prepared and responsible. The real reward for responsible choices is not praise, which is fleeting and hollow. We set our children up for disappointment and unhappiness when we teach them to work for praise. Most of life's greatest accomplishments — loving our spouses, being a good parent, quietly accepting injustice — are never praised. Paula's father taught her well.

More important than what Richard said when Paula did well was what he did on the many occasions when she *not* succeed; he loved her the same. If we treat our children differently when they score well on a test than when they score poorly, they can only conclude that we love them conditionally. They *do* notice. Obviously, when they don't study, we have an obligation to do something about that; but we can learn to do that without disappointment and anger.

FURTHER INSIGHTS ABOUT TEACHING RESPONSIBILITY

Most children resist being taught responsibility. Understandably, they'd rather play than work. And usually, they're unaware of the clever techniques they use.

Asking Questions

When a child is given a task to perform, he commonly asks questions about it. The questions are sometimes genuine, asked for the purpose of gathering necessary information. However, children often ask questions for other reasons:

1. They want to make the job easier for themselves. For example, when we tell a child to clean the kitchen, he doesn't ask questions about how he can do *more* than the usual assignment, only questions that would allow him to do *less*, or put it off. He wants to know what he can get *out of:* "Do I have to wash the pots and pans, too?" "Do I have to do it right now (while I'm watching my favorite television show)?" He doesn't ask, "Would it be all right with you if I scrubbed the stove, mopped the floors, and cleaned out the refrigerator in addition to just washing the dishes?"

2. Children ask questions so we'll do some or all of the work for them.

Years ago, Benjamin and I were doing a plumbing job together.

Me: "Benjamin, I need the channel locks (a kind of tool).
           Would you get them for me?"

Benjamin: "Where are they?"

Again, such questions can be genuine, but I knew that
Benjamin had gotten that tool for me before. He had learned that
when he asked questions like that, I often said something like,
"Oh, I'll just get them myself." He was hoping that I'd do that
again in this situation.

Me: "You'll find them. Think about where you found
           them last time."

3. They ask questions to avoid making mistakes and being
criticized. In the example above, part of Benjamin's motivation
for asking his question was his past experiences with me being
critical and angry when he failed to find the tool I sent him to
get. He wanted to protect himself from that.

When we understand that children often ask questions for the
above reasons, we can better help them to be more responsible.
Joseph (pp. 225-7) asked questions and made excuses, but I did
not solve his problems for him. When he realized that he had full
responsibility for the job, he suddenly came up with solutions.
If I had answered all his questions, helped him do the job, or
delayed the deadline, he would not have learned what he did.
We give our children a valuable gift when we teach them to be
responsible.

**Really Doing the Job vs. Getting You To Stop Bothering
Them**

Until a child learns to be responsible, it's wise to follow up on
any assignment they're given. Otherwise they tend to complete
the job with the least possible effort, so they can *say* they're
done and get you to stop bothering them about it. They won't
learn responsibility with that approach.

Earlier in the day, I had asked Janette to iron a shirt for me. After seeing the finished product, I asked her to come and see me.

Me: "Did you iron my shirt?"

Janette: "Yes."

I took it out of the closet and showed it to her.

Me: "Look carefully at this and remember that I love you no matter what you say and do. If you were giving this shirt a grade for its appearance, what would it be?"

Janette: "Maybe a C-minus."

Me: "You did this job to get it out of your way — so you could tell me it was done and I wouldn't nag you about it. You did the easiest thing for you."

Janette: "Yes, I did."

It's our job to teach children responsibility. If we do it with Real Love, it becomes a rewarding experience for everyone.

Hating the Person Giving the Assignment

If a child persists in not doing a job, despite repeated reminders from his parents, he usually chooses one of two courses:

(1) He takes responsibility for his own laziness (less likely); or

(2) he resents the parent who gave him the task and keeps nagging him about it. He judges the parent to be harsh and unfair. It's much easier to justify not doing a job when you can successfully paint the person who assigned it as an unreasonable and demanding monster.

I told Rob — twice — to change the oil in the car. Three days later, he asked to take the car somewhere.

Me: "Did you change the oil?"

Rob: "Not yet."

Me: "You need to change it now."

Rob: "I can't. I have to be at my friend's house in 15 minutes."

Me: "I guess you'll be late."

He scowled and stomped off to change the oil. Obviously, he didn't appreciate this natural consequence of his irresponsible choice. After a few minutes, I went out to the car.

Me: "You look angry."

Rob: (silence)

Me: (laughing) "Help me understand this. You're angry at *me* because *you* didn't do the job I gave you three days ago, a job which involves taking care of a car that you now want to use?"

Because I had unconditionally loved Rob for a long time, and because I didn't feel irritated at him in this situation, he saw the absurdity of his anger, and it went away. He smiled and finished the job.

The Joy of Responsibility

My eight-year-old son Benjamin had been grouchy for days. He was also behind in his homework, hadn't done his jobs around the house, and was living in a messy bedroom.

Me: "Benjamin, I suggest that you're not happy because you know you're not doing the right things, and you're not being responsible. It's bothering you, even though nobody is pushing you about it. So let's try something. For the next few days, you'll stay busy with your homework and your household jobs. You won't play with your friends or watch television. This is not a punishment. It's an experiment to see how you feel as you're being responsible. I'll help you by asking what you've accomplished several times a day — maybe even every hour. We'll see what happens."

Initially, he didn't like being held accountable, but he soon settled into a routine of doing his work. After several days, he was obviously happier. He quit snapping at his siblings and was much nicer to everyone. We talked about it in a family meeting.

Me: "Benjamin, you look happier than you did last week."

Benjamin: "I guess I do feel better. I like having my homework done."

Children know what's right and wrong. They can feel it. They know that it's wrong to ignore their responsibilities, and they feel bad when they do that. They're happier when they're being responsible.

Years ago, as I talked about assignments being done in family meetings, I sometimes asked, "Now why do we do our jobs?" Of course, the children made a joke of the expected answer, which was, "So we can be happy and strong." Sometimes they mocked me as they rolled their eyes and chanted the answer in unison. In later years, however, each of them has come to appreciate the wisdom of that phrase. One of my teenage sons once came to me and said, "Dad, almost none of my friends at school knows how to work, and I feel sorry for them. They're spoiled and unhappy.

I'm glad you taught us to work, and I'm not laughing about that 'happy and strong' thing anymore."

Children who learn to be responsible really do become happy and strong, and parents who teach their children this quality are wise and loving.

THE RESPONSIBILITY OF PARENTS

Parents are entirely responsible for the happiness of an infant. However, children need to take an increasing responsibility for their choices and feelings. They need to be taught what's right and wrong, and they need to be loved. They don't need to be entertained, pampered, and protected from every discomfort and injustice. A wise parent loves and guides his children and helps them take responsibility for their own happiness. If they leave home without taking that responsibility, they'll be helpless and miserable.

Children often try to give us all the responsibility for their happiness. And we often let them, because we get an intoxicating sense of usefulness and power from being able to "make" them happy. We feel appreciated and important when they smile and thank us.

But we can't keep taking the responsibility for their happiness all their lives. As they get older, they have to make their own choices and learn to be loving and responsible — that's when they find real happiness. We need to constantly and gradually give them more responsibility to prepare them for the day when they'll be independent.

Children often resist being taught to be responsible. They ignore their assignments and act annoyed when we remind them. Most parents find this very unpleasant, and eventually they give up trying to teach responsibility. That is a tragic mistake.

Chapter Summary

We need to teach children to be responsible so *they* can be happy, not for our own convenience.

We teach children to be responsible when we:
regularly give them significant tasks to do appropriate to their age;
love them unconditionally, especially when they are irresponsible;
teach them that they always have a choice and are not victims;
teach them the effect of their irresponsibility on other people;
hold them accountable for their choices; and
sometimes impose consequences for their choices.

Chapter 15

Teaching Children About Relationships

In school, our children are taught a wide variety of subjects: trigonometry, world history, biology, etc. We take that instruction seriously. They attend school between six and eight hours a day, five days a week, for nine months of the year. In most states, children are required by law to do that until they're about sixteen years old. We even make them take frequent examinations to prove that they grasp the material they're taught.

Is it not strange that we go to such great lengths to instruct our children in subjects that most of them will never use in their entire lives, and yet we teach them nothing about the one subject they will use every day? After our children leave school, how many of them will ever need to know the tangent of a triangle? How many will ever be required to know the date of the Magna Carta? Or the physiology of a cell membrane? Not many. But every one of them will become involved in relationships — every day of their lives. And yet we teach them virtually nothing about relationships — not in school, not at home, not anywhere.

Our children are not *taught* what human beings need most. They don't understand how relationships work. And then we wonder why our children get frustrated and angry. We don't understand why they join gangs, why they can't keep a job, why the jails are full, why half of all marriages fail, why people shake their fists at each other on the road, why children are abused and neglected, why relationships seem to come and go like falling leaves, why the newspapers are filled with accounts of violence and war, and so on. There's no mystery in any of this. All these things are *guaranteed* to happen when we don't teach our children the basic principles of love and relationships.

We expect our children to learn about relationships by making countless random mistakes. What a terribly painful, slow, and unpredictable way to learn. Is that how we teach them to drive? Do we expect them to learn trigonometry and biology that way? As I counsel with adults in failing or unsatisfying relationships, they often speak variations on this statement: "If only I'd known." So why didn't someone teach them what they didn't know? What we learn from painful experience about relationships, we tend to keep to ourselves. We don't share that with our children. Or we don't learn anything at all from our mistakes and have nothing to teach them. And the next generation then repeats the same mistakes. How tragic that is.

REAL LOVE

We have the opportunity and responsibility to teach our children about relationships. Not surprisingly, the most important ingredient in that process is Real Love.

We Must Feel Loved and Loving

We can't do anything productive with our children unless we feel unconditionally loved ourselves. Without Real Love, we can only feel empty and afraid, and then we'll use our children for Imitation Love and protect ourselves from them. We certainly can't teach them about relationships when we're doing that.

They Must Feel Loved and Loving

Although I'll be discussing the principles of relationships for the remainder of the chapter, I can't emphasize too strongly how worthless all that is unless a child *feels* loved. If our children don't feel unconditionally loved, they will unavoidably use Getting and Protecting Behaviors, which make healthy relationships impossible, no matter what else we *teach* them about relationships.

THE LAW OF CHOICE

In Chapter 8, I introduced the Law of Choice: *"Everyone has the right to choose what they say and do."* A child cannot have loving relationships or a happy life if he doesn't understand the importance of this law and the two principles that naturally follow from it:

A. Everyone has an *equal* right to choose what they say and do. My right to make choices is no more important than anyone else's.

B. I don't have the right to control or change anyone else's choices, even when those choices greatly inconvenience me.

We must help our children understand that they cannot be happy any time they attempt to control the behavior of other people in any way.

Billy, 8, stomped into the kitchen where his mother, Joanne, was working and threw his baseball glove on the floor.

Billy: "Gerald won't let me use his truck!"

Billy explained that he had been playing outside with his friend, Gerald. Although they had enjoyed themselves for a while, Gerald was now being selfish about his new battery-operated truck.

Billy: "I let him play with everything of *mine*, but now he won't let me touch his truck. He's a pig! It's not fair!"

Joanne: "You can have a big temper tantrum about this, or we
can talk about what you could do next. Which would
you rather do?"

If Joanne had felt critical or angry toward her son, she would
have been completely unable to teach him anything useful. But
she felt loved herself and was genuinely interested in helping
him with a solution. Billy felt her acceptance. He smiled and
said, "What can I do?"

Joanne: "I think I know what you *want* to do. You want to
go out there and take that truck away from him.
Right?"

Billy: "Yes."

Joanne: "In fact, you probably tried that already."

Billy: (smiling) "Yeah."

Joanne: "So let's do that. Both of us will go out there and
knock Gerald over the head and take that truck away
from him. And then we'll tie him up and put him in
the trunk of the car so he can't take the truck back
again."

Billy laughed, thinking that would be pretty fun.

Joanne: "It sounds funny, but think about it. What would
happen to your friendship if you did that? You'd lose
Gerald as a friend completely, wouldn't you? And
remember, when you came in the house, you said
something about 'fair.' To be *fair*, if *you* get to do
that to Gerald, *he* should get to do that to *you* the next
time he wants something that you have — right? So
whenever Gerald wants something you have, he and
his father will knock you down, tie you up, and throw

you in the trunk of their car. Do you really want to start doing things that way?"

Billy: (pause) "Maybe not."

Joanne: "No, you really don't. We've talked about that in family meetings, remember? We talked about the Law of Choice. Everybody gets to make their own choices, and you don't get to control them. I know it feels pretty good for a minute (Imitation Love), but it never works out. Everybody gets angry. It's how people end up hitting each other and going to jail. It's how wars get started. All from trying to control each other. It's awful."

Billy nodded. He was learning.

Joanne: "But there's a more important reason to not take that truck from Gerald — more important than just the Law of Choice. How do you feel when I love you?"

Billy: "Good."

Joanne: "So do I. *I* feel happy, too, when I'm loving you. We always feel happier when we're loving other people — and we're not loving people when we're trying to control them. So do you see how taking the truck from Gerald is not a great idea?"

Billy: "I guess so. But you said we'd talk about what I could do next. What can I do?"

THE THREE CHOICES

Joanne: "You still have three choices. You can:
           (1) live with it and like it;
           (2) live with it and hate it; or
           (3) leave it.

"Let's talk about each one. First, 'Live with it and like it.' You can go back out there and remember that Gerald really gets to make his own choices, *even if his choices are selfish* and you don't like them. He gets to make mistakes just like you do. You can choose to live with Gerald's decision to not share the truck — and *like it*. What's the big deal, anyway? You were getting along just fine without that truck in your life yesterday, weren't you?"

Billy: (laughing) "I never thought of that."

Joanne: "Do you *have* to have that truck to be happy?"

Billy: "I guess not."

Joanne: "Do you want to lose your friend forever just because you can't play with a truck for a few minutes?"

Billy: (pause) "I don't know."

Billy was not going to agree with this just because it made logical sense. He was still understandably irritated that his friend wouldn't share with him.

Joanne: "So that's one choice to think about: you can go out there and live with it and like it. You can keep playing with Gerald and still have a good time. You'll still have plenty to do with your good friend without playing with that one toy.

"The second choice is that you could live with it and hate it. You can keep arguing with Gerald and make yourself miserable. But if you're unhappy, do you understand that it's *your choice*, not Gerald's fault?"

Billy: (with a look of surprise) "No. *He's* the one who won't share the truck."

Mother: "And *you're* the one choosing to be *unhappy* about it. If *I* went out there to play with Gerald right now, would I be angry if he didn't share the truck with me?"

It was obvious that Billy hadn't thought of that. Joanne was trying to teach Billy that other people never make us angry (Chapter 6), a principle that few people understand.

Joanne: "No, I wouldn't be. *You're* angry, but *I* would choose not to be angry, so we can't blame your anger or your unhappiness on *Gerald*, can we? It's *your* choice to be angry and unhappy."

The gears in Billy's brain were working faster than he was accustomed to.

Joanne: "But for now, don't worry about whose fault it is. When you stomped into the house a few minutes ago, were you happy?"

Billy: "No."

Joanne: "Do you want to keep feeling miserable?"

Billy: (pause) "No."

Joanne: "Gerald can choose to be selfish as long as he wants. That's up to him. And if you choose to hate that, you're *choosing to stay unhappy.* How smart is that?"

Billy was thinking.

Joanne: "How often do *you* choose to do things that are different than I would do them?"

They talked about that for a while. Billy often didn't keep his room as clean as his mother preferred. He had to be encouraged to do his homework regularly. He made many decisions differently than his mother would make them.

Joanne:	"If I got angry at you every time you made a choice differently than I would make it, would you like that?"

Billy:	"No."

Joanne:	"I'd be angry at you a lot, wouldn't I?"

Billy:	(smiling) "Probably."

Joanne:	"And I'd be very unhappy myself. That would be stupid. It's dumb for us to be angry at other people when they make their own choices. It only makes *us* unhappy. What do you think?"

Billy:	"I guess so."

Joanne:	"That's what you're doing with Gerald. Sure, he's being selfish. Eventually, he may learn to not do that. But in the meantime, being angry at him only makes *you* unhappy. It only hurts *you*. So the second choice, 'Live with it and hate it,' is stupid. But that's the choice most people make every day. People everywhere are angry at somebody because they won't do something they want.

"Now the third choice: you can 'leave it.' You can decide that you just wouldn't have any fun without that truck. You could come inside and not play with Gerald at all. Maybe you're just feeling selfish enough that you couldn't play with Gerald without thinking about that truck. That's your choice. What do you think?"

Billy: "I'm still mad that he's being selfish."

Joanne: "I understand that. He *is* being selfish. But talking about that all day won't make any difference. He gets to make that choice. Whether you're happy is still your choice completely. No matter how selfish *he* is, *you* still have one of three choices to make. Which one you make will determine whether *you* are happy. That's all that matters. It doesn't matter what *he* has chosen, only what *you* choose. And I'll love you no matter what you do."

Billy was still angry at his friend, so he chose to stay in the house. He made the third choice: "Leave it." He could see that it was wrong to try to make Gerald change his choice, and he knew he wouldn't be happy with the first two choices, so he chose to leave the interaction entirely.

After several minutes by himself, however, he realized that playing with the truck was just not a big deal. He decided to try the first choice, living with it and liking it. He went outside and played with everything but the truck. He learned a lot from this experience with his friend and his mother.

Most human interactions are just as simple as this one between Billy and Gerald. Most conflicts between people of all ages boil down to this: "I want something that you won't give me," or "You're doing something that I don't like." And the three choices apply to all those interactions.

After our children feel loved and understand that they cannot control other people, we need to teach them that they have three choices as they interact with others:

1. Live with it and like it.
2. Live with it and hate it.
3. Leave it.

They do not have a fourth choice: control the other person. If we can teach that to our children, they'll have an incalculable capacity to find happiness in relationships. I'm grateful that my children learned these principles decades before I did.

EXPECTATIONS

The Law of Choice is the foundation of healthy relationships. We simply cannot control other people and be happy. One way we control our partners — mostly unintentionally — is to have expectations of them.

We never have the right to expect that another person will do anything for us. If we all understood that and taught it to our children, the whole world would become a much happier place. Think about every argument you've ever had in your life. They all started and continued because you *expected* something — love, gratitude, support, agreement, respect, praise, loyalty, safety — from the person you argued with.

Marie came home from school, obviously unhappy. She threw her things down on a chair and slumped on a couch in front of the television. Her mother turned off the television and sat down next to her.

Mother: "You want to talk about it?"

Marie: "Not really."

Mother just sat there on the couch with her arm around Marie's shoulder. After a minute, Marie leaned over and put her head next to her mother's.

Marie: "My friends are stupid."

Mother: "How so?"

Marie: "All they think of is themselves."

Mother: "Really?"

Marie: "Yes. They talk about *their* clothes, and *their* boyfriends, and *themselves*. They don't listen to me. It's like they don't care about me."

Mother: "I'm sure they don't."

Marie: "What do you mean?"

Mother: "Very few people have been unconditionally loved enough to really care about anyone else. Your friends are not unusual at all. They don't do this intentionally, but without feeling loved themselves, they *can't* care about anyone but themselves. That's why they're selfish. We've talked about that in family meetings."

Marie: "I didn't think about it like that."

Mother: "Your problem is that you keep *expecting* them to care about you. You keep expecting them to give you something that they *can't* give you, and that's pretty frustrating. It's *your* expectations that are the problem. You think that because they're your *friends*, they *should* care about you, but they still can't. If a group of strangers didn't care about you, that wouldn't bother you — because you wouldn't *expect* them to care about you."

Marie: "So how do I get over this?"

Mother: "Quit expecting anything of them."

Marie: "But I *want* them to care about me. How do I just stop having expectations?"

Mother: "It won't happen overnight, but it will get easier if you remember three things: 1. You really don't have

a right to expect anything from anybody. Everybody
gets to make their own choices. They don't have to
do what you want, no matter how much you want it.
2. Your friends don't *have* what you're expecting, so
it's dumb to expect it. 3. You already have people in
this family who care about you. When you remember
that, you won't feel as desperate to get loved by your
friends."

More important than the words she spoke was the obvious
acceptance that Mother felt for Marie. Marie was touched by
that. In that moment, she felt the enormous contrast between
her mother's love and the conditional, superficial acceptance of
her friends at school. She also learned a lot from her mother's
instruction about the Law of Choice and expectations.

Expectations ruin happiness. When we don't get what we
expect, we're always disappointed. Even when we receive a lot,
if it's less than we expected, we're unhappy because we focus on
what we didn't get. And when we get exactly what we expected,
the best we can feel is satisfied, but not grateful and delighted.
Expectations steal the joy from our lives. When we teach our
children to eliminate them, we add greatly to their happiness.

Marie's mother later explained the three choices in
relationships to her. Marie chose to live with it and like it. As
she began to understand that her friends simply didn't feel
unconditionally loved, she was less irritated by their inability
to love her. She also saw that they accepted her as well as they
could. Marie started to tell the truth about herself to her friends,
and as she did that, she created opportunities for her friends to
learn how to be accepting and loving. As we tell the truth about
ourselves, we actually create wise men and women around us.

Notice what Mother said when Marie first complained that
her friends didn't care about her. Many parents would have
protested, "Oh, sure they care about you." But Mother knew that

it was far more important that Marie be clearly seen, loved, and taught, not just superficially comforted. The truth always works best, and that's what Mother used in her response.

THE LAW OF CHOICE AND
TEACHING OUR CHILDREN THE INCREDIBLY IMPORTANT PRINCIPLE
THAT OTHER PEOPLE NEVER *MAKE* US ANGRY (CHAPTER 6)

Billy and his mother briefly discussed this subject above. We'll address it again here because of the unfathomable damage that anger causes in relationships, and the fact that nearly all of us have a strong tendency to blame our partners for our anger. I suggest that our lives would change overnight if we understood that our anger is *never* caused by other people. Conflict would virtually disappear as we lost our justification for lashing out at others.

Mother heard shouting in the next room and went to investigate. James, 10, and Cynthia, 8, were yelling at each other.

Mother: "You two look angry."

James: "I've told Cynthia to stay out of my room, but she never does. And now she and her bratty little friends have come in and played with my stuff. And ..."

Cynthia: "We didn't touch anything."

Mother asked Cynthia to go to her room while she talked to James. It is never productive to listen to two children accuse each other and defend themselves. In this case, Mother made the decision to have individual discussions with James and Cynthia. Sometimes, she discussed issues with both of them together; children often benefit from the lessons taught to their siblings.

Cynthia and her friends had been in James's room, and while playing, they had stepped on his homework and torn one of the pages, which he would have to re-copy. Mother agreed that Cynthia had violated their agreement to stay out of his room and had caused him some inconvenience.

Mother: "It's obvious that what Cynthia did was wrong."

James was clearly pleased to have Mother "on his side."

Mother: "So I guess she made you pretty mad?"

James: "Yes."

Mother: "No."

James was surprised. He didn't know what his mother was trying to tell him, although he did know he was about to be taught something.

Mother: "Cynthia didn't *make* you angry. She was certainly wrong to come in your room and damage your homework, but she still didn't make you angry. That was *your choice*. Do you understand that?"

James: "No."

Mother: "Do you remember that yesterday Cynthia broke my favorite vase?"

James: "Yes."

Mother: "Do you think that mattered to me as much as your homework does to you?"

James: "Probably."

Mother: "Did I yell at her?"

James: "No."

Mother: "Cynthia didn't *make* me angry. I chose to accept her and love her instead of being angry. You can learn to do that, too. Right now you're thinking of yourself instead of loving her. And that's not entirely your fault. I haven't loved you well enough for you to be able to love her all the time. The more loved you feel, the less angry you'll get when things like this happen, and eventually, you'll hardly ever feel angry.

              "Right this second, do you feel as mad as you did when you first saw what Cynthia did?"

James: "Not really. Actually, I don't feel mad right now."

Although he didn't understand the process intellectually, James had experienced the effect of his mother's love for him. Real Love eliminates anger. Anger is a reaction to emptiness and fear. In the presence of unconditional love, there is simply no *need* for anger.

Mother: "What changed? Not Cynthia — so *she* wasn't the problem. *You* just feel more loved and more loving now than you did moments ago. You were angry then because *you* were not feeling loved, and because *you* were not loving. *You* were the problem, not her, and I'm not saying you were bad. Do you see that?"

James: "I think so."

Mother: "The nice thing about seeing that anger is always your fault is that now you can do something about it. You can get loved and become more loving. When you believe that other people make you angry, you're helpless — other people control how you feel all the time. That's no good."

Our anger is not caused by other people. It is a response to a lack of Real Love in our own lives. If we can teach this principle to our children, it will add immeasurably to their happiness and to their ability to have rich relationships. On the occasions they feel anger, they will understand that they are just empty and afraid, and they will look for opportunities to be accepted and loved, instead of attacking their partners and ruining their relationships.

THE LAW OF CHOICE AND TEACHING OUR CHILDREN THAT WE ARE NEVER VICTIMS

When we don't understand the Law of Choice, we believe that other people have an obligation to make choices that will always benefit us and never harm us. That expectation guarantees that we'll feel like victims, because people *will* make choices that inconvenience us and fail to please us. Victims are very self-centered, forever thinking that people are letting them down or trying to hurt them.

We have many opportunities to teach our children that we are not victims as other people exercise their right to make their own choices. Years ago, my son Benjamin came home from school with a frown.

Me: "You look angry."

Benjamin: "Mrs. Stilton (his seventh grade teacher) picked on me again. All she ever does is tell me to shut up and punish me for stuff I didn't do. It's unfair."

Me: "What happened?"

Benjamin: "The kid next to me was talking, but she thought it was me and made me go to the principal's office. She makes me mad."

Me: "Does everyone have the responsibility to make you happy all day?"

Benjamin: "No, but they can't treat me like she does."

Me: "Really? So people can make their own choices until it's unfair to you?"

Benjamin paused as he realized he was being trapped, but he answered anyway. "Yes."

Me: "You're saying that when people are unfair to *you*, you have the right to make their choices for them. And when you can't, you're angry. Do you see that?"

Benjamin: "Well . . ."

Me: "To be fair, though, *everyone* should have the right to control other people when they're being treated badly. That would mean that anytime someone judges *your* behavior to be unfair, they'd have the right to stop *you*. How would you like that?"

Benjamin: (Long pause) "I wouldn't."

With help, Benjamin saw that he was requiring his teacher to make different choices — essentially to be a different person — whenever she interacted with him. He also saw that his teacher's anger was just her way of protecting herself, and she did that with many people, not just him. He learned that he was not a victim who was treated unfairly. He had simply experienced the consequences of his teacher choosing to protect herself.

Virtually all of us — children and adults — feel victimized when we're treated badly. But we're not victims. We just happen to be inconvenienced as other people search for Imitation Love and protect themselves. Everyone really gets to make their own choices, even when their mistakes inconvenience us. That's the price we pay for living in a world where we get to make our own decisions. The alternative — having our choices made for us — is unthinkable.

We give our children a great gift — a key to happiness — when we teach them that they're never victims. We have many opportunities to do that. Every time a child is disappointed or angry, he's being a victim. He could only be disappointed if he thought other people had an obligation to please him. We need to teach children that other people have a right to make their own choices and mistakes, even the ones that inconvenience us.

Even more important than teaching our children with *words* that they're not victims is giving them enough Real Love that they *feel* loved. Without emptiness and fear, they don't *feel victimized* when people treat them badly, and in those interactions, they can choose to be loving and happy instead of afraid, demanding, selfish, and angry. Such children enjoy profound peace all their lives.

THE LAW OF CHOICE AND SELFISHNESS

Selfishness naturally results when we believe that our choices are more important than the choices of other people.

Years ago, my son Rob was eager to talk about his brother at a family meeting (Chapter 7).

Rob: "Benjamin used my stereo without asking me. It's not the first time, and it's making me mad."

Benjamin: "You weren't home, so I couldn't ask you. And you use my stuff without asking, so you have no right to talk."

Me: "Benjamin, let's finish listening to what Rob is saying first. That's the First Rule of Seeing that we've been talking about (pp. 112-14). Remember that I love you no matter what you did. I'm not going to make you feel bad or punish you in any way. Take your time and put into words what it meant when you used Rob's stereo without asking him."

With help, he saw that his behavior said this: "Rob, I took your stereo because what I wanted was more important to me than what you wanted."

We need to help our children see the occasions when they're being selfish. If we don't, they won't see it and will have a lifetime of empty relationships and unhappiness. Note that I didn't need to tell Benjamin he was wrong, or not to do it again. He knew all that. He only needed to clearly see his behavior. *Our children are basically good*, and they tend to stop doing what they know to be wrong if they can see it and can see a better choice.

TELLING THE TRUTH ABOUT *OURSELVES* IN RELATIONSHIPS

We love to talk about the faults of our partners, and that rarely creates happiness in relationships, as nearly all of us have discovered many times. The only way we can make a real difference in our relationships is to change ourselves, and that starts with telling the truth about *us*. If we can teach our children how to do that, they'll have a powerful ability to avoid conflict in their relationships. As they tell the truth about themselves, they'll create opportunities for their partners to see, accept, and love them, and that's how genuinely loving relationships are formed and maintained. See pp. 195-7 for an example of teaching a child how to tell the truth about himself in a relationship.

Chapter Summary

We have the opportunity and responsibility to teach our children about relationships. We can do that most effectively as we do the following things with our children:

1. Unconditionally love them.
2. Teach them the Law of Choice.
3. Teach them that in any relationship or situation, they have only three choices:
    A. Live with it and like it.
    B. Live with it and hate it.
    C. Leave it.
4. Teach them that we never have the right to have expectations of other people.
5. Teach them that other people never make us angry.
6. Teach them that we are never victims.
7. Teach them to tell the truth about ourselves in relationships

Chapter 16

Teaching Children to Be Happy
and
The Laws of Parenting

The goal of a wise parent is not to raise a child who's obedient, or even responsible and successful. The ultimate purpose of life is to be happy, and that is what loving parents want for their children.

ASSESSING HAPPINESS

How can we know if our children are happy? The answer is much more than seeing smiles on their faces. Children will temporarily appear to be happy if we give them everything they want, if we don't give them responsibilities, and if we never confront them about their behavior. But that's not happiness.

As I said in Chapter 1, happiness is "a profound peace that does not come and go with changing circumstances. Real happiness comes from feeling loved and from loving other people, and that feeling stays with us through struggle and hardship. It does not come from being entertained or getting people to do what we want."

Children are genuinely happy when they're loved, loving, and responsible. Without emptiness and fear, they have no need for Getting and Protecting Behaviors. The absence of these behaviors is therefore one sure sign that our children are truly happy. See p. 56 for some practical, everyday examples of Getting and Protecting Behaviors. Happy children don't get angry, or lie, or act like victims.

TEACHING HAPPINESS

Happiness is a choice. We can teach our children to be happy no matter what is going on around them. The ability to do that is the greatest power on earth and the most valuable gift we can give them.

We cannot teach happiness by command. We can't just tell our children to be happy and expect to be obeyed. But we do that all the time, don't we? When they're being grouchy, we tell them to stop it and put a smile on their face. When they're arguing with their siblings, we tell them to quit it and be nice to each other. When we do such things, our children only learn to be deceptively pleasant, not genuinely loving or happy. Or they learn to hide their unhappiness from us.

Children only learn to be happy when we teach them what we've discussed in Chapters 12-15. We must teach them to tell the truth about themselves, which makes it possible for them to feel unconditionally loved. They must learn to love other people and to be responsible. Children who are truthful, loved, loving, and responsible are happy. In addition, we can add immeasurably to the happiness of our children when we teach them two other important principles: gratitude and the proper role of praise, power, pleasure, and safety.

TEACHING CHILDREN GRATITUDE

Being grateful is a *choice* we make to see what we have, instead of complaining about what we don't have, and that creates joy in every experience. There are few things that contribute more to happiness and loving relationships than gratitude. Without it, we miss all the joy of feeling loved and loving others. We need to teach this quality to our children.

Being Grateful FOR, Not TO

Review the section entitled, "**Praise**" in Chapter 6.

As suggested on those pages, we have a tendency to teach our children to be grateful **to** us rather than to be grateful **for** what they receive. We do that because we *enjoy* their gratitude. It makes us feel important. Such gratitude is not healthy for our children.

In contrast, when they're grateful **for** what they have, they're simply more aware of the love they receive and the happiness they enjoy. That kind of gratitude makes them feel more energized and hopeful. When they're grateful, they don't become distracted by expectations, disappointment, and emptiness.

Loving Them

We can't force children to be genuinely grateful. We can only make them feel obligated. Children can't feel grateful while they feel unloved, empty, and afraid. The most important step in teaching children gratitude is to love them.

Jessica stood in line for two hours, but the concert tickets sold out just before she got to the sales window. She was furious and whined about it all day.

Missing a concert was not the real cause of Jessica's unhappiness. Many people live happy lives without ever attending a rock concert. The real reason for her unhappiness was the fact that she was feeling unloved. When we don't have enough Real Love in our lives, we're on the edge of starvation all the time, and every morsel of Imitation Love seems very important. This concert was such a morsel to Jessica. She expected the concert to fill the emptiness in her life, at least temporarily. When she didn't get what she wanted, she reacted with anger, which made her feel less helpless and victimized.

Jessica's parents eventually took the steps to find love for themselves (Chapter 5). As they felt unconditionally loved, they began to accept and love their daughter. Two years after the event above, Jessica came home after waiting in line again for concert tickets.

Mother: "Did you get the tickets?"

Jessica: "No, they sold out."

Mother: "You must be disappointed."

Jessica: "Sure, a little. But a bunch of us went together and had a great time while we waited. We listened to music and talked. And we'll do something else the night of the concert. It's no big thing that we didn't get the tickets."

The same thing happened to Jessica on two occasions, but her reaction was notably different the second time. Why? Gratitude. On the second occasion, Jessica was grateful for the experience she had instead of complaining about something else she wanted. And her gratitude was a natural result of her feeling loved. When we feel loved, we're genuinely happy and don't need a particular thing or event to please us from one minute to the next. When we're full, we don't have constant expectations and disappointments. Instead, we're grateful for every experience we have. We see everything as an opportunity to learn and be happy. This is not a fantasy. There really are people who live like this, and the joy they experience is profound and consistent.

After children feel loved, we can teach them gratitude with our words, with our own grateful behavior, and by helping them eliminate their selfish expectations of other people. I'll address each of those steps now.

Teaching Them

My daughter Janette came home from school in tears. Her friend Misty had said some unkind things about her to several classmates.

Me: "Do I love you?"

Janette: "Yes, but ..."

Me: "Does Mom love you? Your brothers? Some of your other friends?"

Janette: "Well, yes."

Me: "It's easy to forget about the people who do love you when someone is being unkind to you. You have a lot of people who love you, and that's a big thing. When you remember that, it won't bother you when somebody treats you badly. This is an important lesson to remember: it doesn't matter how many people *don't* love you, only that some *do*. Be grateful for the ones that do."

Notice that gratitude is not a trick of positive thinking. It is simply telling the truth about what we actually have, thereby allowing us to enjoy it. When we remind our children of the love they have, they remember that they already have what really matters, and then the potentially hurtful things people do become less important. When we're grateful, we lose our expectations, fear, and anger; disappointment, demands, and envy vanish.

Janette needed to be grateful **for** the love she was receiving. She did not need to be grateful **to** the people loving her. That would not have made *her* any happier.

Being Grateful Ourselves

With our behavior, we often teach our children to be ungrateful, and they follow that example. We tend to complain about what we don't have instead of appreciating the gifts we do have. We're disappointed and angry when our favorite basketball team loses the game, instead of being grateful for the time we relaxed with friends as we watched it. We complain about traffic instead of appreciating the fact that we're driving instead of walking. We grieve excessively over the death of loved ones instead of celebrating the time we were privileged to spend with them. We complain about having to work instead of being grateful that we have the opportunity and ability to earn what we have. Our children see this incessant stream of ingratitude and naturally follow our lead. They learn to complain, criticize, be cynical, and be miserable.
pleasure

When we feel loved, our vision of the world is no longer distorted by emptiness and fear, and then we see the beauty and joy that really are everywhere. Every experience — however difficult it appears outwardly — becomes an opportunity to learn about loving other people. As we enjoy these experiences, we can share them with our children. We can express our gratitude for the beauty we see everywhere, instead of describing the flaws that can always be found in anything. We can express our gratitude for the difficult times that have taught us valuable lessons, instead of complaining about the inconvenience involved. As we do this, our children learn to do the same.

Eliminating Expectations

Remember what we discussed about expectations on pp. 246-9. Children need help seeing their expectations of other people because those expectations cause nothing but disappointment, anger, and unhappiness. When our children eliminate expectations from their lives, what's left is gratitude, which makes every experience delightful.

THE PROPER PLACE OF
PRAISE, POWER, PLEASURE AND SAFETY

In Chapter 2, I talked about the potential evils of praise, power, pleasure, and safety. "When these things are used as substitutes for Real Love — as they so often are — I call them Imitation Love." Imitation Love in all its forms is distracting, seductive, addicting, and highly destructive. However, praise, power, pleasure, and safety can be healthy, and a wise parent can use them to add to the happiness of his children.

Praise

As I said in Chapter 2 and in Chapter 14, praising our children can be dangerous. When our children do something well and we say, "I'm so proud of you," it's only natural that they feel more accepted and "loved" when they hear that. Almost all children then feel an intense pressure to continue earning our acceptance. That is not Real Love.

I suggest that we don't need to praise our children for the *things* they do. Our goal as parents is to help our children to be genuinely *happy*, which comes from feeling loved and loving others. Since true happiness has little or nothing to do with the accomplishment of *things*, why do children need to be praised for doing them? Again, I submit that they don't, and I further suggest that we believe children need praise only because we ourselves enjoy being praised. It fills our own emptiness in the absence of Real Love. When people feel unconditionally loved, they simply don't *need* to be praised.

Am I saying that we should never praise a child? No. *After* our children have had considerable experience with feeling unconditionally loved, it is possible to praise them without them feeling pressured to please us. When they are certain that we love them, praise become a delight, like dessert at the end of a meal.

However, I suggest that very few children are certain that their parents love them unconditionally. Praising children is a *very* tricky road to walk, and I offer an approach which I have found effective.

My son Rob was an excellent swimmer in high school, winning many regional events and competing at the state championships. We often had conversations like the following when he came home from those competitions.

Me: "Did you have a good time?"

Rob: "Yeah. It was a great meet. Ate some pizza. My friends were all there. We played around on the bus on the way up and back. It was great."

Me: "How did you swim?"

Rob: "Pretty well. In one event, I got my personal best time."

Me: "What did you learn?"

Rob: "The usual. Some people are so serious and competitive. Geez. They just can't have any fun. I'm glad I don't feel that way anymore. I'm glad you don't, either. And there was one guy on the bus who was a real jerk, but I remembered the three choices (Chapter 15) and just stayed away from him."

Me: "I'm glad you had a good time."

I didn't ask whether he won, because *it didn't really matter*. It only mattered that he was happy and that he learned something from his experience — and he did. Someone told me later that Rob won three of the five events he entered and helped his team win the competition. That was an interesting piece of news, but it was not important to his happiness. If a parent makes winning important, that child will look for happiness all his life by earning Imitation Love in the form of praise and power — and he will not find it.

Children don't need our praise. They need our love and guidance.

We need to teach our children what praise means. Praise from someone who is honest and loving can be a useful piece of information about our performance in school, our careers, etc. We can use it to help us judge how we're doing and what our next step should be. However, from someone who does not feel unconditionally loved — which includes almost everyone — praise only means this: "You have done something that makes *me* feel good." When someone praises me, it rarely says anything about *me* at all. They're only telling me what makes *them* feel good. I'm not suggesting that we teach our children to be cynical, but it is a fact that most praise tells us *nothing* about *ourselves*. It only tells us something about the *giver* of the praise. People without Real Love use praise as a way of getting us to do what they want. If we give our children sufficient Real Love and guidance, they won't be deceived by such manipulative flattery.

Power

Without meaning to, our children use power as a form of Imitation Love whenever they control the behavior of another person in any way: when they get angry to take a toy or win an argument; when they threaten to withdraw their approval from a friend to get what they want; when they act like victims to get what they want from us, their parents; etc. They can also get an unhealthy sense of power from seemingly innocent activities like winning at sports. Many athletes thoroughly enjoy *beating* their opponents and exercising a position of superior strength over them. Power is a seductive thing.

The greatest power on earth — real power — is the ability to make our own choices under any conditions. It's the ability to choose to love other people no matter how they behave toward us. Real power has nothing to do with being able to control someone else. That is what we need to teach our children.

One of my children once said this to me: "Dad, I've been around long enough now to see just how unloved and confused most people are. If things get difficult, they react out of fear, and it almost always goes badly. I feel loved almost the time, and when I do, I'm not afraid of anything. No matter what happens around me, I can choose what I do next. That's a pretty powerful feeling."

When we give our children sufficient Real Love, and when we teach them the Law of Choice, and how to love other people, and how to be grateful, they have the power to make the right choices in every circumstance. That is a formidable power indeed.

Pleasure

There's nothing wrong with having a good time. We're here to be happy. Pleasure is only destructive when it takes the place of Real Love. We need to teach our children that pleasure should never be enjoyed at the expense of another human being. When they understand that, pleasure will become a delightful addition to the genuine happiness that comes from the unconditional love in their lives.

Safety

Our greatest fear is that we'll be unloved and alone. When we feel unconditionally loved, and when we love other people, we lose that fear. That is real safety. With the knowledge that we are loved and love others, nothing can take our happiness from us. That's the kind of safety we want to give our children.

HAPPINESS IS A CHOICE

When an athlete has thoroughly trained and prepared himself for an event, winning becomes something he can choose. Without that preparation, he *cannot* choose to win. Winning is impossible. It is the same with happiness. If we teach our children the things we have talked about in Chapters 12-16, they can choose to be happy under any circumstances.

The Law of Happiness

If we plant healthy seeds in good soil and properly care for them, they will grow. If we plant corn and take care of it, we can plan on picking corn at the end of the season. That is the law of the harvest. It is unchangeable. It declares that we reap what we sow. The law of happiness works no differently. It also declares that we reap what we sow. If we are loved, loving, and responsible, we *will* be happy. Our goal as parents is to help our children develop those qualities.

THE LAWS OF PARENTING

To accompany the law of the harvest and the law of happiness, I offer the Laws of Parenting. Interacting with an unhappy child can be confusing and frustrating — there are often so many things going on and so many things for us to respond to. How do we remember what to say and do? The following guidelines are intended to distill all the principles we have discussed thus far in the book, and should give us some clarity and confidence as we teach our children to be happy.

The First Law: My child needs to feel loved.

There is nothing I can do today — no meeting I can attend, no
money I can make, no person I can impress, no fun I can have
— that will be as important as loving this child right now.

See the story of Ryan and Charles in Chapter 9. Before Charles
had his second encounter with Ryan, he knew the First Law.
When Ryan snapped at his brother, Charles knew that the most
important thing he could do right then was to love Ryan. Charles
dropped what he was doing and accomplished that one goal. It
changed Ryan's life — and Charles's, as well.

The Second Law: I can't give what I don't have.

If we don't feel unconditionally loved ourselves, there is no
way in the world we can love our children. There's no sense
pretending to love them. We need to learn to tell the truth about
ourselves to wise men and women and get the Real Love we
need. And then we can share that love with our children and
begin to change their lives. George illustrates this principle and
process in Chapter 5.

The Third Law: If I'm angry, I'm wrong.

If I'm angry, I'm thinking about *myself*. I can't unconditionally
love or help my child, and that's my primary responsibility as a
parent. So if I'm angry, it doesn't matter what my child has done
— I'm wrong. I need to shut up and wait until I can be loving
enough to be a real parent.

In Chapter 5, George applied the Third Law, although at the time
he didn't know the name of it, nor did he completely understand
it. George was angry. Instead of continuing a conversation with
his son in that condition, George stopped talking and talked to
someone who could love him. He resumed the conversation with
his son later.

The Fourth Law: Truth → Seen → Accepted → Loved.

Our children must tell the truth about themselves before they can feel seen, accepted, and loved. We must also tell the truth about ourselves.

In Chapter 13, Diane helped Justin tell the truth about his selfish, unloving behavior. As he did that, he felt seen, accepted, and loved by his mother. If he had lied about his behavior, he would have felt hidden from her — separated and alone.

The Fifth Law: Love, Teach, Faith, Consequences.

Our children need to be loved and taught. "With enough love and guidance, children tend to do the right thing and be happy." (Chapter 10) And then they need our faith in them that they can learn and grow. Occasionally, they need the additional motivation of consequences which are lovingly given to encourage them to make the right choices. They do not need punishment or anger to learn.

The Sixth Law: Happiness comes from being loving and responsible.

The most important things I can teach my child are to love other people and to be responsible.

The Seventh Law: Everyone has the right to choose what they say and do.

This is also called the Law of Choice (Chapter 8). First, *we* need to understand this and not constantly interfere with our children's right to choose, or they will be crippled as individuals. Second, we must teach our children this law, or they will be unbearably selfish human beings and will have terrible relationships with other people all their lives (Chapter 15).

The Eighth Law: Remember what's important.

When a child does something wrong, we get too involved in the specifics of their "crime." When children argue, we tend to get lost in the details about who did what to whom. A great deal of time and energy is wasted over those details when we could be focusing our attention on what really matters: the happiness of our children. Always pay attention to the Laws of Parenting first, not the specific "facts of the case."

In Chapter 11, Christopher's mother avoided getting into an argument about the details of what happened between him and his sister and talked only about what was important to her son. A further discussion of that is found in Chapter 12.

Chapter Summary

Our children will be happy — the greatest gift we can give them — as we teach them to tell the truth about themselves, to feel loved, to love others, and to be responsible.

We also contribute to their happiness by helping them to be grateful and to understand the proper role of praise, power, pleasure, and safety.

When children are adequately prepared, happiness becomes a choice.

The Laws of Parenting are a tool we can use to help our children become happy.

Chapter 17

More About Family Meetings

We began a discussion of family meetings in Chapter 7. Now that we know more about parenting, we can make even better use of these meetings. I suggest that three topics need to be addressed regularly in family meetings, and usually in this order:

Planning and Assignment
Accountability
Feelings and Teaching

There's nothing formal or inflexible about this agenda, but most parents will accomplish more when they remember these components as they guide their family through a meeting. Remember that family meetings only exist as a tool to help families be happier. Adapt the meeting to your family; don't force your family to fit the structure of a meeting.

PLANNING AND ASSIGNMENT

Most events are more successful when they're planned. Our family keeps a large calendar on the living room table, and we refer to it every day as we discuss who is going where, and when, and how they're getting there. For example, if a child is on the swim team at school, the calendar indicates all his practices, competitions, and who is responsible for transportation to those events.

Changes in regularly-assigned household chores (pp. 212-15) are made in this part of the meeting. Assignments are also made for other tasks: fix the broken shelf, get the car serviced, pick up Benjamin and his friend after school on Friday, prune the fruit trees, etc. As discussed in Chapter 14, these assignments are then written and placed where they can be easily accessed.

Purpose

Although planning does make events run more smoothly, and assigning jobs does help children learn responsibility, those are not the only purposes of planning and assignment. A well-planned activity is worthless if children don't feel loved and happy. A responsible but unloved child is not a parenting success. Remember that a family meeting has three goals (Chapter 7), and each part of the meeting should fulfill those goals. It's easy to remember the goal of teaching children responsibility as we talk about planning and assignment, but we must not neglect the other two goals:

1. To create opportunities for parents to see and love their children. As a loving family plans events together, a child sees firsthand evidence that his needs are important to his parents. He feels accepted, included, and loved.

2. To teach children how to love other people. In the planning of events, one person's interests sometimes conflict with those of another. Perhaps two events are held at the same time and transportation to both is impossible. As one person makes sacrifices for the other, he learns more about caring for the happiness of another person, which is the definition of Real Love.

ACCOUNTABILITY

Children tend to learn more and be more responsible when they're required to report to someone else about the work they've been assigned. In our family, we write down every assignment. This ensures that assignments are clear and not forgotten. It creates a better opportunity for children to account for their behavior.

It was Kyle's job to gather trash from each room every day; each Tuesday, he took it to the street, where it was picked up by the sanitation department. Wednesday morning, there was a family meeting before school.

Father: "Kyle, did you empty the garbage yesterday and take it to the street?"

Kyle: "No."

Purposes

When we correctly ask for an accounting of each assignment given to a child, there's no disappointment or anger when a job isn't done. The purpose of accountability is not to control or shame anyone. Again, the real purposes of accountability are the same as the purposes of a family meeting (Chapter 7):

1. Create opportunities for parents to see and love their children. As Kyle's father talked about his irresponsibility, it was obvious from his facial expression and tone of voice that he still accepted and loved Kyle. That has a powerful effect on children, far greater than praise, expensive gifts, or the often hollow words, "I love you." Children don't really feel loved until they're accepted *while* they're making mistakes.

2. Teach children responsibility. Sometimes, simply loving and teaching a child are not enough to change his behavior. Kyle had been loved and taught responsibility, but he still didn't consistently complete his assignment. So his father imposed a consequence for the purpose of helping Kyle consider more carefully his responsibility (Chapter 11). He assigned Kyle to take the garbage to the city dump, quite some distance away. In

the following weeks, Kyle remembered this inconvenience and chose to take the garbage to the street.

3. Teach children to love others. Kyle was too young to drive, so his father assigned Kyle's sister Brooke to take him to the dump. That gave her an opportunity to accept and help Kyle while he was an inconvenience to her. She learned something about Real Love.

Accounting for Success

Accountability is not just a way of identifying mistakes. Children need recognition and discussion of their learning and accomplishments, too.

Father: "Kyle, did you empty the garbage yesterday and take it to the street?"

Kyle: "Yes."

Father: "You've done that for several weeks in a row now. How does it feel?"

Kyle: "I like it. It feels better than being lazy and feeling guilty."

Father: "Choosing to be responsible will help you be happy all your life. You're learning an important lesson. I'm happy for you."

Kyle's father didn't praise him. When we consistently praise our children, they tend to do the right thing only to please us or to avoid our disapproval. That is not a mature motivation that will serve them well as adults. They need to learn to make choices based on what is right or loving or responsible — independent of what pleases us. When they can do that, they have found the secret to happiness. Father recognized that, and when Kyle did the right thing, he expressed his pleasure that Kyle had done what made *Kyle* happy, rather than praising Kyle for doing something that had made *Father* happy.

Children need to feel the joy that comes from being responsible. When they feel that consistently, they tend to be motivated to be responsible on their own, without us constantly pushing them to do the right thing. Family meetings are a good time to point out their moments of success and give them that feeling of responsibility.

FEELINGS AND TEACHING

The third part of the meeting is an opportunity for people to discuss how they feel and what they're learning.

Zachary was eight, Katherine fourteen. They quarreled frequently.

Father: "Are there any feelings to discuss?"

There was no response. Until our children feel certain that they're unconditionally loved, they won't feel safe talking about their feelings. We may need to help them get started.

Mother: "Katherine, you and Zachary seem to be irritated with each other a lot. Would you be willing to talk about that?"

Katherine: "Zachary's always being stupid and trying to irritate me."

Zachary: "I do not. You're the one that picks on me."

Mother wisely remembered the Eighth Law of Parenting: "Remember what's important." She chose to not get bogged down in an argument about who did what to whom, which would have gone nowhere and helped no one. She knew that the central issue in a dispute between children is always the same: they're not feeling loved. Zachary was the youngest child and was often treated like a baby. Katherine disregarded his opinion and left him out of activities because he "wasn't old enough." As a result of that — and other influences — he felt unloved and worthless, and he reacted by attacking her.

Mother helped Zachary see how he was feeling and reacting. She then helped them both see that when Zachary defended himself, Katherine became afraid and reacted by attacking him even more. Mother added that it was her own failure to sufficiently love them unconditionally that led to their emptiness and quarreling in the first place.

As Katherine and Zachary felt accepted by their mother, their fear and anger disappeared. They saw each other more clearly and naturally became more accepting. Notice that all the steps of Chapter 13 — Teaching Children to Love — are illustrated by Mother in this example.

THE REWARD

Miraculous experiences happen in family meetings. We learn to be loving as parents. Children feel loved and learn to be loving themselves. They learn to be responsible. The lives of parents and children are changed forever as they use these meetings to tell the truth and love each other.

Chapter Summary

Family meetings often have three parts:
    Planning and assignment
    Accountability
    Feelings and Teaching

The purpose of family meetings is to teach people to be loving and responsible, not just to accomplish tasks.

Chapter 18

Responding To
Getting and Protecting Behaviors

Children cannot tolerate the pain of feeling unloved, so whenever they feel empty or afraid, they naturally use Getting and Protecting Behaviors (Chapter 3), which make them feel better temporarily. But these behaviors do not make them feel loved or happy. Without Real Love, children are trapped: they can only use Getting and Protecting Behaviors. These are the only tools they have to deal with their unhappiness.

HOW WE REACT TO THE GETTING AND PROTECTING OF OUR CHILDREN

If we have not been unconditionally loved ourselves, filling our emptiness and protecting ourselves become the central pre-occupations of our lives. We then evaluate the success of every interaction — even with our children — according to how much Imitation Love we get. We want people to make us feel good, and if they don't, we're disappointed or angry.

When our children use Getting and Protecting Behaviors — lying, attacking, being victims, clinging, and running — we obviously don't get the love we're looking for. Instead, we feel hurt, used, afraid, and alone — and we hate that. *We then respond with getting and protecting of our own.* That can only have the effect of making our children feel more alone and unhappy, and they naturally respond with more getting and protecting. It's an endless and deadly cycle.

We tend to respond to our children's Getting and Protecting Behaviors with one or both of two opposite reactions: controlling or permissiveness. We respond too much or too little. Which we choose is determined by a combination of which we experienced most as children, which we hate most, which is most effective in a given moment with a particular child, and so on. And many of us alternate between the two extremes, leaving our children dizzy with confusion.

CONTROLLING (ATTACKING, VICTIM)

When our children are lazy, disrespectful, angry, and rebellious, we feel inconvenienced and afraid — if we don't feel loved ourselves. We commonly react by controlling them, which we do by intimidating them with authority, anger, criticism, and punishment, all forms of attacking. Sometimes we act hurt — we act like victims — which again has the effect of controlling them. In short, as we control them, we protect ourselves and get a feeling of power. The reward is shallow and temporary, but it seems better than feeling attacked and helpless as our children use their Getting and Protecting Behaviors.

We learned to do all this from our own parents and others, and we keep doing it because controlling people seems to get us the results we want — even though it's only temporary. But the cost is high. When we control our children, they can't feel unconditionally loved, nor can we teach them to be loving and responsible. And then we have failed as parents.

Another word for a controlling parent is strict, but remember that a more accurate description of a strict parent is *afraid.* Parents who control their children simply don't know how to teach and love them. They don't know how to do anything but control people, and they're terrified of losing control. They're not happy themselves, and they don't raise happy children.

If you're wondering whether you're a controlling parent, consider the two most common ways that parents control their children: (1) anger and (2) rules.

1. Anger at a child is never justified. Anger is always selfish and is used to get what *we* want. It is not used for the happiness of our children.

2. Guidelines are certainly necessary for a happy life. Our children could not learn without them. However, when we find ourselves issuing an abundance of rules to our children, we need to ask ourselves how many of them are making *our* lives more convenient.

PERMISSIVENESS (VICTIM, RUN, LIE)

Another way to avoid the fear we experience when our children manipulate us to get Imitation Love and protect themselves is to give them whatever they want. If we give them money, clothes, entertainment, cars, and free time, and if we don't correct them and make them accountable for their behavior, they won't whine, complain, or dislike us as much. And then we'll feel like "loving" parents.

But it's all a manipulation on our part, because we don't tell them (**lie**) that we're seeking their gratitude and affection, or that we're avoiding their disapproval. And we act hurt (**victim**) when they don't appreciate us. In addition, we're **running** from our responsibility to teach them and correct them (Chapter 11). In short, we're indulging and spoil our children for our own benefit.

When our children manipulate us, they can't feel genuinely loved because what we give them is not freely offered or received (Chapter 3). Permissiveness is therefore as destructive as controlling, since both approaches cause children to feel unloved and empty.

PROPERLY RESPONDING TO GETTING AND PROTECTING

The proper response to children getting and protecting is neither controlling nor permissiveness. And there's no correct middle ground between them. As we move back and forth between controlling and permissiveness, it's all still getting and protecting on our part, and we fail to give our children Real Love or teach them to be loving and responsible.

Remember that children only use Getting and Protecting Behaviors because they feel *unloved*, empty, and afraid. The correct response to each of these behaviors is then obvious. Children who lie, attack, act like victims, run, and cling need to be *seen, accepted, and loved* by us. We'll discuss how to respond to these behaviors individually in Chapters 19-22.

Many parents protest that some anger and controlling are necessary in the process of raising a child. That's not true. People advocate controlling only because they have not seen the power of teaching and Real Love. We've already proven beyond doubt with our own experience that anger, controlling, and manipulating are complicated, ineffective, and exhausting. So why not give it up? Loving and teaching are simpler, easier, and more effective.

As we tell the truth about ourselves and get loved (Chapter 5), we eliminate the blinding effects of our own emptiness and fear. And then we can see, accept, and love our children (Chapter 9).

The Reward

As we learn to love our children while they get Imitation Love and protect themselves, they feel accepted with all their flaws. Filled with Real Love, they don't need to protect themselves any longer. They don't need to get Imitation Love. In contrast, when we react to their Getting and Protecting Behaviors with the same behaviors of our own, we make things much worse.

DON'T GIVE UP

Most children respond in a positive way to being loved. However, some children have been hurt so much and for so long that they don't trust us easily, and they continue getting and protecting despite being loved. We may not see an immediate positive result when we first begin to unconditionally love our children. Understandably, we then have a tendency to give up and go back to controlling and/or permissiveness. Consider this:

1. We don't know what effect our love is having. When a seed is planted, a great deal happens under the ground and out of our sight long before we see a plant sprout from the ground. Similarly, love and faith have powerful effects that are not always visible.

2. Even when we don't immediately see a positive effect from loving our children, giving up is foolish. We've already proven that the other ways of teaching our children — the unloving ways — are worthless. Loving them may not work as quickly as we'd like, but it's still the only approach that has a chance.

3. Even when a child doesn't respond positively, *we* are still happier as we learn to be loving. Loving people is always the best way to live.

Chapter Summary

Children without Real Love are empty and afraid. They react with Getting and Protecting Behaviors, which inconvenience and frighten us. To protect ourselves, we react with Getting and Protecting Behaviors of our own, either controlling or indulging them. But this is not Real Love, and it leaves our children even more empty and afraid.

The only correct response to our children's Getting and Protecting Behaviors is to see, accept, and love them.

Chapter 19

Responding to Lying

Kimberley's mother (p. 21) was angry when she saw the stain on her dress the second time. Kimberley then lied to avoid her mother's anger and the accompanying pain of feeling unloved and alone. It worked, so she naturally continued to lie in other circumstances when she was afraid — as a child and as an adult.

Children everywhere do this. They don't lie to irritate us or because they're bad. They lie because they're mortally afraid we'll attack them or abandon them when we see their mistakes and flaws. Their greatest fear is that they won't be loved, and that fear understandably resulted from the many instances when we *were* disappointed and impatient with them. So they lie about their imperfections to avoid our disapproval. That's what the Wart King did, hiding his warts to avoid the criticism and rejection of other people (Chapter 3).

Ironically, when children lie, they feel even more unloved and alone. A wise parent helps children see their lies and tell the truth because it creates the opportunity for them to feel seen and loved (Truth → Seen → Accepted → Loved, Chapter 12).

PREVENTION

Children only lie to protect themselves from disapproval and to feel accepted. If we accept and love them no matter what they do — Real Love — they no longer have a need to protect themselves and earn our approval. *They have no reason to lie* — and they won't.

In this chapter, let's make a significant change in the story about Kimberley. We'll assume that years before Kimberley stained the dress, her mother had taken the steps to find Real Love for herself (Chapter 5) and had learned how to unconditionally love her daughter (Chapter 9). In that ideal situation, let's imagine one way she could have reacted to Kimberley's behavior.

Kimberley's mother came in the room and saw her daughter playing with the stained dress. Her mother smiled, scooped her up in her arms, and held her.

Mother: "You look like you're having fun."

What our children want most from us is to be loved. Without that, nothing else we give them really matters. However, loving a child does not mean ignoring their unacceptable behavior (Chapters 11 and 14). They still need to be taught and corrected while they're loved.

Mother: Do you remember that I told you not to take food out of the kitchen? This is why — my dress is a real mess now."

She then helped Kimberley treat the stain and put the dress in the washing machine.

Kimberley's mother taught her that she'd made a mistake, but she didn't do it with disappointment or anger. That is the only productive way to teach a child anything. Because Kimberley felt loved as she was being taught, the next time she made a mistake, she freely told her mother about it and they corrected the problem. She didn't feel afraid and didn't need to protect herself with lies. Unconditional love simply makes lying unnecessary.

Mother also taught Kimberley about responsibility as they cleaned the dress together. I recommend reading the Laws of Parenting in Chapter 16 and seeing how Mother demonstrated an understanding of each of them as she interacted with Kimberley.

THE CORRECT RESPONSE TO LYING

There would be no lying in a world where children felt loved. But most children were not raised with unconditional love. For many years, mine were not. So children *will* lie to protect themselves. On those occasions, they need us to *see them*, *accept them*, and *love them*.

INTENTIONAL, CONSCIOUS LYING

Although most lies are unconscious, sometimes children are fully aware of their deception.

Joshua borrowed the baseball glove of his father, Fred, and left it outside. Two days later, Fred found his glove in the grass, soaking wet and damaged. He brought this up in a family meeting, knowing who was responsible.

Fred: "Who left my glove outside in the rain?"

Although Joshua remembered doing it, he joined with the other children in saying, "I don't know."

Joshua lied because he was afraid of Fred's anger and wanted to avoid it. Many of us get angry at our children when they lie, but that only makes them more afraid, and then they have even more reason to protect themselves and are more likely to lie again. In effect, we make them lie when we get angry. But our anger is understandable. When we feel unloved and empty ourselves, our children's lies make us feel like we have no control over them, which makes us uncomfortable — another way of saying afraid. We then attempt to eliminate our fear by controlling our children with criticism, anger, and shame.

The only productive response to children when they lie is to see, accept, and love them.

Seeing

Emptiness and fear are blinding. If we don't feel loved ourselves, we can't clearly see our children — we can only see what we want from them and what we're afraid they might do to inconvenience, embarrass, or hurt us. When we feel loved (Chapter 5), seeing them is easy.

Fred knew Joshua was lying, and years before he would have angrily confronted his son, making him feel bad. However, in the previous year, Fred had learned to tell the truth about himself to some wise people and had begun to feel unconditionally loved.

Feeling loved in that moment, Fred saw Joshua clearly. He knew that Joshua lied only because he was feeling empty and was afraid of his father's disapproval. He also knew that Joshua needed his acceptance and love more than anything else. Fred remembered the First Law of Parenting: My child needs to feel loved.

Fred: "Josh, did you leave the glove out?"

Joshua: "No."

Fred: "Two days ago, I saw you play with it and leave it on the lawn."

Joshua hung his head.

Fred: "You lied to me because you thought I'd love you less if you ruined my glove. Your fear is *my* fault because I *have* loved you less on many occasions when you made mistakes like that. I've yelled at you, said critical things, and told you in many ways that you were defective. You lied to avoid that happening again here. Your lie is still wrong, but it is understandable."

Fred clearly saw his son and the *cause* of his mistake, instead of only seeing what Joshua had done *to him* by lying. That was only possible because Fred felt loved himself.

Notice that part of seeing a child is requiring him to tell the truth about himself (Chapter 12). A child can't continue to lie and feel loved. Fred understood the Fourth Law of Parenting: Truth → Seen → Accepted → Loved.

Accepting and Loving

Fred crossed the room and sat next to Joshua.

Fred: "You were careless with my glove, but mistakes like that are unavoidable as you learn to be responsible. As you see your mistakes and feel loved, you'll make them less. And as you feel moved loved, you won't feel afraid and won't need to lie. I care about your happiness much more than a damaged glove."

As Fred really saw Joshua, accepting him was easy. He taught Joshua that being irresponsible and lying were wrong, but he did it without disappointment and anger. He understood that Joshua needed to be taught and loved, not criticized. He had faith that with acceptance and guidance, Joshua would become responsible and honest. Anger is never necessary in teaching a child.

UNINTENTIONAL LIES

Let's replay the story above with one change: when Fred asked about the glove at the family meeting, Joshua really didn't remember leaving it outside. When he denied it, his lie was *unintentional*. Most lies are like this.

Fred: "Joshua, did you leave my glove outside?"

    With a genuinely puzzled look on his face, Joshua said, "I don't think so."

Fred: "Josh, other than myself, who is the only person in the family who ever uses my glove?"

Joshua: "Me, but . . ."

Fred: "I'm not saying you intentionally lied about this, but when you answered, you were only interested in getting yourself out of trouble. You were not honestly trying to remember whether you left the glove outside. So relax. I'm only trying to teach you something here. Do you remember playing ball with your friends two days ago?"

Joshua: (pause) "Yes."

Fred: "You lost your own glove last month, right?"

Joshua: "Yeah."

Fred: "And you needed a glove to play with your friends, didn't you?"

Joshua: (pause, starting to get the point) "Yes."

Fred: "So what's the likelihood that you used my glove?"

Joshua could see that his father was not angry, and he felt accepted and safe because of that. Feeling loved, the blinding effect of fear was eliminated, and he could actually remember what happened more clearly. Fear is crippling to the mind.

Joshua: "I remember now. I did use the glove and I don't remember putting it back where I got it."

At this point, Joshua did not need to be criticized, shamed, or punished. He had already seen and told the truth about his behavior, and that is what leads to feeling loved and learning. Fortunately, his father had faith that with guidance and love, Joshua would learn about telling the truth, feeling loved, and being responsible — and he did.

Chapter Summary

Children lie only to protect themselves and to get Imitation Love. When we unconditionally love them, they have no need to do those things and therefore no need to lie.

When children lie, we need to point that out to them as we accept and love them.

Chapter 20

Responding to Attacking

Attacking is any behavior where we protect ourselves or manipulate people to get what we want by making them afraid. We attack each other with anger, criticism, irritation, intimidation, accusations, authority, guilt, and even passive resistance or withholding affection.

WHY WE ATTACK PEOPLE

When a man is healthy and well-fed, forcing him to live for two days without food would be inconvenient and mildly uncomfortable, but not dangerous. Such a man could tolerate many stresses: cold weather, physical exertion, etc. However, these same experiences could be fatal to a man who was starving and sick. When our health is already compromised, little things can become life-threatening.

The same is true with our spiritual and emotional health. When we're filled with Real Love, we have what matters most. We're strong, unafraid, and easily able to tolerate the inconveniences and injustices that inevitably accompany interaction with other human beings. But without Real Love, we're starving and sick. In that condition, every experience becomes a possible source of pain and fear. Most of us are in that position — including our children.

When we're in pain and helpless to do anything about it, we feel powerless and miserable. One way to feel less helpless and afraid is to attack people. Attacking makes us feel strong and also scares off many of the people who could hurt us. In short, we attack people because we're empty and afraid.

WHY CHILDREN ATTACK THEIR PARENTS

Children are younger, less experienced, and less powerful than almost everyone around them. They can be used and hurt quite easily, and they feel that. To a child, virtually everyone is a potential threat. Naturally, they protect themselves from people who are more powerful and who can hurt them. Attacking is one Protecting Behavior they frequently use.

But why would they attack **us**, their parents, after all we've done for them? Because they feel even more powerless with us. We've changed their diapers, wiped their noses, dried their tears, and seen them at their weakest moments. We know all about their flaws and fears. We therefore have the ability to hurt them more easily than other people can. We can destroy them with a word or glance — and we often do. In addition, they depend on us for food, shelter, and love. They feel utterly controlled by us. When we use them or do hurtful things to them, the effect is devastating. When they're afraid, they defend themselves with great energy, using all the Protecting Behaviors, including attacking.

Ashley, 15, was heading out the front door when her father saw her.

Father: "Where do you think you're going?"

Ashley: "To Brittany's house."

Father: "At this hour?"

Ashley: "It's not that late."

As her father spoke, he walked closer to the door. The scowl deepened on his face and his voice grew louder.

Father: "On a school night it is. And you didn't get anybody's permission, young lady."

Ashley: "She just lives a block away."

The volume of the conversation was quickly rising.

Father: "Did you hear me? Shut the door and get back in here."

Ashley: "You never let me do anything! I hate living here!"

Father: "You get in your room and stay there!"

Ashley slammed the door and stomped back into her room. Ashley attacked her father when she raised her voice, when she said she hated "living here," when she slammed the door, and when she stomped her feet as she went to her room. If she had been physically larger than her father, and if there had been no negative consequences to her action, she would not have hesitated to push him out of the way and leave the house. She also used the Protecting Behaviors of acting like a victim ("You never let me do anything") and running (she sulked all the next day).

Ashley was not a "bad" child. She simply felt unloved, empty, and afraid. When her father confronted her, she protected herself. That does not justify her unacceptable behavior, but it does explain it. Without feeling loved, Ashley could not have chosen to behave any better than she did.

HOW WE FEEL ABOUT ANGER FROM OUR CHILDREN

Ashley's father did not feel unconditionally loved. When Ashley was a little girl, she smiled at him, held his hand, did what she was told, gave him kisses, made him laugh when she did cute things, and said, "I love you." In fact, she was the only reliable source of "love" in his life, and he adored her for that.

Although Ashley's father loved the attention and affection she gave him, she did *not* give him Real Love (pp. 86-7). Real Love is genuinely caring about the happiness of another person. It's something we learn to give as we're unconditionally loved ourselves. Ashley was not unconditionally loved by her father and couldn't possibly have given him something she never got herself.

With their smiles and expressions of affection, children are *really saying* this to us: "I feel good when you feed me, clothe me, shelter me, and make me feel safe. And I'll be so happy if you keep doing all that." Children don't unconditionally love us. They *need us* — and that's how it should be (Chapter 6).

When we're empty ourselves, we can't give our children the Real Love they need. Instead, we're busy looking everywhere to get affection for ourselves — including from our children. When children are cooperative and affectionate, we *hear them say* this: "I love you. You're the most important person in the world to me. I'm grateful for you with all my heart, and I'll do everything I can to make you happy."

In summary, although our children express that they *need* us, we hear them say that they *love* us. It's natural that we hear that because that's what we *want* to hear. It's what we want to hear from everyone. And then the unthinkable happens — our children become angry at us. When that happens, all our hopes for praise, gratitude, and love are crushed. We feel betrayed and afraid. That's how Ashley's father felt.

HOW WE REACT TO ANGER FROM OUR CHILDREN

When we feel empty and afraid, a child's anger is frightening, although we tend to deny that. Naturally, we then protect ourselves, just like everyone else does in the face of anger. Without thinking about it, we use the Getting and Protecting Behaviors with our children.

Attacking

As a child, Ashley tried very hard to earn her father's love. She did all the right things to please him. She tried not to make mistakes, but mistakes are inevitable, and as she made them and saw her father's unintentional reaction to them, she learned the unbearably painful lesson that her father's love was *conditional*. That's a terrible thing for any child to learn. And then she had to work harder and harder to get the acceptance she craved, and to keep from being criticized. Increasingly, she gave up trying to please him and reacted to his anger and controlling by expressing her own anger. Unable to feel Real Love, at least she enjoyed the feeling of power she got from being angry.

The moment Ashley's father saw her going out the door, he felt out of control. She was disobeying him and he didn't know what to do about it. His automatic reaction was to protect himself from feeling helpless and afraid. He unconsciously used anger, which is an attack. He also used anger as a Getting Behavior, to get respect and power. When she reacted with anger, his own anger only increased.

We attack our children more than we realize. Criticism and anger are forms of attack. Even when we're "just" disappointed, we communicate that our children are defective, and they feel the painful withdrawal of our affection. We express our disappointment in words, sighs, the shrug of a shoulder, and our tone of voice. All these behaviors wound the heart of a child, leaving him more alone, more afraid, and more likely to attack us to defend himself. To a child, the effect of anger is only a tiny step past that of disappointment.

Even though anger at our children is selfish and counter-productive, we still do it because it does get some results. When we get angry, they often do what we want: they move faster, respect us (fear us, actually), and give us a moment of peace and quiet. But what a price we pay for doing this! Children who act out of fear don't learn to be responsible or loving. They only learn to protect themselves: they hide their mistakes (lie), get angry (attack), act like victims, and avoid us and other people (run).

Lying

Every time we're angry at our children, we're lying. We're saying, directly or by implication, that something they've done has "made" us angry. The truth is, we're angry because *we* don't feel loved and are protecting ourselves.

Acting Like Victims

After Ashley slammed the front door and then the door of her bedroom, her father felt hurt by his daughter's behavior. He thought, "How could she treat me like this, after all I've done for her?" In other words, he felt like a victim.

Attacking — controlling, blaming, anger — is exhausting and often ineffective. At times, we give it up and try another approach: we act like victims with our children. We often say out loud a variation on the words that Ashley's father was thinking: "How could you talk to me like that after all I've done for you?" We make them feel responsible for hurting us. For some parents, acting like victims is not used *after* attacking; it's their primary Getting and Protecting Behavior. It's the one they learned as children.

By acting like victims, we can often manipulate our children and make them stop doing what's "hurting" us. And we feel self-righteous in the process. But the price is very high, because once again our children feel unloved and alone.

Running

For several days after their angry interaction, Ashley's father avoided speaking to her. He wasn't even aware that he was doing it.

When we avoid our children, we're using the Protecting Behavior of running. And when we don't feel loved ourselves, it's understandable that we avoid our children when they're angry. It's unpleasant being around children who attack us. Running gives us the temporary sensation of safety, but it also leaves our children feeling unloved and alone — again. All of our Getting and Protecting Behaviors have that result.

HOW TO REACT TO ANGER

Children only attack us because they feel unloved, empty, and afraid. Knowing that, the most effective response to their attacks is obvious: they need to be seen, accepted, and loved. When they feel loved, they're no longer afraid and have no *reason* to protect themselves by attacking.

As I've said before, parenting is not a technique. We can't simply memorize the right words to say or things to do and expect to help our children. Nor can we just decide that we're going to start loving our children when they're angry instead of defending ourselves and controlling them. We must first feel genuinely loved ourselves before we can lovingly respond to our children (Chapters 5 and 9).

Ashley's father did that. He learned to tell the truth about himself and associated with wise men and women who accepted and loved him.

Seeing

As Ashley's father began to feel loved, he was no longer blinded by need and fear all the time, so there were occasions when he saw her clearly. He saw that she was empty and afraid because she didn't feel loved. He saw that she wasn't "bad" or intentionally troublesome, just afraid and doing what she could to feel less helpless and alone.

Accepting and Loving

Months after the incident described above, Ashley was leaving the house when her father saw her.

Father: "Where are you going?"

Ashley: "To Brittany's house."

Father: "We had agreed that you would talk to me or your mother before you left the house. Did you do that?"

Ashley slammed the door and shouted, "You never let me go anywhere!"

She was in the process of stomping off to her room when Father stood in her path. He put his arms around her and said, "I'm not angry at you. I just want to know where you are all the time." He continued to hold her gently and repeated that he was not angry at her. He also told her that he loved her, and slowly, her anger went away. Ashley had never felt her anger leave like that, and she began to cry.

Ashley: "I'm sorry I slammed the door. I was mad."

Father: "I don't care. You thought I was angry at you. I certainly have been angry at you a lot in your life, and I feel bad about that. I have a lot to learn about loving you."

What a wonderful experience. Instead of trading Protecting Behaviors — as they had done in their previous experience and many times before — Father told the truth about himself and loved his daughter; Ashley told the truth about herself and felt loved. These experiences are life-changing.

When Father saw Ashley clearly, he found it easy to accept her. How can we be angry at someone who's only afraid and protecting himself — even if it inconveniences us?

Feeling loved himself, Ashley's father began to care about her happiness and change the way he interacted with her. Other examples of parents who learned to respond productively to attacking from their children are found in Chapters 9 (Patricia) and 11 (Bob's mother).

When our children attack us, they're simply protecting themselves or trying to satisfy their own needs by finding Imitation Love. Unfortunately, these selfish behaviors inconvenience and injure us. When we feel loved ourselves and love our children unconditionally, we understand that anger is always a reaction to fear, and our primary concern is for *their* happiness, not how they affect *us*. When they're inconsiderate or hurtful, we want to know what's missing in *their* lives that would cause them to behave that way, instead of feeling hurt or angry ourselves.

Loving our children doesn't mean approving of wrong behavior. We still need to teach them the truth (Chapter 12) and correct them (Chapter 11).

Early Recognition

It's best to not wait until our children are shouting at us to recognize that they're using attacking as a Getting or Protecting Behavior. Any time our children are angry, they're attacking, and they generally begin using that behavior at a very young age.

Ruth watched her four-year-old son playing with some toys that required putting parts together. He was having difficulty making the parts fit, and after several minutes he began throwing parts against the wall. In years past, she would have told him to stop throwing things, but she had recently been learning about Real Love, and she realized that this was an opportunity for her to see and love her son. Telling him to "stop it" would have ignored the message he was communicating with his behavior. He was telling her that he felt unloved and alone. Ruth knew that children who feel loved don't get angry and throw things. She had also learned from her first two children that saying "stop it" and controlling children was not a productive way to go.

Ruth stopped what she was doing and walked over to her son. She kneeled down, looked him in the eye, and told him that she loved him. She then sat on the floor and played with him. She didn't put the toys together for him. That wasn't the problem that mattered. She gave him what he really needed: a feeling of being accepted and loved. His frustration disappeared.

Children who are loved and taught don't need to get Imitation Love and protect themselves. They don't need to attack other people — or throw things against walls. We need to watch our children for signs of anger. In Chapter 15, Billy was angry at his friend, James and Cynthia were angry at each other, and Benjamin was angry at his teacher. In each case, their parents noticed their child's irritation, brought it to their attention, and discussed it. We have countless opportunities to respond to our children's attacks other than when they attack *us*. And the proper response is always the same: we need to see, accept, and love them. As we do that, we give them the ability to choose to feel loved and be loving all their lives, instead of angry and miserable. That is a gift of infinite worth.

Chapter Summary

Children attack us and others only because they're afraid and don't feel loved. When we love them unconditionally, they have no need to protect themselves by attacking.

When children get angry, we need to point that out to them as we accept them and love them.

Chapter 21

Responding to Victims

Please review pp. 51-4. When our children don't feel loved, acting like victims is one way they can get Imitation Love and protect themselves from being hurt. Victims blame other people when things go wrong, and they believe that other people are responsible for making them happy.

WHAT CHILDREN GET FROM ACTING LIKE VICTIMS

Our children get a great deal from the victim behaviors described in Chapter 3. That's why they use them.

(1) If they can convince us that we are the cause of their discomfort, they know that we'll feel guilty and will then be more likely to give them what they want. Children learn this at an early age. I've watched many children crying and sulking in a store because they didn't get something they wanted. The parent didn't want to feel guilty — or be seen as unloving — so he or she surrendered and bought what the child wanted. Those children will repeat variations on that extortion with their parents and other people for the rest of their lives.

(2) They protect themselves from further injury. When children look wounded and helpless enough — by pouting or crying, for

example — we often feel sorry for them, and then we're less likely to criticize or otherwise hurt them.

(3) They avoid responsibility. Children don't have be accountable for their own behavior if they act like victims and blame everything on their parents, teachers, and others.

(4) They enjoy the power of condemning those who "mistreat" them. Children normally feel quite helpless and weak around adults — especially their parents — but when they can condemn the unfair behavior of their parents and others, they feel strong and in control.

WHY WE TEND TO GIVE OUR CHILDREN WHAT THEY WANT
WHEN THEY ACT LIKE VICTIMS

Most of us have a natural tendency to help anyone who is treated unfairly. We root for the underdog. Look at the sympathy and support we give to disaster victims, abused children, war-time refugees, and even endangered animal species. To our credit, much of our motivation comes from genuine compassion. However, when children act like victims, we often give them what they want for selfish reasons.

If we don't already feel loved ourselves, we feel guilty when our children claim to be injured by us. We then give them what they want because we're afraid *not* to. If we don't give them what they want, we're afraid that they will withdraw their approval and affection from us. We also don't want to look bad in the eyes of other people. In fact, in our society, it's quite politically incorrect for us to withhold our support from any person or group who claims to have been treated unfairly. We want to be seen as concerned and loving.

When our children claim to be injured by someone else, we have an especially good opportunity to look like loving parents.

We can rise like a white knight to their defense, feeling self-righteous and powerful as we take the side of truth and justice. For example, many times I have seen parents who had not previously shown any serious interest in their child's schoolwork. However, when they heard that their child had supposedly suffered some injustice at the hands of a teacher, they became crusaders in defense of their child. Such parents rarely have a genuine interest in helping their children. They're getting an unhealthy sense of power from supporting a child acting like a victim. Children don't need that kind of support.

We feel important, even indispensable, when we save our children from uncomfortable circumstances. In those situations, we briefly feel more connected to them and less alone. In other words, we sometimes save our "victimized" children in order to feel more loved ourselves.

Not all parents respond to a child who is acting like a victim by giving him what he wants. Some parents are irritated by victim behavior, and punish a child when he whines and cries. However, at least one parent in a family does reward victim behavior occasionally, or the child wouldn't have a reason to do it. When a child has parents who sometimes reward victim behavior and on other occasions punish it, life can be very confusing.

THE TERRIBLE CONSEQUENCE OF CHILDREN ACTING LIKE VICTIMS

As we discussed in Chapter 3, Real Love can only be felt when it is freely given and received. When children act like victims, they are manipulating us and others for whatever attention they get. Anything they receive cannot feel like Real Love. While they act like victims, they can only feel empty and alone.

If we allow our children to act like victims, we guarantee that they will be unhappy. We cripple them when we respond to their victim behaviors with sympathy, rescuing, spoiling, anger, or any of the other Getting and Protecting Behaviors.

THE PROPER RESPONSE TO CHILDREN WHO ACT LIKE VICTIMS

As I said in Chapter 18, all children who demonstrate Getting and Protecting Behaviors are simply telling us that they don't feel loved. The solution is obvious: they need to be seen, accepted and loved.

We need to learn to identify the victim behaviors of our children and help them see those behaviors in themselves. When we feel unconditionally loved ourselves, we can share that with our children. As they feel loved, they will no longer have a need to get Imitation Love and protect themselves by acting like victims. Those victim behaviors will simply disappear without our ever doing anything to *make* them go away. No child claims to be wounded when he is genuinely happy and healthy.

HOW WE REACT TO CHILDREN WHEN THEY ACT LIKE VICTIMS WITH OTHERS

It is tempting to save our children from injustice. It seems like the compassionate thing to do. But sometimes when we do that, we teach them that the world is obligated to treat them "fairly," and that can be a crippling belief.

Lewis came home upset.

Lewis: "My teacher is stupid. I was supposed to turn in my English paper this morning, but I didn't have it because I was sick yesterday. I couldn't help being sick, but she still gave me a zero on the assignment."

Father: "That's not fair. You were in bed all day yesterday. Did you tell her you were sick?"

Lewis: "I tried, but she wouldn't listen."

Father: "I'll call her and straighten this out."

Lewis's father thought he was being supportive, but the truth is, he did some very unproductive and selfish things instead — none of which were done intentionally:

(1) He helped Lewis feel like a victim. He taught his son that we should always get what we think is fair, which is a foolish and dangerous notion. In the first place, our idea of fairness is often completely mistaken. We tend to define "fair" as whatever benefits *us*. What we think is fair is often quite unfair to everyone else. In addition, children need to understand that all our lives, we function in relationships and systems — families, friendships, schools, jobs, and politically-defined societies — where it's entirely the right of someone else to define what is "fair." Employers often determine what is fair. The judicial system establishes what's fair. If we allow our children to believe that they always have the right to determine what is fair, they'll experience endless conflict and disappointment in their lives.

(2) Lewis's father had often been treated unfairly in his own life, and he understandably hated the sense of helplessness and loneliness that had accompanied those incidents. Defending Lewis gave him a chance to vent his frustration and anger at all the people who had "victimized" him in the past. Sympathizing with Lewis became a selfish way for *him* to feel powerful, instead of a way for him to see and love his son.

(3) By offering his support to Lewis, Father won his son's affection. He unconsciously *used* his son to feel more important and "loved." He saw it immediately in Lewis's face when he said that he'd call the teacher and straighten things out. He often used people in that way, saying and doing things so they would like him and make him feel better. Most of us do that, and we're mostly unaware that we do it.

By responding to Lewis as he did, his father missed a valuable opportunity to teach his son some important lessons about responsibility and accepting the consequences of his choices. We'll discuss those shortly. He also missed the chance to teach his son about the right that all people have to inconvenience us as they learn from their choices and mistakes, a lesson that Benjamin learned in Chapter 15. In addition, he could have talked to Lewis about the fact that other people never make us angry. Every time we interact with our children, we have the opportunity to teach them many important principles.

RESPONDING TO A VICTIM PRODUCTIVELY

Children don't need sympathy. They don't need someone to cry with them or spoil them. That doesn't make them feel more loved or loving, which is what leads to genuine happiness, the ultimate goal of life and the aim of every loving parent. Children also don't need to be criticized or to be told to "stop it" when they're acting like victims. What they need is to be seen, accepted, and loved.

When Lewis received a zero on his school assignment, he knew that would make him look stupid. He also knew from past experience that he'd be criticized and would feel less accepted by everyone, including his parents. He immediately and unconsciously protected himself by angrily blaming his *teacher* for treating him unfairly. When he did that, he was using two Protecting Behaviors: acting like a victim and attacking. He also blamed his *illness* for his incomplete assignment, another way of acting like a victim.

Now let's change the interaction between father and son in one significant way. Let's suppose that years before this event, Lewis's father had taken the steps to finding Real Love for himself (Chapter 5). Therefore, in this new scene, when Lewis complains about his teacher, his father feels loved and isn't blinded by emptiness and fear. He is able to see his son clearly and give him what he needs.

Lewis came home upset.

Lewis:	"My teacher is stupid. I was supposed to turn in my English paper this morning, but I didn't have it because I was sick yesterday. I couldn't help being sick, but she still gave me a zero on the assignment."
Father:	"I know you were sick yesterday, but how long before that did your teacher give you the assignment?"
Lewis:	(after a long pause) "A week."
Father:	"So you could have done the assignment on the same day it was given — a whole week ago — couldn't you?"
Lewis:	"Well . . ."
Father:	"If you had done that, it wouldn't have mattered at all that you were sick yesterday, would it? You could still have turned your work in on time. The real reason you got a zero is that *you* chose to put off doing your assignment. Your teacher gave you plenty of time to do your work, don't you think?"
Lewis:	(weakly) "Yeah."
Father:	"Most of us blame other people for our problems without thinking about it. It's easier than admitting we're responsible ourselves. If *we* admit that we're completely responsible for our mistakes, we're afraid we'll look stupid.
	(laughing) "You just made a mistake. Next time you'll remember this zero and will choose more wisely. I still love you — (laughing again) even with the zero."

Lewis's father taught him a wonderful lesson. Without making him feel worthless, he taught him that he was entirely responsible for the consequences of his behavior. He taught him that he was not a victim.

HOW WE REACT TO CHILDREN WHEN THEY ACT LIKE VICTIMS WITH US

Kate's mother talked to her as she was leaving the house on a Saturday morning.

Mother: "Did you do those two loads of laundry I asked you to do yesterday?"

Kate: "There wasn't time. And I can't do it now because I have to leave for cheerleading practice."

Notice that both of Kate's sentences were spoken by a victim. When she said, "There wasn't time," she was blaming something other than herself for her situation, and that's the definition of acting like a victim. And when she said, "I can't do it now because I *have* to leave," she was implying that any attempt to stop her from going to cheerleading practice would be *unfair*. She was threatening to become an even bigger victim if anyone dared to interfere with her plans.

Mother: "Well, please try to do the laundry when you get home."

Kate's mother took the easy way out and accepted her daughter's excuses. Most of us hate conflict, and to avoid it, we often allow our children to act like victims. We don't like to keep giving those boring, repetitive, and often difficult lessons in responsibility that our children hate as much as we do. When we take this lazy course and fail to teach our children what they need to know, we are running, a Protecting Behavior. We run because we're uncomfortable when we have to confront our children with their behavior. We understandably don't like it when our children withdraw their affection from us when we teach them and correct them.

Sometimes we don't run. Instead, we become irritated when our children make excuses for their behavior. We express our anger at them so they'll stop making excuses and will do what we want them to do. But that doesn't help them to be responsible and loving, either.

RESPONDING TO A VICTIM PRODUCTIVELY

Let's suppose that Kate's mother had already learned how to tell the truth about herself and had found people who loved her unconditionally (Chapter 5). In the following interaction, she is therefore happy and doesn't need to buy the approval of her daughter. She isn't afraid to teach her daughter the truth even though she knows that Kate might not like it.

Mother: "Did you do those two loads of laundry I asked you to do yesterday?"

Kate: "There wasn't time. And I can't do it now because I have to leave for cheerleading practice."

Mother: "I gave you that assignment more than twenty-four hours ago. In that entire time, did you watch television at all?"

Kate: "Yes, but . . ."

Mother: "Did you talk to anyone on the phone?"

Kate: "I talked to Kris for a little while, but . . ."

Mother: "And I answered the phone when Sharon called for you."

Kate: "I forgot about that."

Mother: "So you chose to do at least three things — probably
             more — instead of the laundry I assigned you. When
             I asked about the laundry a moment ago, you told me
             you couldn't do it now because you *'had'* to leave for
             cheerleading practice. When Sharon called, did you
             tell her that you *'had'* to do the laundry before you
             could talk to her?"

Kate: "No."

Mother: "Clearly, you repeatedly *chose* to not do the laundry.
             Your obligation to do your assignments here at
             home is at least as serious as your commitment to
             cheerleading. We've talked about that before, but
             talking hasn't been enough. Obviously, you need
             some help understanding this, so I'll help you by
             requiring that you do the laundry right now."

Kate: "But I'll miss practice if I do that. They can't do the
             routines without me there. That would hurt the whole
             team. You can't do this to the team."

Mother: "*I'm* not doing this to the team. *You* are. If you had
             chosen to be responsible and done what you were
             asked to do yesterday, this wouldn't be happening.
             This is a result of *your* choice. You can tell the team
             it's my fault, of course, but you'll know that's not
             true. In the past, I have allowed you to go to practice
             many times when your work wasn't done, and you
             only learned that you could do whatever you wanted.
             That was my mistake. I'm choosing not to make that
             mistake again this time."

Kate was not happy about missing practice, but she found it
difficult to stay angry at her mother when it was obvious that she
wasn't angry at Kate.

Kate's mother employed many principles that we have talked about thus far. She saw her daughter clearly. She saw that she was irresponsible and behaving like a victim, but she nonetheless accepted and loved her. She then taught Kate the truth about herself and imposed consequences that would help Kate choose more wisely the next time she had to make a decision about responsibility.

This kind of firm and loving interaction is impossible for us as parents unless we feel loved ourselves. When we tell our children the truth about themselves and impose consequences, they often become angry and communicate that their anger and pain are all *our* fault. If we don't feel loved, we unavoidably use Getting and Protecting Behaviors of our own, and the possibility of a loving interaction goes straight down the drain.

RESCUING

See the story of the toddler on p. 53. If we run to our children and offer them our sympathy whenever they fall (physically or emotionally), they learn to whine and complain whenever they're frightened, or even inconvenienced. They expect to be rescued, and if we do that every time they indicate a need, we cripple them.

Our children don't usually need to be rescued. They need to be loved, supported, and guided. Let's see how the story of the toddler could change with a mother who understood Real Love.

Joan watched as her toddler fell, smacking both hands hard on the floor. She did not get up from her chair, nor did she look frightened or startled. Sudden movement and a look of panic from parents are enough to make most children cry.

Joan: "Wow, that was quite a noise. Come here and let me look at you."

He walked over to Joan, where she lovingly touched his hands and face as she inspected them for signs of injury.

Joan: "You're all right. Go off and play now. I love you."

Joan's child did not need to be picked up and treated like a baby. He was quite capable of getting up by himself. What he needed was to be reassured that he was safe and loved. We need to remember that as our children get older and fall down in other ways. If we rescue them, we teach them that they *are* victims. We teach them that they don't have to live with the consequences of the choices they make. We rob them of opportunities to learn about responsibility and the right of other people to make their own choices.

We need to love our children as Joan did, and teach them that inconvenience and pain are part of living. When we do that, children don't expect everything to go their way. The inevitable discomforts of life become insignificant instead of frightening. We give our children a great gift when we teach them to avoid the deadly trap of acting like victims.

LEARNING TO RESPOND TO VICTIMS

Linda called to ask if I would help with her five-year-old daughter, Cindy. The child was endlessly demanding, insisting on everything she wanted in a shrill, high-pitched voice. If her demand was not instantly satisfied, she repeated it louder and louder until she got what she wanted, usually within seconds. Her mother felt like all she did every day was fill this child's orders. As a result, Linda couldn't go anywhere, couldn't have a quiet conversation on the phone, couldn't complete a task without interruption, and always felt frazzled and burdened.

Clearly, Cindy did not feel loved, so she naturally screamed at the top of her little lungs for whatever attention she could get. She learned at an early age that the more she acted like a victim, the more attention she got.

What Cindy needed was to be unconditionally loved. With Real Love, she would have no need for her demanding behavior. I explained this to Linda, and she was one of those courageous parents who accept their responsibility for the happiness of their children. She was willing to do whatever it took to find Real Love for herself and to help Cindy.

In the meantime, while Linda was learning how to find Real Love for herself, what could she do about her child's fits of temper? Children only act like victims because that behavior gets them what they want. While we're learning how to unconditionally love them, we can at least teach them that acting like victims no longer works to get them the immediate rewards they're accustomed to. I made some suggestions to Linda, and the next day she had an opportunity to use them.

Cindy's sister was playing with a toy that Cindy wanted, and Cindy shrieked, "Give me that!"

In the past, Linda would have insisted that the sister give up the toy to make Cindy happy. But not this time.

Linda: "Your sister is using that, so you can't play with it right now. You can play with any other toy in the house, but not that one."

Linda remembered the Law of Choice, so she knew that Cindy didn't have the right to take the toy from her sister. She also tried to remember that Cindy was just empty and afraid, and was using Getting and Protecting Behaviors. She was not intentionally being difficult.

Cindy: (squeezing her fists while jumping up and down) "I want it now. I want it! I want it!!!"

It is tempting for a parent to give in at this point and make an angry child "happy." Linda wanted Cindy to like her, and she wanted to give her the toy. But Linda remembered the Fifth Law of Parenting: "Love, Teach, Faith, Consequences." She knew that doing the same old things with Cindy had never been productive, and she made a commitment to having real faith in loving and teaching her daughter. She recognized that Cindy could only feel unloved and alone if she was allowed to keep acting like a victim. It takes a truly loving parent to stop that behavior. Linda decided to use a consequence to help Cindy not choose this particular behavior in the future.

Linda hugged Cindy and said, "I love you very much, but you can't act like this and stay out here with everyone else. If you want to scream and have a fit, you can, but you'll have to go to your room. You can scream all you want in there."

Cindy was stunned. Her mother had never behaved like this before. But Cindy didn't know another way to get what she wanted, either, so she began to whine and scream again. Linda picked her up and took her to her room and closed the door. Cindy soon stopped crying. Children rarely have tantrums by themselves for long. They behave badly to *get* something. When it doesn't get the desired results, there's no reason for the behavior to continue.

After several minutes of silence, Linda asked Cindy if she wanted to rejoin the family. Linda had to take Cindy to her room several times that day, each time telling Cindy that she loved her. Within two weeks, Cindy had stopped screaming to get what she wanted. She had learned that demanding and screaming simply didn't work. Her mother had changed a very old pattern of behavior. In the months and years to come, Linda learned how to unconditionally love Cindy, and that changed Cindy's life far more than the technique described above.

TEACHING CHILDREN HOW TO RESPOND
TO OTHER PEOPLE WHO ACT LIKE VICTIMS

All their lives, our children will interact with people who act like victims. We need to teach them enough about this behavior that they can understand it when they see it and react in ways that are healthy.

Glenn came in the house with an obvious scowl on his face.

Father: "What's bothering you?"

Glenn: "Mark (his friend) is mad at me."

Father: "About what?"

Glenn: "You remember those tickets you got?"

Glenn's father had been offered four tickets to a professional baseball game. He was taking a friend from work and Glenn. In addition, he told Glenn to bring along *one* of his friends.

Father: "Sure."

Glenn: "Mark got real mad at me when he found out that I asked Michael to go with me to the game with us instead of asking him. But I could only ask one person to go. What else could I do?"

Father: "Now Mark's making you feel guilty about it, isn't he?"

Glenn: "Yes."

Father: "We've talked about this in family meetings. Mark is trying to get what he wants from you by using a particular kind of Getting Behavior. What is it?"

Glenn: "He's acting like a victim."

Father: "Yes. He's acting like you did something to hurt him. Did you?"

Glenn: "I'm not sure."

Father: "No, you didn't. You believe you might have hurt him only because he *acts* like you did. Have you taken the right to be happy away from him?"

Glenn: "No."

Father: "On the night of the game, are you going to be doing anything to keep him from having fun?"

Glenn: "No."

Father: "Does anyone ever *make* us angry?"

Glenn: "No."

Father: "If he felt completely loved, would he be angry about this?"

Glenn: "Probably not."

Father: "So is this your fault that he's mad at you?"

Glenn: "I guess not."

Father: "Then are you through feeling guilty about it?"

Glenn: (smiling) "Yeah, I guess so."

Father: "All your life people will try to tell you that you're responsible for making them unhappy, but that doesn't make it true. Remember that. On the other hand, that doesn't mean you shouldn't care about their happiness. We should always *care* about the happiness of other people and do all that we can to *help* them be happy. But that doesn't mean we're responsible for *making* them happy.

"You keep doing your best to be a friend to Mark. He's only doing this because he doesn't feel loved. If he wants to stay angry, he will. But hopefully, in time, he'll get over this."

When we love and teach our children, they can see why people act like victims. We can help free our children from the chains of guilt, obligation, and manipulation that characterize so many unhappy relationships.

Chapter Summary

Victims constantly complain about what people do **to** them and what people should do **for** them. To a victim, everything is unfair, and they feel quite justified in manipulating others to keep themselves safe and to get what they want. Our children do this with us and others, and it usually works.

Victims don't need sympathy or to be rescued. They need to be seen, accepted, and loved.

Chapter 22

Responding to
Running and Clinging

RUNNING

When our children feel unconditionally loved by us, they naturally want to be with us. How could they *not* want to be with us when we make them happy? But when we're not unconditionally loving, that is a horrifying prospect for a child who is already feeling empty and unloved. It's therefore understandable that our children tend to emotionally and physically run from us when we add to their emptiness and pain instead of giving them the Real Love they need. Running protects them, but it also leaves them feeling alone and unhappy.

TELLING THE TRUTH ABOUT RUNNING

Running is so common among our children that we have come to accept it as normal. We need to recognize when our children run from us and accept our responsibility for it.

When Emily, fourteen, came home from school each day, she went straight to her room, where she listened to music and talked on the phone. The idea of looking for her parents and having a conversation with them never entered her mind. She only came out of her room to eat dinner or watch television, and she only spoke to her parents when they spoke directly to her.

Mother: "How was school today?"

Emily: "Okay."

Emily obviously didn't want to talk about what she did at school that day, or her answer would have been much longer than one word. But Mother wasn't satisfied with Emily's answer.

Mother: "What did you do that was interesting?"

Emily: "Nothing."

Emily wasn't just being quiet or moody. She wasn't "just acting like a teenager." She felt empty and unloved, and she knew that engaging in a conversation with her mother would only make her feel worse. She was actively avoiding a conversation with her mother.

David was also fourteen. When he came home from school, he immediately looked for his father and hugged him — as he did most days. They talked for several minutes. David spoke about his interaction with an angry classmate, a boy known to cause trouble with other students. David thought he handled the situation pretty well, mostly because he felt loved and had learned a lot about relationships in family meetings. His father expressed his delight with what David was learning, and he re-confirmed his love for his son.

David and his father often interacted like this. Children who feel Real Love from their parents are irresistibly drawn to the source of that love. We need to honestly ask ourselves how often our children come to us and share their lives as David did. If they don't, they're telling us that they don't feel unconditionally loved by us. They're running from us. We don't need to feel guilty about that, but we do need to tell the truth about it so we can start to do something about it. Only when we recognize that our children are avoiding us can we begin to get Real Love for ourselves (Chapter 5) and share it with them.

HOW WE REACT TO RUNNING

If we lack Real Love in our own lives, we tend to take it personally when our children withdraw their attention, cooperation, and affection from us. We feel unloved and become afraid that we haven't been good parents. We then we react with Getting and Protecting Behaviors.

Lying

When we're afraid our children are withdrawing from us, we often unconsciously pursue them and attempt to buy their affection:

We give them money, cars, free time, entertainment, clothes, etc. We give them whatever it takes to get them to like us.
We avoid criticizing them, so they won't be angry or further withdraw from us.
We avoid giving them responsibilities, or we don't hold them accountable for the ones they do have, knowing they'll be irritated with us for bothering them.

It may be embarrassing to admit that we do these things, but we still do them. It's painful to feel unloved by our own children. Most of us feel quite alone in the world, and as I said in Chapter 6, it is a commonly held belief—an intense hope, really—among many of us that our children are the one group of people in the whole world who truly love us. When we feel their "love" slipping away, we'll do a lot to get it back, including buy it.

These behaviors we use to purchase their love are all lies because we hide — usually unconsciously — our intent to earn

their affection. Initially, children like to be bribed, but they really
can feel the absence of Real Love when we dishonestly purchase
their attention and cooperation. And then they feel unloved and
alone.

Attacking

When Emily (p. 319-20) avoided her mother's questions, her
mother became afraid for the reasons we've discussed. She
reacted by attacking her daughter.

Mother: "That's what you always say: 'Nothing.' There can't
           be nothing happening with you all the time. I'm tired
           of you sulking and acting like you're not a part of the
           family. I want you to start treating me with respect
           and answer my questions."

When we don't feel loved ourselves, we unintentionally
count on our children to love us, and when they pull away from
us, we feel afraid and helpless. When we get angry and criticize
them — when we attack them — we feel less powerless. We
also think we can control them and keep them from withdrawing
from us.

When we attack our children, we do get some of what we
want. We make them afraid and often get some kind of temporary
attention or cooperation. But it doesn't last, it isn't freely given,
and it makes them feel even more alienated from us. The price
we pay for attacking them is terrible.

Being a Victim

On one occasion when Emily failed to respond to her mother's
questions, her mother said: "We've worked hard to give you
a good home and everything you need. We've taken care of
you all your life, and then you thank us by sulking and being
uncooperative. I feel hurt and disappointed when you act like

this." Mother was acting like a victim. Another time, Mother said, "We used to have such great talks together, and I miss those. I wish you'd share more of your life with me." Again, this is the statement of a victim, with a dash of clinging—another Getting Behavior—thrown in.

When intimidating (attacking) doesn't succeed in keeping our children from pulling away from us, we often act wounded, hoping to get sympathy and cooperation. If we make them feel sufficiently guilty, we can often get their attention, but then they feel the awful and inappropriate burden of being responsible for our happiness. They feel even more unloved and alone, and they respond with more Getting and Protecting Behaviors.

Running

We can manipulate our children and get their attention, but it's a lot of work and we still don't feel Real Love from them. Eventually, we weary of dealing with their getting and protecting, and we finally just avoid them. That's running.

Emily's mother became tired of manipulating her daughter, and eventually she threw up her hands in despair and just let Emily retreat into her room every day. Mother chose to run. It was easier than confronting Emily or learning to give her the Real Love she didn't have.

HOW TO RESPOND TO RUNNING

When our children withdraw from us, they're not trying to hurt us or show us disrespect; they only run to minimize the pain of feeling unloved and empty. It's a Protecting Behavior. Since our children run because they have insufficient Real Love in their lives, the solution is obvious: they need to be loved — by us. When we get loved ourselves (Chapter 5), we can see their fear and accept them. As we care about their happiness (Real Love), they begin to feel that and want to be around us. They simply stop running from us.

It takes time for our children to trust that we love them and to stop running from us. If we expect that to happen overnight, we'll become frustrated and will unavoidably express our impatience to our children. That will only heighten their distrust. We need to have faith that loving and teaching them will be enough to stop their Getting and Protecting Behaviors, including their running.

How can we love them? See some of the examples of loving in Chapter 9. There are many other examples of parents loving and teaching their children throughout the book.

CLINGING

Clinging is a Getting Behavior. When we feel unloved and empty, we tend to cling tightly to anyone who gives us attention. An obvious example is a toddler who won't let go of his mother, physically clinging to her. In an infant, that's normal, but later it becomes a sign that a child doesn't feel sufficiently loved. A child who does feel loved doesn't need to cling. He feels secure that he's loved and doesn't need to have that constantly proved to him.

As children get older, they cling in other ways. They come to us to be praised for every little thing they do. Some children ask for help and approval about everything, making no decisions on their own. They're afraid to be away from home. They can't learn to be independent and strong when they cling to us in those ways. Many children continue to cling to their parents even after they get married, which makes a healthy marriage impossible.

How We Respond to Clinging

Many of us enjoy having our children cling to us. It makes us feel useful and important. Sometimes we even put ourselves in a position where our children have to come to us for advice and permission. We manipulate them for praise and power. We actually train our children — however unintentionally it may be

— to cling to us. We give advice constantly and make ourselves indispensable in their lives. We enjoy the gratitude and attention we get so much that we can't let that go. And our children come to believe that they can't make any decision alone.

Some parents resent the burden of a clinging child. They push their children away emotionally. That usually ends the clinging and prompts the child to use other Getting Behaviors.

The Effect of Clinging

A child who clings to his parents can't be an independent and happy human being. He becomes an extension of his parents, constantly trying to please them rather than learning from his own experiences. He is weak, and although he enjoys the approval of the parents he pleases, what he gets from them is Imitation Love, not the deeply satisfying experience of Real Love. He therefore never feels genuinely happy. I have known many such people, as children and as adults. They are frightened and empty, incapable of healthy relationships.

How to Prevent Clinging

Infants *need* to cling to their parents. They need a tight physical and emotional attachment to learn that they are loved, safe, and connected to the people around them. We need to provide that connection. However, children of all ages also have a constantly developing need to explore things on their own and learn who they are as independent creatures. If we hover over them and attach ourselves to their every move, they can't learn who *they* are. They come to believe that they exist only as an extension of *us*, and that is not healthy. That is how clinging begins and develops.

When your baby is fed and dry and comfortable, put him down and allow him to investigate the world on his own. That's how he acquires self-confidence. Allow him to do that as soon as possible after birth, and continue that attitude for the rest of his life. In this way, children are encouraged to explore the world and gradually separate themselves from us in a healthy way. I'm not advocating that children be pushed away from us and frightened. However, when a child feels satisfied and safe, we need to give them the opportunity to experience the world independently. That's how they learn to not cling to us.

How to Respond to Clinging

Most of us didn't know about unconditionally loving our children when we started out as parents, so we made many mistakes. Perhaps we've already created a clinging child. What do we do now?

The response is the same for clinging as for all Getting and Protecting Behaviors (Chapter 18). Clinging children need to be seen, accepted, and loved. See the example of the toddler on p. 53. Although we discussed it as a victim behavior, the child was also clinging to the support of his mother. The mother on pp. 311-12 responded beautifully to a similar situation.

Lucy had a relaxing evening planned with some friends after a long week filled with work and raising children. She was looking forward to it. As she was walking out the door, her six-year-old daughter, Natalie, came running up to her and said, "Mommy, please don't go!"

What do most parents do at this point? We tend to reward this clinging behavior with a kind of sympathy that isn't healthy: "Oh, please don't cry. You'll be okay. I promise to come back soon." Some of us even *apologize* for leaving our children at home. And we prolong our departure from the house, which teaches the child that he can change everyone's schedule by acting like a victim. Some parents take their children with them everywhere they go to avoid these scenes. Other parents just respond with a Protecting Behavior: they get angry at the inconvenience and yell at the child to be quiet. None of these approaches gives children what they need.

Lucy had learned some things about unconditionally loving her children.

Lucy: "When I leave the house, do I come back?"

Natalie: "Yes."

Lucy: "Every time?"

Natalie: "Yes."

Lucy: (smiling) "And does Miranda (the babysitter) ever beat you with a stick while I'm gone?"

Natalie: (laughing) "No."

Lucy: "What time are you going to bed?"

Natalie: "Eight-thirty."

Lucy: "I'll see you in the morning when you get up. I love you."

Children need to be seen, accepted, and loved. They do not need sympathy and coddling. The latter simply don't help them.

Many children continue to ask for help doing tasks that they already know how to do. That is another kind of clinging. They need to be instructed and loved. They do not need to be rescued and have their problems solved for them. If we keep doing that, we only make them dependent on us. We make them weak.

Another common example of clinging is children who stay financially and physically dependent on their parents far too long. We'll talk about that in Chapter 26.

Chapter Summary

Children run from us to protect themselves when they don't feel unconditionally loved by us.

We often react to their running with our own Getting and Protecting Behaviors, when they really need us to teach and love them.

Children cling to us when they're afraid of not being loved. We need to see, accept, and love them.

Chapter 23

Being Right

As we learn to tell the truth about ourselves and feel loved, teaching and loving our children become increasingly productive and effortless. However, in the process of learning, we *will* make many mistakes. There will be times when we feel unloved and afraid, and then we'll naturally go back to the Getting and Protecting Behaviors we're familiar with. On those occasions, we'll hurt our children, and we'll tend to do two things: feel guilty and/or lie.

GUILT

It's foolish to feel guilty when we do the best we can with what we know, even when that causes inconvenience and pain for our children. We all learn at the cost of inconveniencing the people around us. While we're imperfect, there's no other way to learn. And we simply can't behave now with the wisdom we're going to acquire in the years to come.

LYING

All our lives, we've been praised when we did the right things, and we've been criticized when we didn't. So now when we make mistakes, we often hide them in order to avoid the disapproval of our children and others. Other words for hiding are "lying," "making excuses," and "being right." Although we get a temporary sense of safety and power when we claim to be right, it's deadly to our growth and happiness. We can't have a desire to learn and change — the first step in the process of feeling loved and loving others—while we insist on being right.

WHY WE HAVE TO BE RIGHT WITH OUR CHILDREN

With our children, we have an especially strong need to be right. We think that in order to teach them, we have to know more than they do and make fewer mistakes — or no mistakes. It's generally accepted that the teacher should be superior to the student. We're afraid that if we admit that we're wrong, we'll look foolish to our children and lose their respect, which is a form of Imitation Love that we enjoy. So when we make mistakes with them, we tend to maintain that we're right. We lie.

BUT WE *ARE* WRONG

We hide our mistakes so we won't look weak and confused, but the truth is we **are** weak and confused. As we learn anything, we have to be weak before we're strong. We learn to hit a baseball only after failing to hit it many times. We learn to play the piano only after hitting many wrong notes. We *must* be wrong many times before we can consistently do almost anything correctly. Similarly, we learn to be loving parents by making many mistakes.

By this time next year, I hope to know much more than I know now. Certainly, I know more this year than I did last year. That's what learning is for. Compared to next year, therefore, I *must* be relatively stupid now. We have a terrible time accepting that word, don't we? There's no shame in *being* stupid. What is truly foolish is to *remain* stupid because we're too proud to admit our ignorance and insist on hiding it. Then we can't do anything about it.

Are you ashamed of the fact that you soiled your diapers when you were a baby? Of course not. It was unavoidable as you learned to control your body. All ignorance and learning are like that. We have to be weak and foolish as we learn. It's not something to be embarrassed about or hide. And yet we're still ashamed of ourselves as we learn. We think we should magically become wise without mistakes. So we hide them, claiming to be right. Sadly, learning then becomes impossible. How can we learn something when we claim to be right about it already? In our desire to avoid looking bad, we stay the same — alone and unhappy.

One thing we commonly insist we're right about is that we love our children unconditionally. But their behavior proves our claim is false. When they use Getting and Protecting Behaviors — when they're angry, withdrawn, rebellious, having sex, arguing with their siblings, using drugs, getting in trouble at school, and so on — they're loudly declaring that they *don't* feel loved. They're reacting to *our* inability to give them the Real Love they need. Until we see that, and until we want to change ourselves, we'll never be better parents, nor will our children be happy.

HAPPY OR RIGHT?

If we want to be right, we can always find some justification for our belief in every interaction with our children. When Charles spoke harshly to his son Ryan (p. 133), he thought he was right: "Ryan shouldn't talk to his brother that way. And I was right to tell him to do his homework. If I don't tell him, he doesn't do it." Charles chose to focus on how he was right, and in some ways he was: Ryan *was* wrong to be angry at his brother, and he *did* need to do his homework. But remember the Third Law of Parenting: "If I'm angry, I'm wrong." Charles was utterly *wrong* to be angry at Ryan, and the negative effect of his anger far outweighed the possible benefit of showing Ryan his mistake.

When children make mistakes, it *is* our job to correct them. But no matter how important the principles we're teaching, or how wrong they are, if we're disappointed or angry with them, *we are wrong.* Are we willing to admit we're wrong? Until we are, our children will continue to be unhappy.

When we insist on being right, we get a sense of power and safety, but the benefit is shallow and brief. Justifying ourselves and being right makes no one happy. We learn to be happy ourselves and to make our children happy as we tell the truth about the mistakes we make. Would we rather be happy or right? Do we want to be loving parents and have happy children? Or do we want to be right? We can't have both.

IT'S FUN TO BE WRONG

Mike had told his eight-year-old son, Philip, three times that day to clean his room, and it still wasn't done. Mike angrily confronted Philip in his room.

Mike: "How many times have I told you to clean up this pigsty? I'm getting sick and tired . . ."

Philip shrugged his shoulders, looked down at the floor, and was obviously miserable. Fortunately, Mike had started the process of telling the truth about himself to wise men and women several months before this (Chapter 5). He was beginning to experience the genuine happiness that comes from feeling loved and loving others. As he started speaking to Philip, Mike felt that this was very different from the times that he had recently felt loved and loving. He did not like how he felt as he talked to his son.

Mike stopped talking and thought about what he'd been learning. He knew that his anger meant he was feeling unloved and afraid. As he remembered how it felt to be loved by wise men and women, he didn't feel as empty and afraid anymore.

Instead of selfishly wanting something from Philip, Mike saw that Philip was just being lazy and irresponsible, a very natural condition for a child feeling unloved and alone. And Mike knew that his son could not learn anything about responsibility while he was being yelled at and feeling bad.

Mike hugged his son and said, "Philip, I was wrong to yell at you. I love you even when your room looks like a pigsty." Philip couldn't believe what he was hearing. Mike looked him in the eye, smiled, and added: "Of course, you still need to clean this room — now. And if you get done in time for dinner, you might even get something to eat."

Mike could easily have insisted he was right in being angry. After all, Philip did need to be more responsible. It's especially easy to think we're right when the person we're talking to is obviously wrong. Mike had done that a hundred times before. But if he'd done that again here, he would have felt bad the rest of the day, like we always do when we're unloving with our children. Mike and Philip would then have avoided each other, and they both would have felt alone. We all know that feeling.

But Mike said he was wrong, and that changed everything. He loved and taught his son instead of being angry and right, and they were both amazed at how good they felt, even after Mike required that Philip clean his room and imposed a consequence for not completing the task. It's always easier and more fun to be wrong than to insist on being right.

I stopped in a doorway to listen to an argument between my daughter Rachel and son Joseph. Earlier in the day, Joseph listened to an audiotape that belonged to Rachel and she attacked him for not asking her permission. Now, hours later, they were discussing the event.

Rachel: "I was wrong to yell at you. I didn't even need the tape; I was just being selfish.

Joseph: "No, it was my fault. I should have asked you before
             I used it. I was only thinking of myself."

Rachel: "But I was worse. I was the one who started
             yelling."

I burst into laughter. I never thought the day would come
when two of my children would each insist on taking the greater
responsibility for an argument between them.

Rachel and Joseph both enjoyed the amazing freedom that
comes to all of us when we admit that we're wrong. Insisting
that we're right — accompanied, as it usually is, by anger, lying,
and acting like victims — is a huge burden. Being wrong is the
beginning of telling the truth, learning, and feeling loved.

Chapter Summary

We don't like the criticism we received in the past when we
were wrong, so we often hide our mistakes and insist that we're
right.

Being right makes it impossible to learn and grow, and it isolates
us from the love of other people.

Chapter 24

Teaching Children About Sex

Every day, our children are taught — by actors, authors, television producers, politicians, movie directors, comedians, and their own friends — that casual and indiscriminate sexual activity is normal, even admirable. People who are sexually attractive and sexually active are portrayed as role models. Our children are encouraged to be sexually appealing with their choice of clothes, make-up, hairstyle, cars, music, speech, and behavior. They're told in a thousand ways that having sex will make them feel worthwhile and happy. Tragically, they usually have no one to tell them the truth about sex.

THE DECEPTION OF SEX

Between two people who feel unconditionally loved and are mutually committed to a lifetime relationship, sex is a delightful addition to the happiness they already have. But in the absence of Real Love, sex cannot create happiness. Millions of people prove that every day when they succeed in getting the sex they want, only to discover — once again — that it doesn't bring them the genuine happiness they hoped it would. Many people become completely immersed in an addiction to sex, but no matter how much they get, they're still alone and miserable. Clearly, sex is not enough to make us happy.

Without Real Love, sex can only be Imitation Love, in the form of praise, power, and pleasure.

Praise

If we don't feel unconditionally accepted, it feels great to hear someone say, "I like you. You make me feel good." Unfortunately, that is the definition of Imitation Love, and it's what we hear when someone finds us sexually attractive. Without Real Love, we pursue that excitement with great energy. Let me borrow a story from *Real Love—The Truth About Finding Unconditional Love and Fulfilling Relationships*:

Brenda was fifteen years old. Although her parents did their best, they had no idea how to love her. As a result, she felt worthless and alone. But a sixteen-year-old boy at school, Matt, thought Brenda was beautiful, and he communicated that profusely as he looked at her and talked to her. That was more attention than she'd ever received, and for the first time she could remember, she felt worthwhile.

Matt was not primarily concerned for Brenda's happiness. He liked how *he* felt when she looked at him, talked to him, and allowed him to touch her. When Matt's expressions of affection became increasingly sexual, Brenda cooperated without hesitation because Matt made her feel important, and she was willing to do anything to keep that feeling. It's little wonder that she ignored her parents and others who warned her about the dangers of her behavior.

Children without Real Love are strongly attracted to anyone who praises their sexual desirability. They feel accepted, important, and lovable.

Power

Real power is "the ability to make our own choices under any conditions. It's the ability to choose to love other people no matter how they behave toward us (Chapter 16)." That power only comes after considerable experience with feeling unconditionally loved. In the absence of Real Love, however, a pleasant illusion of power can come from the ability to influence the behavior of other people, and sex often provides a great deal of that. Children feel powerless most of the time, a feeling they hate. But they discover that when they attract and satisfy people sexually, they can strongly influence the behavior of those people, a power they enjoy very much.

Brenda had very limited influence over the behavior of her parents, siblings, teachers, and friends. That lack of power made her feel unimportant and helpless. But she learned that when she offered sexual pleasure to Matt, she could get him to do almost anything she wanted. It was more power than she'd ever had, and it felt wonderful. Again, it's no surprise that she was reluctant to let go of that feeling when people told her she was being "bad." And she continued to use that power with other boys and men long after her relationship with Matt was over.

Pleasure

The physical pleasures of sex — sight, sound, touch, taste, and smell — are intense. For a child whose life is otherwise empty, sex is a very rewarding experience.

THE DANGER OF SEX

Real Love is the only thing that will ever make us happy. Without it, however, the praise, power, and pleasure of sex are so exciting that children — and adults — interpret this feeling as "happiness."

That is the biggest danger of sex, that we can use it to deceive ourselves and believe that we're truly happy. Without Real Love, we're desperate for anything that might relieve our emptiness, and we get enough Imitation Love from sex that we're temporarily satisfied. And then we continue to use sex as a temporary distraction from the pain of feeling unloved, hoping it will eventually bring us real happiness. Blinded by the praise, power, and pleasure of sex, we have no reason to look for the path of telling the truth about ourselves and finding Real Love and genuine happiness.

It can be difficult to teach children that sex has great potential for harm, especially when so many people around them seem to be having such a great time using sex. Without Real Love, sex is like jumping off a cliff. The jump itself *is* exciting — but then we hit the bottom.

Relying on sex for happiness becomes an addiction like any other — to drugs, alcohol, power, praise, or money. It helps us forget the emptiness of feeling unloved, but it turns us into prisoners, lost and starving as we try to fill ourselves with something that can never make us happy. Few activities have caused more emptiness and misery than sex without Real Love.

SOLUTIONS TO THE DANGER

Parents can do a lot to help children see and avoid the dangers of premature sexual activity.

Love Our Children

The most important thing we can do to protect our children from the negative consequences of sex is to give them Real Love. The biggest reason young people experiment with sex is that they're not happy. They're looking for anything that will make them feel less unloved, powerless, and alone. For those who are alone and unhappy, sex provides an exciting connection to someone, however superficial and brief.

When our children are filled with Real Love from us, they don't have a desperate need to seek Imitation Love. They're already happy and are not tempted to participate in the compulsive and endlessly frustrating effort to find happiness in sex.

Only in marriage

The dangers of sex are drastically reduced when it's limited to a married relationship. From the beginning of time, societies have prescribed marriage as they recognized that indiscriminate sex has a destructive effect on stable relationships and families.

We need to explain to our children that sex outside marriage can be enormously distracting and hurtful. When a genuinely loving parent teaches this principle, children listen.

Jack and Charlotte had a discussion with their fourteen-year-old daughter, Susan, about sex. They did not say, "Susan, come here, there's something we want to talk to you about." That formal approach tends to make children uncomfortable. They just started talking one day when they were all together in the same room. This was not the first time they'd spoken about sex.

Charlotte: "I've noticed that you've been spending more time with boys lately, and you look like you're having a good time."

Susan: "Yeah, it's fun."

Charlotte: "I remember what that was like. It *is* fun. You'll notice that many boys will want to touch you — physically and sexually. We've talked about that before."

Susan: (smiling) "I've noticed that."

Charlotte: "Sex is a wonderful addition to the happiness that married, loving partners enjoy. But sex outside marriage is very confusing."

Jack: "In our family, you know what it's like to be unconditionally loved, where people care about *your* happiness, instead of just using you to make *them* feel good. When boys try to touch you sexually, they're *not* doing it so that *you'll* be happy."

Susan: (laughing) "No, I didn't think so."

Jack: "Remember that. If you ever settle for anything less than somebody who cares about your happiness in a physically intimate relationship, you won't be happy."

Charlotte: "Sex without Real Love and without the commitment of marriage never adds to your happiness. It will ruin your relationship. If a young man pushes you to be sexually active with him, he's telling you that he wants something for himself at your expense. You don't want a guy like that. But you'll be tempted, because then he'll like you temporarily and will make you feel important."

Susan: "You don't have to worry. You guys have shown me what real love is. And I see what it's like for the girls at school who have sex. They're *not* happy. I'll wait for a guy who can love me like you two love me — and like you two love each other."

   If I gave you a hundred dollars every time I saw you, you'd love that, and you'd look forward to seeing me. But you'd also be confused. You'd find it very difficult to know whether you really liked *me* or only the money I gave you. The money confuses things. So does sex — in the same way. If we have sex with someone before we're certain of Real Love and committed to them for a lifetime, we just can't be sure that our relationship is not based on Imitation Love, which always fails.

Sex is easily confused with love. The praise, power, and pleasure temporarily feel good, but our emptiness and fears are still there, making us blind and unhappy. This is something we can teach our children. Even in marriage, sex can be misused and be distracting, but marriage has the advantage of being a relationship where two people make a commitment to stay together while they learn to be unconditionally loving (*Real Love—The Truth About Finding Unconditional Love and Fulfilling Relationships*).

MORE PREVENTION—GUIDELINES FOR DATING

Children can't possibly understand the consequences of sex. If our children asked us about the pharmacologic effects of cocaine, which of us would suggest that they go out on the street, buy a bag, and take a hit to find out for themselves? Ridiculous. And yet we send them out to meet potential sexual partners completely unprepared for the consequences. Once a child has experienced sex, the sensation is not easily forgotten or abandoned. Sex is easily as addictive and harmful as any drug. As wise and loving parents, we must tell our children about that. We need to teach our children about sex, as Jack and Charlotte did above. Sometimes we must impose limits on their exposure to sex, which we'll discuss below. These limits can only be applied to children whose behavior is still primarily our responsibility. Controlling the choices of adult children is not appropriate.

The Purpose of Dating

Until a child is prepared to make the lifelong commitment of marriage, the only purpose for dating is to practice establishing and developing relationships. Dating provides a place where young people can (1) practice telling the truth about themselves, (2) learn to see the truth about others, and (3) learn to unconditionally accept people and care about their happiness. Dating is an opportunity for children to practice the principles they learned in Chapters 12-16.

Age for Dating

It has been proven that children who start dating at an early age
are much more likely to have sex at an early age. Those children
have a much higher incidence of promiscuity, pregnancy, and
sexually transmitted disease. They also experience all the
distractions of sex as a form of Imitation Love — praise, power,
and pleasure — which makes it virtually impossible for them
to experience a genuinely loving relationship based on the truth
(Chapter 15). When love-starved children are put together in
dating situations at an early age, they can only share what they
have: their bodies, drugs, anger, emptiness, and unhappiness. If
we do nothing about it, they *will* use and hurt each other. They
don't do it intentionally; without sufficient love and guidance,
there's simply nothing else they have to offer each other.

Children lack the experience and judgment to know when
they're ready for dating. Parents need to determine that age limit
and teach it to their children long before they reach it. I suggest
that children not be allowed to date before age sixteen. A child
younger than that has nothing to gain by dating and a lot to
lose.

Type of Dating

When children are put together one-on-one early in their dating
experience, they feel a pressure to develop an intimacy that's
inappropriate for their level of maturity. They naturally try to
imitate what they see on television and in movies, where sex is a
normal activity in dating, even very early in a relationship. They
can only be hurt by their attempts to follow those examples.
Until children are older, say eighteen, they learn more about
loving relationships, and they learn more safely, when they date
with groups of friends, rather than dating in pairs.

Going Steady

There is enormous pressure for children to "go steady," to have a dating partner that belongs entirely to them. That provides a lot of Imitation Love. They feel worthwhile when someone is willing to commit to such an exclusive relationship. It gives them a feeling of approval (praise) and power. It also gives them the security (safety) of having someone they can rely on to "love" them.

Steady dating encourages intimacy that children are not prepared for. It is unwise until they're prepared for a committed, mutually loving relationship, like marriage.

Age Difference

When a nineteen-year-old boy dates a fourteen-year-old girl, it's very likely that the older boy will exploit the sexual inexperience of the younger girl. It's not malicious, just natural when people try to fill their emptiness with Imitation Love. I suggest that young people not be allowed to date anyone more than two years older than they are.

Drinking and Drugs

People have a hard enough time with relationships under the best of conditions. Nothing good can happen on a date where children have their senses distorted by drugs or alcohol. Wise parents make it very clear that *any* use of drugs or alcohol on a date is intolerable. Parents who are flexible on this subject are playing with explosives.

SEXUAL PRACTICES

People who are given limits on any pleasurable activity naturally explore how close they can get to the limit. When children are told that sexual intercourse has dangerous consequences, they often experiment with every sexual activity other than intercourse. What about necking? What about fondling? And so on.

Imagine that you're driving on an icy mountain road at night, and you learn that to your immediate right the cliff drops off to the valley floor one thousand feet below. How fast do you want to drive on this icy road, and how close to the edge do you want to get? When the consequence is death, we don't explore how fast we can go, and we concentrate on staying as far from the edge as possible. How hard do you shake a bottle of nitroglycerin? You don't shake it at all. Children need to be taught that this is also true with the many sexual practices short of intercourse. Any activity which distracts us from finding and giving unconditional love is harmful.

Sex can be a beautiful expression of affection between people who unconditionally love each other, but that's often not how it's used. Very persuasive and pervasive voices in the world teach us that sex is harmless, just a healthy expression of natural desires. We can easily look around us and see where that attitude has led. Sex has become an obsession and source of unhappiness for millions of empty and miserable people. We take sex far too lightly, vastly underestimating the destructive effect it's having on our children — and on us.

Masturbation

I can't begin to count the light-minded references I've heard to masturbation. People giggle about it and refer to it with words and gestures on television and in movies. It's portrayed as a totally normal and acceptable activity — like eating a snack or taking a nap. According to the definition of right and wrong on p. 16, masturbation is wrong. I've seen that statement met with enormous hostility, but only by people who do masturbate — usually compulsively — and who are defending themselves. Masturbation is wrong because it distracts people from the pursuit of Real Love. Anything that does that is deadly.

I read that pornography is the single most common product sold on the Internet, and its primary purpose is to provide stimulation for masturbation. People become easily, quickly, and powerfully addicted to that pleasure, just as they do to any drug. It distracts them from the truth and from finding loving relationships. I've seen its destructive effect in the lives of many, many people.

OPPORTUNITIES TO TALK ABOUT SEX

We don't discuss sex sufficiently with our children. They see and hear references to it everywhere they go, but they don't hear the truth about it. That's our job.

If our children watch television and movies, we need to frequently watch with them. Because sex is depicted and referred to so often in the media, we can use those opportunities to discuss sex, assisting our children in making wise sexual decisions for the rest of their lives.

Chapter Summary

In the absence of Real Love, sex is a vast source of Imitation Love: praise, power, and pleasure. Sex can be so exciting that it fatally distracts us from finding Real Love.

We can help our children avoid the dangers of premature sex by genuine loving them, teaching them about abstinence before marriage, and by limiting their dating practices.

Chapter 25

Drugs and Alcohol

Alcohol is simply a drug, so I will refer to alcohol and drugs interchangeably.

THE REASON CHILDREN USE DRUGS

Human behavior is not complicated. If we have sufficient Real Love, we're happy. If we don't, we're empty and afraid. Without Real Love, we use Getting Behaviors to find Imitation Love to dull the pain of our emptiness, and we use Protecting Behaviors to keep from being hurt. Understanding human behavior is usually that simple.

A child will do anything to avoid feeling unloved and alone. He'll lie, attack, act like a victim, cling, and run. Using drugs is a form of running. Drugs provide a distraction from the pain of feeling empty and alone. While a child is under the influence of alcohol, marijuana, cocaine, amphetamine, etc., he feels less criticized, rejected, afraid, and unloved. Those are the worst feelings in the world, and he'll do whatever it takes to get rid of them, even if the means required are illegal and irritating to his parents.

THE COST OF USING DRUGS

The physical effects of using drugs are well-documented. Dozens of books and thousands of articles have been published on the subject. Our children have heard uncounted lectures in school and elsewhere about how dangerous drugs are to their health. I will not attempt to add to that information here.

I suggest that the health risks of using drugs are actually quite small compared to the emotional and spiritual harm experienced by those who use those substances. Considering the number of people who use drugs, and the volumes they consume, a relatively tiny number of people suffer significant physical injury. The incidence of non-physical trauma is much higher.

Feeling loved is the most important thing in the world for a child. Drugs give him immediate relief from pain and fear, but they also make it impossible for him to feel Real Love. Even when his parents learn how to unconditionally love him, he can't feel that if he's being influenced by the distracting and numbing effect of drugs. Children using drugs can't consistently tell the truth or be responsible. They can only feel empty and afraid, enduring a life ruled by Getting and Protecting Behaviors.

PREVENTING DRUG AND ALCOHOL USE

I was a drug addict for years. I can tell you from personal experience that it's much easier to prevent drug use than to stop it. The most important thing we can do to prevent our children from using drugs is to unconditionally love them. Children use drugs to get relief from emptiness and fear. They don't have a need to do that when they're filled with Real Love.

HOW MUCH ALCOHOL IS ACCEPTABLE?

The older I get and the more I see the consequences of the decisions we make, the more astonished I am at how utterly blind we are to the effects of alcohol in our society. We are cane-tapping, eyes-shut, seeing-eye-dog, run-over-by-a-bus-in-broad-daylight blind. More than half of our teenagers who die in car accidents die because they were drinking. And yet we still laugh at beer commercials on television. Is that funny? What do our children learn from that? 10-20% of the adults in this country are addicted to alcohol and drugs. That means they use those substances in a way that their lives are seriously affected in a negative way. That's a loose definition that doesn't even include many of the emotional and spiritual effects I mentioned earlier in the chapter. I suggest that the real incidence of addiction is much higher.

And yet we continue to allow our children to drink *a little*. I strongly propose that allowing our children to drink alcohol a little is exactly like allowing them to use cocaine a little. The two drugs are equally dangerous. Allowing our children to drink alcohol a little is like allowing them to drive without a seatbelt. Sure, they might not get in a wreck, just like they *might* not become an alcoholic. What parent could possibly be foolish enough to take that chance? There isn't an alcoholic in the world who planned on becoming an alcoholic when he took his first drink.

There isn't a single good reason to allow a child to drink alcohol. If he wants to make that decision for himself when he's moved away from home, that's up to him. But that's one choice that a parent can make for a child while he's at home. Alcohol is a drug. It makes a child less able to tell the truth, feel loved, be responsible, make wise decisions, love other people, and be happy. Do we need to know more about it than that?

STOPPING DRUG AND ALCOHOL USE—AN EMERGENCY

Suppose you found your child lying on the floor, motionless and not breathing. If you knew the technique, you would immediately start CPR (cardiopulmonary resuscitation). However, chest compression that's vigorous enough to move blood to the brain can sometimes result in bruised and even broken ribs. Knowing that you might break a rib, would you still be willing to do CPR on your child? Of course you would. A broken rib is insignificant compared to death.

Similarly, using drugs is potentially fatal to our children emotionally, spiritually, and physically. Stopping drug use is an emergency. Are we willing to risk some pain — bruise some emotional ribs — to save their lives? Are we willing to risk their anger in order to give them a chance at real happiness? Many of us are not. We want our children to be happy, and we want them to be drug-free, but we're not willing to do emotional CPR. Most of us are not willing to offend our children and take the risk that they might not like us.

Walter called me at home and told me that his sixteen-year-old son Brandon had been drinking alcohol in increasing quantities every day, despite many warnings and confrontations. His behavior was becoming dangerous to himself and others.

Me: "You need to admit him to a drug treatment center."

Walter: "He won't go."

Me: "Legally, he's a minor. In this state, you can admit him for treatment whether he wants to go or not."

Walter: "Oh, I couldn't do that. He'd be furious at me."

Me: "Then you've decided to actively help your son stay an alcoholic and be miserable. You may even contribute to his death."

Walter protested that he really did want to help, but words mean nothing. With his behavior, he clearly said he was not willing to help his son. Two months later, Walter's son died in a car accident; he had been driving while intoxicated.

Once a child is dependent on drugs, he can't judge whether he functions normally or not. He can't decide whether he needs help, so we have to make that decision for him. If we're not willing to do the difficult things required to help a child who's using drugs, we're helping him kill himself.

What do we do when a child is over eighteen and can legally make such decisions for himself? See the approach to adult children in Chapter 26.

THE EXAMPLE WE SET

It's impossible for our children to seriously listen to us talk about drugs when we smoke and/or drink alcohol. Sure, those vices are legal, but they're still drugs used to escape the pain of feeling unloved and alone. Our children follow our example.

Chapter Summary

The use of alcohol and drugs is so distracting and deceptive that those who use them can't feel Real Love even when it's given to them.

Preventing drug use is best accomplished by loving a child, who then has no need to use them. Helping a child stop using drugs is an emergency.

Chapter 26

Families

The most important role for families is to provide a place where people — especially children — can feel unconditionally loved and learn how to love others. Nothing else a family does will compensate for failure to do this. If a child doesn't feel loved, it doesn't matter how well he is clothed, or how well he does in school, or how good he makes his parents look. To be happy, he must feel loved and learn to love other people.

SIBLINGS

Siblings give each other marvelous opportunities to learn how to be loving, but we often fail to understand that and don't use those opportunities. We even interfere with them when they occur. For example, we see their quarrels as something we need to stop, instead of using them to teach valuable lessons.

Stopping arguments

Children argue with each other because they feel empty and afraid. They argue to protect themselves and to get Imitation Love in the form of praise and power. When we interfere with their arguments, we're saying this: "Even though you feel empty and afraid, I want you to feel loved and be loving instead."

That's impossible. Insisting that angry children be more loving with each other is like demanding that they be taller or smarter. It's like telling a drowning person to stop being afraid and stop struggling to save himself.

In the first interaction between Ryan and his brother (Chapter 9), their father stopped the argument. That gave him a moment of peace and quiet, but the boys only learned this: when we fight, Dad gets irritated and stops us. That's not a lesson that will lead to genuine happiness in a child's life. Children then learn to stop arguing only because they're afraid of the anger of their parents, not because they're learning to be responsible or loving.

Diane (pp. 201-4) didn't make the mistake of stopping her children's argument. Instead, she saw, accepted, and loved them. In addition, she taught them how to see and accept each other, giving them a invaluable gift.

Justice vs. Loving

Erica and Michelle both knew they had to complete their assigned chores in the house before they could play. When it was time for their favorite television program, Erica had done her jobs, but Michelle had not. Michelle was sent to finish washing the dishes, and she wasn't happy about it. After she left, Mother spoke to Erica.

Mother: "Would you be willing to help Michelle?"

Erica: "Me?! That's not fair! She didn't do her work. I did mine, and now I have the right to watch television."

Mother: "Yes, you do, and I'm not going to make you help her. I'm only suggesting that you have an opportunity to learn something about loving your sister. This is entirely up to you. If you decide to stay here and relax, you're entitled to do that. I'll never say another word about it."

Erica did stay and watch television for a while, but then she went to help Michelle. Later that night, she talked to her mother.

Erica: "Michelle was surprised when I went to help her, especially when she found out that you didn't make me do it. And I enjoyed it more than I thought I would. I'm glad you suggested it."

Mother: "Did you help her partly because you would have felt guilty if you hadn't?"

Erica: (smiling) "Yes."

Mother: "I know how that feels. In the future, do the right thing because you *want* to. If you had stayed there and not helped your sister, I would not have said anything. You just said that you enjoyed helping Michelle. Remember that feeling the next time you're trying to decide whether to do something loving or not. The more loving you become, the happier you'll be. *That* is the reason to do the right thing, because it makes you happier. It also makes other people happier. You're learning an important lesson. I'm glad for you."

A child can't easily give Real Love to his parents (Chapter 6) because Real Love must be freely given. A child feels too indebted to his parents, and needs them too much, for him to give them his love freely. With siblings, that sense of debt, obligation, and fear is much less. Siblings therefore provide each other a great opportunity to learn about unconditional love. As children learn to love their brothers and sisters, they learn to love people in general, and that guarantees a lifetime of happiness.

DIVORCE

By 1990, the divorce rate in the United States was 50%. Unfathomable numbers of children are raised by single parents, step-parents, lovers of parents, grandparents, and so on. However, *it is not the number of parents, nor their marital status, that determines the happiness of a child*. It is simply not true that a child must be raised by two married parent to be happy. Similarly, it is not true that divorce makes children unhappy.

What makes a child unhappy is the absence of unconditional love in his life. Period. The reason that children of divorced families have more problems is that families without unconditional love have more problems with everything: divorce, alcoholism, child abuse, etc. It's *the lack of love* that causes both the divorce *and* the unhappy child. It is not the divorce that causes the unhappy child.

Divorce *can* be a traumatic experience for a child — but only if the child has no source of Real Love. If a child doesn't feel loved, *everything* is frightening and painful, and divorce is just one more intolerable event. However, if a child is filled with Real Love, divorce can become a fairly minor experience.

Children need to be unconditionally accepted and loved. It would be ideal if a child could always get that from both his natural parents. But in many cases that's impossible, and fortunately, it's not necessary. Real Love from *any source* eliminates a child's emptiness and fear.

So how do we deal with our children when their other parent leaves? If we're already giving them Real Love, the effect of the divorce will be small. We only need to continue loving them. If they seem afraid, angry, or otherwise difficult, they're simply not feeling loved. It's not a "divorce problem." It's a deficiency of unconditional love, and the only solution is for us to learn more about telling the truth and finding Real Love for ourselves

(Chapter 5). We'll then be able to give our children what they need most.

BLENDED FAMILIES

When divorced parents marry another spouse, that creates many new interactions — with step-parents, new siblings, new grandparents, new environments, etc. It also changes the way children interact with their natural parent. Blending families can be very complicated and difficult — but it doesn't have to be.

The solution to blending families can be simple. If parents and step-parents have Real Love in their own lives (Chapter 5), they can offer it to their children and step-children. That's what they really need to be great parents and to create happy families.

Children often resist the initial attempts of step-parents to get close to them. They only do that because they don't feel unconditionally loved, and they're afraid of being unloved and hurt again. They use Protecting Behaviors to keep them safe from injury. Those behaviors — lying, attacking, acting like victims, and running — are often irritating to step-parents. But step parents are irritated by a child only if they (the step-parents) are also unloved, looking for affection, and expecting love from their step-children.

If you're trying to *get* your step-children to behave in a certain way toward you, your relationship with them is guaranteed to be difficult. If you feel disappointed or irritated as you interact with them, you can be certain that you're trying to get them to make *you* feel good, and that selfish desire can only make them feel empty and unhappy. Find love for yourself first (Chapter 5) and then learn to give it to your children and step-children (Chapter 9). It's the only effective approach.

PARENTING AN ADULT CHILD

When a child is three years old, it's obvious that his parents need to love, guide, and instruct him, and sometimes they must even make decisions for him. However, this process can become confusing as a child gets older. When do parents need to back off and quit making choices for him? When should they stop giving instruction entirely?

From the time they were born, we knew our children had to grow up and move out on their own. Parents who don't help their children to become independent are selfishly using them to get Imitation Love for themselves. Such parents enjoy a sense of power when they control their children. They enjoy the feeling of being needed and important.

How to Let Them Go

It would be unwise to control our children until they're 21, and then suddenly kick them out of the house and expect them to wisely make their own choices. We need to prepare them gradually and steadily to be independent. They must be allowed to make more and more decisions for themselves, and then the day will come when they can easily make all their own decisions. Leaving home will then be a natural step. In Chapter 15, we talked about how to teach them to be responsible, a very important part of becoming independent.

When to Let Them Go

There's no standard age when every child is ready to make all his own decisions. However, when children have been taught responsibility from an early age, they're usually prepared for independence by the time they're out of high school. Children who are taught nothing about responsibility may not achieve real independence all their lives.

From the time they were young, I told my children that when they finished high school, they would be on their own as far as a place to live and the responsibility to support themselves financially. It's helpful to set a specific age or date, because then they know what to expect and can prepare for it. They're less likely to then feel abandoned or punished when the day comes that they have to move out on their own.

Most of us allow our children to live at home far too long. There are a number of reasons for that indulgence:

1. We want to avoid the confrontation that results from telling a child he has to leave. Children can make us feel very guilty about that.

2. We don't want to look harsh and unloving to other family members and friends.

3. We don't want to lose our position of authority, power, and importance, which includes the gratitude and affection we receive from our children. We enjoy being indispensable in our children's lives. Many of us feel worthless when the "nest" is empty and we lose our role as protectors and providers.

But it hurts everyone involved when a child stays home too long. We may think we're being kind when we keep taking care of adult children, but it makes *them* weak, and *we* often accumulate feelings of obligation and resentment about this care-taking that never ends.

I allowed one of my children to live at home for more than a year after high school. It was the wrong thing for him. He wanted the independence of making his own choices, but he also liked the advantages of having things provided for him at home — food, housing, transportation, insurance, etc. Who wouldn't? I began to see that he wasn't learning and growing while he was enjoying the irresponsibility of childhood, so I finally told him to find his own place to live. After leaving, he sulked and avoided me for several months, but then he came and talked to me. He said he had been learning some things that he could not have learned if he'd stayed at home. He knew that leaving home was the right thing to do.

Financial Support

Many young people continue to receive financial assistance from their parents for long periods after leaving home. Parents think they're being kind, and certainly the children enjoy the generosity and relief from their own responsibility. But we often cause harm with our "kindness."

Our children learn and become stronger as they struggle and earn what they get. When we financially support them for too long, we rob them of those important lessons. Many of us protest, "But if I didn't help him (or her), he wouldn't make it." Ridiculous. They won't starve. What we mean is that without help, our child would have to work hard and might resent us for not making his life easy. Or he wouldn't be able to drive a nice car and live in a nice apartment, and then we'd look uncaring and might feel guilty.

We learn responsibility as we live within our means. For years, I lived in some tiny and simple places in my adult life, and I don't regret a minute of it. Happiness is not determined by the material things we have. In fact, if we enable our children to have too many nice things, they become distracted by them and forget that the only source of genuine happiness is Real Love.

We may decide to help children with part of their education after high school, but we should not feel obligated to do that. Many parents feel pressured by social custom to completely put their children through college, but that may not be a wise thing for all children. Remember that some children just do less as we do more for them, and that doesn't help them grow. They need to be increasingly responsible for their own finances. How that's done may be different for each child in the family, according to their abilities and needs.

I offer one approach that has worked well in our family. I do not propose that it would work for everyone. After high school, our children are financially independent from us. We don't pressure them to continue schooling, but if they choose to continue their education, we do help them with that. The first six months after high school, we pay for their tuition, books, rent, food, and utilities. They pay for their clothing, entertainment, and transportation. The second six months, we only pay for tuition, books, and rent. Increasingly, we wean them from financial support until they're entirely independent in one or two years.

Advice

We love to give advice, to our children and to others. If we're not filled with Real Love, giving advice makes us feel wise, important, and powerful. And we feel especially justified in giving advice when we're "right," when the direction we offer is clearly better than the path being chosen by the child we're advising. Yes, we do have more experience and may even know more than our children. But that's not enough reason to give adult children advice.

With few exceptions, don't give advice to an adult child unless he asks for it. Our counsel may be correct, but when we offer uninvited direction, what the child hears — and what we usually mean — is this: "Without my help, you are incapable of making the right decisions." That's a very damaging message, far outweighing the potential good of the advice we give.

Children learn from mistakes. Let them make their own. It doesn't matter that our advice is right. Learning to make decisions is more important than actually making one decision correctly.

While my nineteen-year-old daughter was in college, she met a man with whom she quickly developed a close relationship. After a month of dating, they decided to get married. She called to get my opinion.

Rachel: "Dad, some people are saying that we're rushing into this, that we ought to get to know each other better. Others are saying that we should wait until we both finish school and are more financially secure. What do you think?"

Me: "For nineteen years, I've taught you how to know what's right and what's wrong. You know how to tell the truth about yourself, how to be responsible, and how to love other people. You also know how to look for those qualities in a partner. That's all I can teach you. You'll make this decision just fine on your own."

We can only teach our children so much, and then they have to do the rest themselves. It's a great blessing to them when we learn to be quiet early rather than late.

Resentment, Distance, and What We Can Do

Many of us are now in the position of having adult children who are clearly emotionally distant from us, and we wonder what is wrong. Almost without exception, there is no mystery to that. If our adult children avoid us, or seem emotionally withdrawn, they do not feel unconditionally loved by us, and it's very likely that they never felt loved by us. We can make all the excuses in the world and point to how much we *tried* to love them, but the fact is that they don't *feel* loved. Certainly, we loved them as well as we could, but it's virtually impossible that we loved them *unconditionally*.

Even though we did our best, if we didn't unconditionally love our children when they were young, we seriously hurt them. It's then only natural that they would choose, as adults, to avoid us. Why would they want to expose themselves to the risk of being hurt by us again?

When we feel unloved ourselves, we want our children to forgive us for all our past mistakes and to love us right now. We can do a lot to change the feelings of our adult children toward us, but we need to remember two important things as we interact with them:

1. We cannot insist that our adult children love us. The same rule applies here as when they were young (Chapter 6): it is not their responsibility to make us happy. It's true that we brought them into this world, changed their diapers, fed them, wiped their noses, and took care of their every need for many years. But those were all things that *we* chose to do, and they obligate our children in no way to do anything for us. Ever. They do not have to pay us back.

2. We're not responsible for making our adult children happy, either. We can't undo the mistakes we made in the past, nor can we take responsibility for the poor choices *they* have made on their own since childhood.

All we can really do now with our adult children is to accept and love them, with no expectations or disappointment. But we do need to admit that we did not unconditionally love them as children, and that we did hurt them. That's hard for many of us to acknowledge, but we need to tell that truth — first to ourselves, then to some wise men and women (Chapter 5), and eventually to our children. As we do that, we can begin the process of learning to love our children. We begin to fill their emptiness and heal their wounds. We also become free from our own guilt.

Alice came to me in tears and said her 30-year-old son Chuck was always avoiding her. He never called, and he stayed in the next room when she came to his house to see her grandchildren. He only spoke to answer her questions, and then only briefly.

Alice: "It hurts me that he treats me like this, but he doesn't seem to care."

Me: "It's not his job to love you (Chapter 6). It's your responsibility as his mother to love him unconditionally."

Alice: "I do."

Me: "I know you do your best, but the fact that he avoids you is like a billboard on his forehead saying, 'I don't feel loved by you.' If he did feel accepted, he wouldn't avoid you."

Alice: "But I do accept him."

Me: "Does he have any habits you don't like?"

Alice: "Yes, he smokes and drinks, and obviously, that's bad for him."

Me: "Do you ever tell him that?

Alice: "Sure. A good mother wouldn't stand by while her son is doing something that could kill him."

Me: "How about his job? Does he have a good one?

Alice: "No, and he could do a lot better if he wanted to. I keep making suggestions, but he doesn't do anything about them."

It was obvious from her words and the expression on her face that she didn't accept her son. And he felt that disapproval every time he saw her. That's why he avoided her. It's true that smoking and drinking aren't healthy, but he knew that very well without her reminding him every few days. And maybe Chuck could have done more with his career, but adults get to make those decisions for themselves. He didn't need or want her constant advice about his health, or job, or anything else, certainly not after he'd repeatedly made it clear that he didn't want to hear it. He only needed her unconditional acceptance, and she didn't give him that.

Me: "Try going a week without giving him any advice at all."

Alice: "But he's making bad decisions."

Me: "Alice, I love you, but what your son chooses to do with his life is none of your business. If you feel compelled to tell him what to do, or even make silent judgments about him, and if you find it difficult to stop doing that, you're trying to control him. It's his life, and you don't accept that — nor do you accept him. After all the advice you've given him, has he changed and done what you want?"

Alice: "No, but . . ."

Me: "So it's not helping him, is it? And now your own son hates being around you. So far, how do you like the results of doing this relationship your way? Are you happy? Does your son feel loved and happy? Is *your* way working?"

We keep trying to control our adult children, and the result is unhappiness for everyone. Many of us can't stop being critical and giving advice. However, with great faith and courage, Alice did stop. She learned to tell the truth about herself and found unconditional love in her own life (Chapter 5). With that, she became happy and lost her need to tell her son what to do. After several months, she came to me in tears — happy ones this time — to say she felt more loved and loving than she ever thought possible. In addition, her son had quit avoiding her. Children of all ages respond best to being accepted, not criticized.

The only goal of wise parents is to love and guide their children, and to help them be happy. As children mature, they move past the point of needing our guidance and only need our unconditional acceptance.

Spouse

When your child gets married, a new family unit is formed. That unit doesn't directly include you. Don't give advice to your child about their spouse unless you're asked. It's none of your business.

GRANDCHILDREN

I hear these questions frequently: "How can I get my grandchildren to be more _____?" "How can I get it across to my son that he needs to _____ with his children?"

The answer? "You don't." Your child's children are not yours. You may have great ideas about how to raise them. Fine. Write a book. Give advice to your child about his children only if you're asked. With rare exceptions (cases of sexual abuse, for example), grandparents do not have the right to interfere with the efforts of parents, even when they're certain their advice is good. Parents learn by making mistakes. Our children must be allowed to make those mistakes with their children, just as we did with *them* while *we* learned to be parents. It may be difficult to sit back and watch our children make mistakes with their children, but that's how it has to be.

We need to have faith in our children (Chapter 10) that they'll learn to be great parents. They learn that best when we support and love them, not when we criticize them or contradict what they teach their children. If our children feel unconditionally loved by us, they *will* be good parents, because they'll have what their children need more than anything else — Real Love. And if our children feel unconditionally loved by us, they'll *ask* us for advice on the occasions when they need it.

Our grandchildren need the same thing all people need. They need what we often didn't give our own children: Real Love. If we simply love them, we give them the greatest gift of all and can have a powerfully positive effect on their lives.

BEING AN ADULT CHILD

As adult children, it's our responsibility to respect and love our own parents. Some other things are not our responsibility:

1. To obey them. As young children, it was important that we obeyed our parents. They were wiser and had the responsibility to teach us. As adults, we have to learn and grow from our own choices.

2. To make them happy. Many parents place the responsibility for their happiness on their adult children. They make them feel guilty if they don't visit or call, etc. — as Alice did on pp. 363-5. It's never our responsibility to make other people happy — including our parents — only to unconditionally accept and love them. Our parents have to make their own choices about feeling loved, being loving, and being responsible — and that's what will determine their happiness, as it does with everyone else.

3. To listen to their advice. I'm not suggesting that we should ever be rude to our parents, but some parents continue to offer advice long after it's appropriate. On those occasions, we may need to lovingly indicate that we don't need to hear any more.

Correcting our Parents

As we become adults, we often realize how many mistakes our parents made with us. At that point, some of us make three common mistakes:

1. We feel victimized and angry. What a waste of time, energy, and happiness! We can stay miserable thinking about our parents' mistakes, or we can move on with the rest of our lives. Which is more likely to make us happy?

Let's assume the worst, that your parents made every imaginable mistake and are responsible for every moment of unhappiness that you've had in your life so far. Now what? That's over. From now on the responsibility for what you do to find love and happiness is yours alone, not theirs.

2. We want our parents to admit their mistakes. For most parents, that's just too difficult and painful. They can't discuss that subject without feeling attacked and defensive. When that's the case, it's arrogant and hurtful for us to insist on it.

3. As we realize what we didn't get as children, many of us insist that our parents give us that love now. But most of our parents didn't ever get Real Love for themselves. They were therefore *incapable* of giving it, something they consistently proved throughout our childhood. And in most cases, they still can't. Many of us then protest, "But they're *supposed* to love me — they're my parents." The fact that they're our parents doesn't magically give them the ability to love us. If they didn't get it themselves, they can't give it to us. We can't get milk from a bull, no matter how thirsty and insistent we are.

The effect of Real Love is miraculous from any source. We can tell the truth about ourselves to wise men and women all around us (Chapter 5). We do not have to be loved by our parents to be happy.

Chapter Summary

Families are a place where people get unconditional acceptance and learn to love others. That is the purpose of all interactions between family members.

Parents must teach children how to make their own decisions and eventually allow them to be independent.

Chapter 27

What We're Really Saying

For reasons we discussed in Chapters 3 and 19, we lie frequently and mostly unconsciously. But when we lie, we hide ourselves and therefore can't feel seen or loved — and that makes it impossible for us to love our children.

Following are some of the lies we commonly tell our children and others, along with what we really mean — the truth. Read them slowly, and try not to feel guilty or defensive. Talk with a wise friend and recognize how often you tell these lies. Then practice telling the truth. This will create opportunities for you to be seen and accepted (Chapter 5). As a result, you'll feel more loved and will become a more loving parent.

The chapter will be laid out this way for each lie:

1. **The Lie**
2. **The Truth** — what we're really saying, but don't have the courage or insight to put into words.
3. **Discussion**

In the beginning, it can be frightening to tell the truth about ourselves, even about little things. But the risk is actually very small considering the alternative: when we lie, we always feel unloved and alone.

"HOW MANY TIMES DO I HAVE TO TELL YOU ...?"

We say this when we've repeatedly told a child to do or not do something. It's always said with an impatient tone of voice and a frown on our face.

The Truth

"I can't believe you're so stupid — but you must be, because I have to keep telling you the same things over and over. My life is so empty and unhappy that I require everything around me to go smoothly or I get upset and angry. So when you don't listen to me, or when you inconvenience me in any way, I don't think about teaching and loving you. I selfishly attack you and try to make you do what I want."

Discussion

When we feel unloved and empty ourselves, it's easy to forget that our role as parents is to teach and love our children. When we don't have any love to give, we require them to make *our* lives easier, or at least to not inconvenience us. When they fail to meet that expectation, we attack them. When we say, "How many times do I have to tell you ..." our children finish that sentence in their heads with the words, "you idiot," or something similar. It's a terrible thing for a child to hear.

"STOP THAT!"

We say this to our children about a lot of things:

The Truth

"Stop fighting."	really means	"When you feel empty and affraid, Be loving instead of defending yourself."

"Be quiet."	really means	"Because I'm feeling selfish and irritable, you have to stop making the noises that all children make at your age."
"Can't you hold still?"	really means	"Stop moving around and acting like the child you are. Behave like an adult."
"Do you have to make that much niose with your gum?"	really means	"Stop having fun or doing anything that could possibly disturb the peace and quiet of My Royal Highness."
"Whatever you're doing in the next room, stop it."	really means	"Stop breathing. Everything about you bothers me.

Most of the time when we say, "Stop it" to our children, what we really mean is this: "Stop being yourself. Quit acting your age and inconveniencing me. Stop failing to give me what I want from you and being such a huge disappointment to me."

Discussion

Every time our children interact with us or anyone else, they're communicating something important about themselves (the Third Rule of Seeing, Chapter 7). How could we be more foolish than to interfere with that communication, and yet that's just what we do each time we say "Stop it." We need to listen to them and see them instead of insisting on getting what *we* want.

Making noise, wiggling, arguing, and being foolish are part of being a child. When we feel loved ourselves, those things don't bother us at all. We also need to see their Getting and Protecting Behaviors as a sign of their emptiness and fear, not as an inconvenience we should eliminate. When we understand that, we see how selfish and harmful it is for us to say "Stop it." Again, this does not mean we should ignore inappropriate behavior, only that we need to change it by teaching and loving our children rather than simply controlling them.

FROWN

Mostly we're unaware of how often these expressions of disappointment and disapproval appear on our faces. But our children are quite sensitive to these silent and lethal communications.

The Truth

"You disgust me. Right now, my life is less happy as a result of you being in it. You are inconvenient and irritating, and I wish you were different."

Discussion

It's a hard thing to admit, but our children really do hear all that each time we frown at them — and it's actually what we mean. When we don't feel loved ourselves, we have enormous expectations of our children to make us happy (Chapter 6). That's natural, but it's wrong. Our children even try to shoulder the responsibility we give them to make us happy, but they simply can't do it. When they fail, our disappointment is crushing to them.

"GIVE MOMMY A KISS."

We commonly ask for some sign of affection from our children, especially at bedtime or as they leave the house for school, etc.

The Truth

"I feel unloved and alone. When you smile and kiss me, I feel important and less lonely. I don't consistently get that feeling anywhere else, and I need it. I ask for love from you because you're less likely to refuse me than the other people in my life."

Discussion

Although it's our responsibility to love and teach our *children*, most of us still have expectations that our children will love *us* and make us happy. We prove that with our requests — often demands — for respect, obedience, courtesy, and affection. We confirm our expectations every time we're disappointed in them or angry at them. Our children are not responsible for our happiness (Chapter 6).

"I LOVE YOU."

When we say these words to our children, we are not aware of any lie. We give our children the best we have. We fail to love them unconditionally only because we don't have sufficient Real Love to give them.

The Truth

"I *need* you. I need your gratitude, respect, and affection. If I genuinely loved you, I'd care about *your* happiness first, but that's not my primary interest. I prove that with my disappointment and anger each time you fail to meet my expectations. I tell you I love you because:

1. "I know I should. That's what loving parents are supposed to say. I look good if I say it and bad if I don't."

2. "You're more likely to say it back to me, and I like that."

Discussion

When we tell a child we love him without having Real Love ourselves, we can only be saying it for the selfish reasons above. The deception is not intentional. But children can tell if we love them by how we *behave* — our smiles, frowns, silence, tone of voice, and the time we spend with them. When they see that we disapprove of them, control them, and otherwise conditionally accept them, they actually come to resent us saying "I love you" — because they know it's not true.

In our defense, I suggest a third reason that we say, "I love you" to our children, even though we don't feel unconditionally loving toward them. I believe that we all *want* to be more loving toward our children, and we fail only because we don't know how to go about it. I think that on many occasions when we say, "I love you" to them, we're expressing our desire, our goal, our wish that we *could* love them better, make them happier, and be the mother or father that we've always wanted to be.

"WHERE ARE YOU GOING?"

We ask this — usually with an accusing tone — when a child is going out the door and we don't know their plans.

The Truth

"You are so foolish and irresponsible that you couldn't possibly choose how to spend your time wisely without my supervision. In addition, I feel powerless when you make decisions on your own and don't tell me. I feel left out and unloved, and I don't like that."

Discussion

We feel disrespected and out of control when our children don't tell us where they're going and what they're doing. So we *insist* on being informed. We forget that the reason they don't tell us their plans is that they fear the criticism and disapproval we've given them many times when they *have* shared their plans. I'm not saying we shouldn't know where our children are. Of course we should. But we demand it in such a way that they feel violated and controlled, not accepted and loved.

If our children feel loved, they'll feel comfortable telling us where they are all the time. But what if they don't feel loved? And what if a child is going out the door without our knowing where he's going? What is an appropriate way to ask a child where he's going? Just ask: "Where are you going?" It's not the *words* that matter. What's important is that we're not disappointed or angry with them — that's what hurts them.

"YOU ARE SO . . ."

When parents get angry, they often use incomplete sentences, choked off by irritation and frustration.

"You ..."
"I ..."
"I'm so ..."
"I could just ..."
"I can't believe you ..."

The Truth

"Because I'm selfish, I'm angry that you've inconvenienced me. I really want to say something mean and hurtful, but I know that's wrong, and I don't want to look bad. So I'll just start the sentence and let you finish it in your head with something awful. That way, I won't look completely unloving and out of control, but you'll still get the disapproving and angry message."

Discussion

Our children fill in the blanks of these incomplete sentences with the worst imaginable words, and it hurts them.

SILENCE

This comes in many forms:

The disapproving glance.

Physical avoidance of a child. We often don't realize how much we stay away from our children when we're angry at them. We certainly don't hug them as much when we're angry.

Failure to speak to a child. When our children enter a room and we don't speak to them, they notice that — and they should. How many things in this world are more important than our children? How long does it take to speak a child's name or say hello, and what excuse can we offer for not doing it? They interpret our silence as a lack of caring.

Lack of interest in their activities. They know we care about them as we ask about what they did each day, and they know we don't care when we don't ask. Caring does not mean prying and insisting on information that a child is obviously reluctant to give.

The Truth

"I usually don't know what to say to you. And I'm lazy, so I take the easy way out and say nothing. Sometimes I'm silent because I'm disappointed and angry. On other occasions, I'm avoiding my responsibility to teach and correct you, because you always act annoyed when I say anything to you."

Discussion

We often use silence as a Protecting Behavior. We use it to run from difficult conversations. But it leaves our children feeling more alone and unloved.

"I JUST DON'T KNOW WHAT TO DO WITH YOU."

We say this when we're frustrated at our children. They repeat the same foolish behavior, and we don't know what to do next.

The Truth

"It's obvious that you don't feel loved, or you wouldn't act like this. But I don't know how to love you and teach you, and then I feel stupid and helpless. So I shift the blame — and hopefully the discomfort — to you."

Discussion

When our children behave in a way that frustrates us — meaning that we can't control them — we blame the problem on them. If we can reassure ourselves that something is wrong with *them*, we don't have to consider the more painful prospect that *we* need to change.. It's a cheap way of making ourselves comfortable, and one that causes great harm to our children.

"THIS ROOM IS A PIGSTY!"

The Truth

"Something is wrong with *you*. I cannot accept you with this flaw."

Discussion

It's true that many pigs live in conditions more sanitary and attractive than some children. However, we forget that a clean room is far less important than a child knowing he's loved. When we say "This room is a pigsty!" with anger, a child can only hear that something is wrong with *him*. Children need to be loved more than anything else, and when we're angry, they can only sense that they are *not* being loved.

We do need to teach children to be clean and responsible (Chapter 14), but never with anger and a lack of acceptance. We also need to remember that eventually, children need to be allowed to make their own decisions about how they keep their own rooms (127).

"DON'T YOU TALK TO ME LIKE THAT."

We often say this when our children dare to question what we say or when they don't give us the respect we demand.

The Truth

"I feel unloved and alone. Without Real Love and genuine happiness, it feels good to get the Imitation Love of respect (power and praise). After all I've done for you, you at least owe me that. And I'm in a position of authority where I can demand respect from you, something I can't do with most people."

Discussion

A child speaks disrespectfully only to defend himself or to relieve his sense of helplessness. If we saw him clearly, we'd give him what he really needs — our unconditional acceptance and guidance — instead of insisting on respect for ourselves. It's true that children need to be respectful. It's part of being considerate, grateful, and happy. However, we rarely insist on respect for the benefit of our children. We do it for ourselves. We can teach genuine respect and gratitude to children only as we love them (Chapter 16).

"HOW DO YOU EXPLAIN THESE GRADES?"

We say variations on this when our children perform in an unsatisfactory way in many areas, not just their grades.

The Truth

"I'm so disappointed when you perform badly. When you fail, I feel ashamed and worry that other people will think I'm a lousy parent. Even without their opinion, I feel like I've failed as a parent. I feel stupid and helpless when you're a failure — and I hate that. I wish you were smarter, worked harder, and didn't make me uncomfortable like this."

Discussion

The instant children feel our disappointment for not meeting our expectations, they know they're not unconditionally loved. Criticizing our children's performance never makes them happy and rarely improves their performance.

Ironically, even children who are praised for success often become miserable — sometimes many years later — because they know the praise they receive is conditional. They know they'll be criticized and have their approval withdrawn if they perform badly, so they feel trapped by the obligation to succeed all the time.

"YOU MAKE ME SO MAD."

There are few lies more common than this one.

The Real Truth

"I'm completely selfish and hate being inconvenienced. I want to control you and stop you from ever getting in my way. You can make your own choices and mistakes with everyone else, but not with me. When you fail to recognize that the world revolves around me, I get angry."

Discussion

See Chapter 6 for more about anger.

"MY SON IS BECOMING A REAL PROBLEM."

We say this to friends and family when they wonder why we look angry and distracted, or when they hear about our child's misbehavior.

The Truth

"My son is angry because he feels unloved and afraid. The only person who could be responsible for that is me. I've always loved him less when he didn't do what I wanted, so he doesn't feel unconditionally accepted. The real problem is not my son, but the fact that I don't know how to love him. But I can't say all that — it would make me look like a bad parent. So I blame his behavior on him and act like a victim myself."

Discussion

We love to blame our children. We roll our eyes and look for sympathy from other parents — and we usually get it. It's our responsibility to love and teach our children. It is not their responsibility to make life easy for us.

Chapter 28

What They're Really Saying

Children lie for the same reason the rest of us do — to protect themselves and to get Imitation Love. But when they lie, they can't feel seen or loved. Following are some of the lies our children commonly tell. We need to know what they're really telling us so we can see them more clearly and help them tell the truth about themselves. Only then can they feel accepted and loved (Chapter 12).

The chapter will be laid out this way for each lie:

1. **The Lie**
2. **The Truth** — what they're really saying.
3. **Discussion**

"I DIDN'T HAVE TIME."

This answer is given to the question, "Did you finish that job I gave you?" It's one of many variations on the victim's general response, "It wasn't my fault."

The Truth

"I'm being lazy and irresponsible. I didn't want to do the job you assigned me, so I put it off and did what I wanted to do instead. But now I'm blaming it on a lack of time so you won't be as angry at me."

Discussion

This lie is told by many of us every day. In truth, it's rare that we lack the time to do what we're supposed to do. We have time to do what we *want* to do: talk to our friends, watch television, relax, and so on. When we say we didn't have time to complete an assignment, the truth is almost always that we chose to do what we wanted instead. There's an example of a mother explaining this to her daughter on pp. 309-11.

Unfortunately, when we confront a child about a task they haven't completed, the tone in our voice communicates this: "What's the matter with you? Why are you always so irresponsible and unreliable? I don't like you when you're like this." That's why they lie to us — to keep from hearing that message of disapproval.

We do need to teach our children the importance of being responsible, but *how* we teach them is critical. When we love them unconditionally while we teach them, they feel safe enough to tell the truth and learn. They don't *need* to tell us lies like the one above.

An Example of
A Child Telling the Truth

Me: "Joseph, the garbage in my room hasn't been taken out in two days. Why is that?"

Joseph: "I was just being lazy. I've been playing around and putting off doing my jobs around the house."

Because Joseph felt loved, he didn't feel guilty about making a mistake and felt safe telling the truth. It's a wonderful feeling to tell the truth about our flaws and be accepted with them.

"I LOVE YOU."

Children are taught from an early age to say this to their parents and others. When they do, they're rewarded with smiles, hugs, and "I love you, too."

The Truth

"I *need* you. I count on you for my physical and emotional support. I say I love you because it's obvious that you like me more when I do that. And I'm afraid that if I don't tell you I love you — especially after you've said it — you'll be disappointed or angry with me."

Discussion

We like it when our children express their affection and gratitude to us, and unconsciously, we manipulate them to do that. We don't realize that it places a heavy burden on them. For reasons we've discussed (Chapter 6), children don't have the responsibility to love us, and with rare exceptions, they don't have the ability to offer us Real Love.

"HE HIT ME (OR IN SOME WAY TREATED ME UNFAIRLY)."

This is a frequent accusation one child makes about a sibling, usually with a bit of acting involved and a hope of getting the offender in trouble.

The Truth

"I was selfish and did something I knew would irritate my brother (or sister). He told me to quit it, but I kept it up until he finally got sick of it and hit me. I did plenty to provoke his attack, but I don't want to admit that because then I'll get in trouble."

Discussion

Children have learned that if they can successfully paint themselves as the victim of another person's abuse, they'll be free of blame and punishment (Chapter 21). They also gain power over the person who hurt them. We need to identify this behavior and respond in a way that does not reward them for acting like victims.

"NOTHIN'."

Children commonly say something like this when their parents ask them about their activities while away from home. An example of this is found on pp. 196-7.

The Truth

"I don't want to answer your question, because whenever I tell you what I'm doing with my life, you do one or more of the following things.

(1) You criticize what I've done.
(2) You tell me what I should have done differently.
(3) You ask a bunch of questions I don't want to answer.
(4) You don't really hear what I say.

I feel like you don't care about me, and that you ask questions because: (1) you feel obligated to look like a concerned parent, or (2) you want to find fault with me, or (3) you just want to satisfy your own curiosity."

Discussion

When our children avoid answering questions about what they're doing, they're clearly communicating that they don't feel unconditionally loved by us. When we push them to answer, we prove once again that we're not listening to them or caring about their happiness.

"I FORGOT."

This is the answer a child gives to a question about why he didn't do an assigned task. There's an example of this on pp. 220-1.

The Truth

"I didn't want to do that assignment. So I did what I wanted instead and let the assignment completely slip from my mind."

Discussion

Children don't forget to do the things they want to do. They don't just forget to eat. They don't forget what time school is over, or when summer vacation starts, or when their birthday is. They forget the things they don't want to do.

SILENCE

Children — especially as they get older — are commonly quiet around their parents. Most behave like Emily (pp. 319-20), who avoided her parents, rather than David (p. 320), who often talked with his mother and father. We tend to explain this as moodiness, shyness, or just being a teenager. We need to look deeper than that.

The Truth

"I'm afraid that if I speak, you'll criticize me and make me feel bad, like you've done many times before. So I stay quiet and protect myself."

Discussion

When children feel loved by us, they're naturally drawn to us and talk to us frequently. Children who are quiet are almost invariably communicating that they don't feel accepted and loved.

"I THOUGHT YOU MEANT . . ."

This is spoken in response to a question like this: "Why didn't you finish the whole job I assigned to you?"

The Truth

"What you asked me to do required more work than I wanted to do. I was lazy and chose to interpret your request in a way that involved as little work as possible."

Example and Discussion

Parent: "I asked you to wash the dishes."

Child: "I did."

Parent: "But there are dishes all over the dining room table."

Child: "I thought you only meant the dishes in the sink."

We've all done things like that, at home, at school, and at work. We did less than someone requested not because we didn't understand, but because we didn't *want* to understand. We didn't want to consider the interpretation that meant more work for us.

Many times, children (and adults) have said to me, "But I really did think you meant . . ." That's rarely true. I used the following illustration with my children twice, after which they quit saying, "I thought you meant . . ."

Let's suppose I go to a particular store every week and each time, the owner makes a mistake in the amount he charges me. I keep a written record of these mistakes and after a year, I finally present it to him. He claims — with apparent sincerity — that many of the prices are printed too small and sometimes he can't see them clearly. Can I know if he's telling the truth? Yes. If his mistakes are approximately half in my favor and half in his favor, his explanation is believable. However, if all the mistakes are in his favor, the problem is not his vision. He's a thief and a liar.

Notice that when children say, "I thought you meant," they have invariably done *less* than was requested of them. Their confusion never causes them to do *more* than they were asked. That's not a lack of understanding. It's lazy and selfish, and most of us do that as adults. We hear what we want to hear. We're often not consciously aware of our deception, but it's still a lie. When our children do this, we need to help them see it.

". . . BUT . . ."

Listen to a conversation between a parent and child who disagree on an issue. You'll hear the word "but" spoken many times:
"I agree with you, *but* . . ."
"Yes, *but* . . ."
"*But* you . . ."

The Truth

"I'm not really listening to you. I'm only interested in being *right*, avoiding blame, and getting you to shut up and stop lecturing me. I stay quiet for a few moments while you're talking, but what I'm really doing is thinking of my next response and getting what I want."

Discussion

Most children do not listen well. Neither do most adults. Our
children want to avoid being responsible and wrong, so they
tend to say "but" as we're making them accountable or teaching
them anything. We need to help them see that when they say
"but," they're almost always trying to be right and excusing
their behavior. That's important for them to see, because if they
believe they have not made a mistake, they will not change and
are certain to make that mistake again. As we learn to love them
unconditionally, they feel safe and loved, and then they don't
need to protect themselves with "but" any longer.

Chapter 29

Questions

I receive a great number of letters from parents with questions about their children. In this chapter, I'll respond to several of them. With each answer, I'll assume that the reader has read *Real Love in Parenting*. Remember that it's always the primary goal of wise parents to:

(1) love their children — Chapter 9;
(2) teach them to be loving — Chapter 13; and
(3) teach them to be responsible — Chapter 14.

"BUT IT'S MY TURN TO . . ."

"My children seem to fight over everything. As soon as one of them has something, the other one wants it, and the fight is on. And then I have to break it up. I'm tired of it, but what can I do about it?"

It's inevitable that two children will occasionally want to use something at the same time — a toy, the bathroom, the phone, the television, etc. In fact, children seem to be irresistibly attracted to any object being enjoyed by another child.

Many years ago, my oldest sons, Jonathan and Michael, were arguing over who had the right to play with a toy outside. I heard both of them loudly claiming, "But it's my turn." Jonathan was much bigger than his brother, and I thought I had to defend Michael, so I took the toy from Jonathan and gave it to Michael.

I was wrong to settle that dispute the way I did. Determining who plays with a toy is meaningless. Far more important to children is developing the ability to see and love each other. As our children argue over their right to use something, we have an opportunity to teach them how to love each other. That means we need to let them settle most interactions themselves. Children learn from making those choices. They learn little or nothing from decisions that we impose on them.

I offer a few examples of helping two children who are arguing. These approaches work even better if you've had previous discussions with your children about relationships and loving each other (Chapters 15 and 13).

1. "I've taught both of you how to love each other, and I'm confident you can solve this disagreement. I want you to talk about this until you've made a decision that you're both happy with. Then come and tell me what you decided and what you learned." It's amazing how quickly children can solve a problem when they know that the problem must be solved and that someone else isn't going to do it for them.

2. "You two frequently fight about the time you spend in the bathroom as you get ready for school. I want you to stay here at the table until you work out the exact fifteen minutes you want to have the bathroom for yourself each morning. Then we'll coordinate what you decide with everyone else at the next family meeting."

3. "If you can't agree on a television program you want to watch, turn off the television and talk about it until you can agree." Children can become effective diplomats when the need arises.

Sometimes one or more of the children involved in a disagreement are simply too young or otherwise unable to participate in a reasonable discussion like one of those above. In that case, the parents do have to settle the dispute, as the mother did on pp. 312-14. Cindy was too immature and too demanding to come to an agreement with her sister, and eventually, her mother had to actually carry her to her room.

HAIR AND CLOTHING

"My son's hair is a disgrace. My husband forced him to get it cut six months ago, and then he wouldn't speak to us for months. Now it's grown out and looks terrible again, and he refuses to cut it. And his clothes! I'm ashamed to be seen with him in public. I've bought him some nice clothes, but he won't wear them. What can I do with him?"

Children have a healthy need to be independent and strong. But when they don't feel loved, their need for independence can sometimes turn into rebellion, from which children get (1) a sense of power, (2) the praise of their peers, and (3) an opportunity to punish their parents (attacking).

One way children express their independence is with their hair, clothing, jewelry, etc. When a child feels unconditionally loved, he's not likely to do bizarre things with his grooming and what he wears because he doesn't need the power and praise that come from those things.
However, even a child who feels loved will occasionally experiment with an odd appearance. Most of the time, we can ignore such experiments, but sometimes we do need to offer guidance in addition to loving him.

How do we know when to step in? When do we interfere with their choices and tell them what they will do with their hair or what they will wear? Those are very personal things to tell a child. As I said in Chapter 8, we need to reserve the times we interfere with our children's choices for the occasions when the consequences would be *unnecessarily* damaging if we did not interfere. That is usually the case only when they are quite young.

I usually allowed my children to choose how they styled their hair. However, when my son Benjamin was eight years old, he wanted to cut his hair in a way that was clearly associated with a group known for drug use and rebellion. He had no intention of behaving like those people. He just liked the appearance of their hair.

Me: "You can't have your hair like that."

Benjamin: "Why not? My friends do."

Me: "I know. And it wouldn't make you a bad person. Certainly I wouldn't love you less. But everywhere you go with your hair like that, there would be consequences you couldn't have thought about. Teachers and other people would assume things about you that are not true, and they would treat you in ways you wouldn't like. You know that we let you make most of your decisions, but the consequences of this one are too severe."

Because I had trusted Benjamin with many other decisions, he knew I was not trying to control him. That made it much easier for him to accept my decision about this one thing (11:10). And he already knew that I loved him, so getting the approval of his friends with his hair was not critical to him.

My son Joseph was fifteen when he began to wear his hair in a way so unusual that everywhere he went, people looked at him and whispered. At his age, I decided that he *could* make that decision. Eventually, he cut his hair more conventionally, but in the meantime he had felt entirely accepted by me. A child can have no greater feeling than to be accepted and loved no matter what he does.

Although the original question was about a boy's hair and clothing, I want to say a word about girls' clothing. A fourteen-year old girl can't possibly understand what goes through the minds of boys and men when she dresses in a way that calls attention to her body. Parents need to help their daughters understand that and sometimes make decisions for them when the consequences would be unnecessarily dangerous.

CLEANING UP

"My ten-year-old makes a mess wherever he goes, and I'm sick of cleaning up after him. I've tried to get him to clean up after himself, but he won't do it. I get angry, but that doesn't help, either. And I can't just leave the messes sitting there. What should I do next?"

Starting at an early age, children need to clearly understand that it's *their* responsibility to clean up their own messes. Parents who clean up after their children think they're doing them a favor, but they're really teaching them that other people are responsible for taking care of them. For example, in many families, when a child spills a drink all over the table, his mother rushes to clean up the mess. That teaches the child to be irresponsible. Children need the opportunity to clean up after themselves. Marcus was only two years old (pp. 216-17), but he was capable of learning that lesson.

If a child consistently neglects his responsibility, consequences may need to be imposed (Chapters 11 and 14). A child who leaves his belongings in the room where the television is may have to be restricted from using that room before he'll seriously consider picking up his things. He may even have to be restricted from *eating* until he cleans up after himself. A child who leaves the car a mess may need to have his driving privileges revoked in order to learn the consequences of choosing to be irresponsible. If he's not old enough to drive, he may need to be told that he can't be taken anywhere in the car — other than to necessary places like school, obviously. A child who hasn't cleaned up a messy room by bedtime may benefit from spending an uncomfortable night on the hard floor of the messy room.

There are many creative consequences that we can impose to motivate children to choose to do the right thing. But we must remember that the moment we become angry, consequences become punishments and no longer teach children anything beneficial.

BEDTIME

"I hate bedtime around here. Some nights it seems like I put the kids to bed twenty times. They get up over and over, and sometimes they don't actually go to sleep until hours past their bedtime. By then, it's way past *my* bedtime. Unless I get angry and spank them, they just won't stay in bed. What else can I do?"

I don't know many parents who haven't wanted to handcuff their children to the frame of the bed. I remember once thinking that putting kids to bed is like trying to get the toothpaste back in the tube — they just keep coming back out no matter what you do.

So let's get practical. One night, just when you think they're all in bed, one of them comes back into the living room with one of those stupid excuses — again. Now what? When in doubt, start with the Laws of Parenting. The First Law states, "My child needs to feel loved." Yes, you know that, but right now you just don't have any love to give, which reminds you of the Second Law: "I can't give what I don't have." Besides, you've been trying to love this child all day, and right now you only want to get him into bed and get some peace and quiet for once. You're beginning to get annoyed. That's understandable.

The Third Law: "If I'm angry, I'm wrong." Now you feel even worse. You can't give your child the love he needs and your anger will make him feel even more unloved. What can you do? Move on to the Fourth Law: "Truth → Seen → Accepted → Loved." If you're feeling irritated with this child who won't go to bed, at least tell the truth about it. If you can tell the truth to someone capable of seeing, accepting, and loving you — a wise man or woman — that would be great. Your anger will melt away, and you'll be able to interact with your child quite differently. If not, at least tell the truth to yourself — that you're feeling empty and selfish — and laugh at yourself that you're expecting this child to behave like an adult.

Now perhaps you're ready to move on to the Fifth Law: "Love, Teach, Faith, Consequences." You may not be perfectly loving at this point, but at least you can be mildly accepting and can teach your child something useful.

Children need to be clearly taught what their bedtime is. They need to understand that it isn't a guideline. It's a *law*. You then need to do your part to prepare them for it. You need to help them get ready for bedtime well before it arrives. If you don't help them to get undressed, get their teeth brushed, get tucked in, get a last-minute drink, etc., well before the appointed time, you have guaranteed that they won't get in bed on time.

You can also make it a great deal more fun if you love them as you make these preparations with them. I know that some parents are busier than others and can't do everything. But if it's possible, *help* them do all those things. Read to them. Hold their hands and look into their eyes and talk to them (Chapter 22) as they get ready for bed. What they want more than anything in the world is to know that you love them. If they're certain of that as they go to bed, it's *much* more likely that they'll go to bed when you tell them to. Very few parents do all the above before they complain about a child who doesn't go to bed on time.

So what do you do if they *still* get out of bed past the appointed time? Because that does occasionally happen even when you do everything right. My daughter Rachel was two years old when she decided that she would not stay in her crib one night. She ran into the living room where we were reading and shouted "Hi!" No matter how many times I put her in her crib, she still crawled out and came into the next room. This was at the same time she was mastering the word "No!" No discussion could persuade her to stay in her bed.

I was becoming angry, and when Rachel began to cry, I realized my approach was wrong. I took her by the hand to the garage, where we found an old bathroom door handle, the kind that uses a button to lock the bathroom door from the inside. Rachel watched me as I installed that handle on her door in such a way that I could press the button and lock her door from the outside. When I finished my installation, I sang her a song, told her I loved her, and explained that she would not be able to leave her room. I then pressed the button and locked her in.

Of course, Rachel soon attempted to leave her room and realized she was a prisoner. She was furious and began screaming at the top of her lungs. I waited for maybe a minute and opened the door. I asked her if she wanted me to unlock her door. After sobbing for several heart-rending moments, she finally said, "Yes," and I told her that I would unlock her door only if she stayed in her room. She did, and immediately fell asleep, exhausted.

She didn't get out of her crib the next night, but the night after that she slowly appeared in the next room after her bedtime. I gently said to her, "Would you like me to lock your door?" She shook her head and ran back to her room. I followed her to her crib, hugged her, and told her I loved her. She smiled and went to sleep. She never got out of her crib again.

Consequences always seem harsh in the beginning. But the alternative is far worse. Allowing our children to become irresponsible is unspeakably unloving on our part. Rachel did not like being locked in her room for that sixty seconds, but she knew that I loved her, and she benefitted enormously from learning obedience and responsibility.

Parents often say to me, with an air of helplessness, "But what can I do?" Teaching children requires action. There is always something we can do. It may require installing a lock. If you don't know how to install a lock, you can install a very inexpensive latch on the outside of the door. Or you can simply put a heavy object against the door. But a child must learn that bedtime means bedtime.

As they get older, children need more opportunity to choose their bedtime. We prescribed bedtimes for our younger children. As they became more responsible (not just as they became chronologically older), we allowed them to choose when they went to bed. However, they also had to be up and alert for the family meeting in the morning. If they were sleepy during the meeting, or if they missed it, an early bedtime was imposed for that night — sometimes very early.

PUNCTUALITY

"My kids don't get up on time and don't arrive on time for anything. I yell at them. I buy alarm clocks. We rush around and arrive late for everything. I'm out of patience. Now what?"

Obviously upset, 8-year-old Nathan came to his mother at 8:15 a.m.

Nathan: "I missed the bus."

Mother: "Yes, you did."

Nathan: "Why didn't you get me up?"

Mother: "I believe you have a watch and an alarm clock, don't you?

Nathan: "My alarm clock didn't work."

Mother: (laughing) "Alarm clocks are pretty dependable. Either you didn't set the alarm, or you turned it off and went back to sleep. The clock is right next to your bed, isn't it?"

Nathan: "Yes, and I remember that I set the alarm last night."

Mother: "Then you must have turned it off this morning and gone back to sleep. You'll have to put the clock farther away from your bed so you have to get out of bed to turn it off. We've talked about this before, remember? This isn't the first time."

Nathan: "Okay, I will. But we have to get going so I'm not late for school."

Mother: "We? I already have plans for the morning, and taking you to school isn't part of them."

Nathan: (stunned) "But how will I get to school?"

Mother: "Walk."

Nathan: "It's a long way!"

Mother: "You walk farther than that to your friend's house almost every day."

Nathan: "If I walk, I'll be late."

Mother: "Then run. In the future, you'll be more likely to get up on time, won't you?"

Nathan moved his alarm clock so he would have to get out of bed to shut it off, and he was more aware of his responsibility to get up on time without someone helping him.

Children need to experience the natural consequences of their choices. It is not unkind on our part to allow that. If we rescue them from those consequences, they'll have little reason to learn responsibility. If we don't lovingly teach our children to be responsible now, other people (employers, etc.) will teach them later, and it's very unlikely that those people will teach them with unconditional love. Learning to be responsible as an adult can be quite painful and expensive.

Our children also need to understand that their punctuality has consequences for other people. If a child is late to a class or meeting, the people around him feel rushed to help him get there. And other people have to wait on his arrival. It's arrogant and selfish to think our time is more important than the time of others, but many of us do that a lot.

PLANNING AND ATTENDING ACTIVITIES

"We seem to have kids going a hundred places at once. They don't tell me about things till the last minute, and then I get irritated. What can I do to better coordinate things?"

What children choose to do with their time affects the whole family. If a child wants to attend an event, that affects the person who has to transport him to the event, the person picking him up, and sometimes other people who need to go places at the same time. Children need to see the effect they have on others, and occasionally they have to make sacrifices for the benefit of the family.

Our family keeps a record of all events on a large calendar that everyone can refer to during the week. If a child doesn't plan something with the family and put it on the calendar, and remembers it only at the last minute, he may not be able to go to that activity. That's a natural consequence that effectively teaches him to be more responsible.

In addition, if a child's jobs aren't done, he can't go to an event, even if it was planned and important to him. Initially, children may be angry about that natural consequence, but they also remember it and are more likely to choose wisely the next time.

PROPERTY

"What should I do when my children won't share their things with each other?"

Children need to have things that belong to them. It gives them a sense of independence as well as an opportunity to learn responsibility. They also need to learn how to treat the things that belong to other people.

Benjamin was wrong to take Rob's stereo out of his room without permission (pp. 254-5). He needed to learn that he had violated his brother's property rights. Despite Benjamin's transgression, however, Rob's anger was still not justified. On pp. 201-4, Sarah had a right to require that Justin ask her permission before using her shampoo. However, that did not justify her failure to love her brother.

Parents often settle property disputes by simply taking an object from one child and giving it to the other. Far more important than who has possession of the object in question is what each child learns, and parents need to constantly balance two principles:

1. The child who owns the object does have the right to possess it. It's his, and other people should be required to ask permission before using it. Children should not be forced to share what is theirs simply because that would eliminate conflict, or because it would make things easier for a parent, or even because it would be loving. Children can't be forced to be loving.

2. On the other hand, children need to understand that loving and sharing are more important than protecting personal property.

BEING ALONE AT HOME

"At what age can I start leaving my children at home alone without a babysitter?"

Children need to feel independent, and that only happens as they have experience with making their own choices. As soon as a child is capable of understanding what to do in emergencies—calling the neighbors, calling 911, and so on—parents need to do small errands away from the house while leaving him or her at home for short periods. Children blossom as they realize they're being trusted to take care of themselves. Only you can know at what age a given child is capable of handling this responsibility. Some children are prepared at a much earlier age than others.

By the age of twelve (much earlier with some), most children should not require a babysitter when their parents are gone for hours. They're quite capable of learning the phone numbers to call, what to do if there's a fire, and so on. They need to know how to make choices and manage things without constant supervision.

BED WETTING

"What should I do about my child who wets the bed?"

Some children wet the bed because of a medical condition. However, many children wet the bed because they don't feel loved. What we call "stress" in adults is the feeling of being unloved, empty, and afraid. Stress has been identified in countless studies as a significant risk factor in the cause of a huge portion of adult physical disorders: high blood pressure, heart disease, ulcers, headaches, back pain, depression, cancer, and so on. It's no surprise, then, that feeling unloved affects the bodies of children, too, causing them to wet the bed, among other things.

A child who wets the bed doesn't need to be shamed. He doesn't need to be told that bed-wetting is undesirable and inconvenient for his parents. He already knows that. He only needs to be loved and to take responsibility for it. If his bed is wet in the morning, the natural consequence is that he gathers up his clothing and sheets and washes them. Children can learn to wash clothes at a very young age.

WATCHING TELEVISION

"How much television should my children watch? How should I screen violence and sex?"

Learn how to unconditionally love your children. Don't allow them to watch material that interferes with them feeling loved and loving other people. I suggest that children not watch television until they've completed their assigned jobs around the house. If parents follow those guidelines, children won't be harmed by watching television.

MONEY AND WORKING OUTSIDE THE HOME

"How should children pay for their own expenses? Should they get an allowance? Should they get a job?"

In our family, we discuss the expenses of each child as they come up, and then we pay for the ones that seem appropriate:

clothing, a new basketball, dues for the swim team, a night out with friends at the movies, prom night, etc. A child who feels loved and learns to be responsible with his jobs also tends to be responsible where money is involved. Children who are loved, loving, and responsible are aware that their spending affects the entire family, so they don't usually make requests that would spend the family's money foolishly. And they manage their finances just fine after leaving home.

There are other ways to teach children financial responsibility:

1. An allowance, from which they pay certain expenses: entertainment, clothing, etc.

2. In some families, children are paid for doing extra jobs around the house, like painting, landscaping, etc. This does not mean being paid for routine jobs that are given to every family member: bedrooms, bathroom, kitchen, etc. That approach would rob children of an opportunity to feel a sense of service toward the family.

3. Some people advocate that a child get a job outside the home. I can't prescribe an answer for everyone, but I can suggest some advantages and disadvantages:

Advantages

An outside job can teach a child to be independent. It gives him his own source of income, and he learns to be responsible for that. He also learns that there are people in the world other than his parents who require him to be responsible and accountable. Without that experience, many children think that only their parents are "mean" and make them work.

Disadvantages

Nothing in life is more important than feeling loved. If a child is just learning that, any time spent away from the family may detract from opportunities to be seen and accepted. The job can also become a source of Imitation Love — praise and power. In addition, jobs outside the home often cause schedule conflicts in the family and strain transportation resources. And jobs can interfere with a child's schoolwork.

"IT'S NOT FAIR"

"When I give my children something to do, they often say, 'that's not fair.' I don't always know what to say when they say that. They hate it when I say, 'Too bad. Life's just not fair.' What do you say to your children?"

On a Saturday, my sons Jonathan and Michael were given different assignments in the yard to complete before they could play with their friends. Jonathan thought his job was much harder and would take longer to complete than the work I had given his brother. He was right. Jonathan was older, and I thought he would benefit from the larger responsibility.

Jonathan: "This isn't fair."

Me: "What's not fair?"

Jonathan: "I have more work to do than Michael does."

Me: "You *do* have more work to do, but what's not *fair* about it?"

Jonathan looked at me like I was stupid. Did I not understand the meaning of the word *fair*?

Jonathan: "Why should I do more work than he does?"

Me: "Tell me *why* you're working in the yard today?"

Again, he looked at me like I was stupid.

Jonathan: "I guess somebody has to do the work."

Me: "But why are *you* working? *I* could do it all."

Jonathan: (smiling) "I wish you would."

Me: (laughing) "I bet you do. There's a reason that I have you working out here, and contrary to what you think, it's not so I have to do less of the work myself. What's the reason?"

Jonathan: "I know what you want me to say: so I'll be happy and strong."

Me: "As funny as you think that is, that's exactly right. You can only learn to be responsible by working. There's no other way. Where do you get the food you eat every day?"

Jonathan: (rolling his eyes) "From you."

Me: "And the clothes you wear?"

Jonathan: (rolling his eyes and sighing) "From you."

Me: "And how do you think I learned to earn a living for that stuff? I learned to be responsible by working. It all starts by doing the kind of thing you're doing right now. It really does. And there's always something unfair happening. I work harder than lots of the people I work with. So what? As a result of working harder, I've learned to be more responsible than many of those people. I also get paid more than many of the people I work with. How nice for me — and for you, huh?

"The harder you work, the more responsible you'll learn to be. You'll also learn more about how to love the family as you do more for us. The reason you work is to learn. The more you work, the more you learn. So the question is this: do you want to work more and be more responsible and more loving, or work less and be less responsible and less loving?"

Jonathan was beginning to see that insisting on fairness was more selfish and more irresponsible than he had previously supposed. No child could swallow such a discussion all at once, but he was thinking about it. I emphasize that any trace of anger from a parent makes a discussion like this impossible.

Children often complain that things aren't fair. What they really mean is they didn't get what they wanted. All our lives, we're in positions where we get less of something than the person next to us, or our burden is heavier than someone else's. The only way for us to eliminate such "injustice" is to control the choices of everyone around us. But a world where people can control the choices of others is unthinkable. What we really need to learn is to be responsible and loving. Compared to that, occasional injustices are meaningless. In fact, it's often from the "unfair" experiences that we learn to be responsible and selfless. That's what we need to teach our children.

DISAGREEMENTS ABOUT THE CHILDREN

"When I try to teach my children something, or tell them they can't go somewhere, or that they can't do something, my husband often interrupts me and contradicts what I'm saying in front of them. Or the kids will go to him later and get him to change what I told them. How can I be a good parent when he's interfering with everything I'm trying to do?"

Always remember our responsibilities as parents: to love and teach our children. When we argue with our spouse, let's examine what happens to those to objectives:

To love our children. Two parents who unconditionally love each other can certainly disagree about many things, but the moment they become irritated with each other, children sense that. How can our children feel loved or learn to love other people while we are providing an example of unloving anger?

To teach our children. What principle can we possibly teach our children while we're in a state of disagreement? We can only confuse them, and in many cases frighten them.

If you disagree about a decision regarding your children, put the decision off until you do agree. If your spouse says something to a child that you disagree with, do not voice your contradictory opinion where the child can hear it. Wait until you can speak to your spouse alone, preferably when you can speak without anger. If you speak to your spouse while you're angry, you will not like how the conversation goes. You've already proven that, haven't you?

You'll make many mistakes as a parent. If you make a bad decision with a child, and you realize that fact later in a discussion with your spouse, go to the child and admit it. Change your decision if possible. Your child won't think you're a fool. He'll feel closer to you and loved by you.

If your spouse continues to contradict you in front of your children, do not respond with anger. That only makes things much worse. Do not respond by acting like a victim. Note the victimy tone of the question above: "How can I be a good parent when *he's* interfering with everything I'm trying to do?" You cannot feel happy and loving — which is what your children need — when you're feeling and acting like a victim. Read *Real Love—The Truth About Finding Unconditional Love and*

Fulfilling Relationships, learn to tell the truth about yourself, and find Real Love in your own life (Chapter 5). Then share that love with your children. Even if your spouse contradicts you, *you* can still feel loved and loving. You can still be a great parent.

Afterword

To learn more about the basic principles of Real Love, read *Real Love — The Truth About Finding Unconditional Love and Fulfilling Relationships*, found at http://www.gregbaer.com/book/book.asp.

For a workbook that multiplies the practical effect of the *Real Love* book, read *The Real Love Companion — Take Steps Toward a Loving and Happy Life*, found at http://www.gregbaer.com/book/book.asp.

To learn more about how to share Real Love with others, read *The Wise Man — The Truth about Sharing Real Love*, found at http://www.gregbaer.com/book/book.asp.

To learn how the principles of Real Love apply in marraige, read *Real Love in Marraige — The Truth About Finding Genuine Happiness in Marraige*, found at http://www.gregbaer.com/book/book.asp.

To learn how to use Real Love in parenting, read *Real Love in Parenting — A Simple and Powerfully Effecitve Way to Raise Happy and Responsible Children*, found at http://www.gregbaer.com/book/book.asp.

For a set of three 60-minute CDs that describe the princibles of Real Love in an abbreviated fashion, listen to *The Truth About Love and Lies*, found at http://www.gregbaer.com/tapes/tapes.asp.

For the complete audio recording (eight hours of listening) of *Real Love — The Truth About Finding Unconditional Love and Fulfilling Relationships*, get the seven CDs at http://www.gregbaer.com/tapes/tapes.asp.

For a video recording (150 minutes, two DVDs) of a presentation by Greg on the subject of Real Love — before a life audience — watch *The Healing Power of Real Love*, found at http://www.gregbaer.com/tapes/tapes.asp.

For more information of any kind, write to us at mike@gregbaer.com.